HIGHWAY DESIGN AND CONSTRUCTION

By the same author

HIGHWAY TRAFFIC ANALYSIS AND DESIGN, Revised Edition

Highway Design and Construction

R. J. SALTER

University of Bradford

Second Edition

MACMILLAN

First edition 1979
Reprinted 1986
Second edition 1988
Reprinted 1991

Published by
MACMILLAN EDUCATION LTD
Houndmills, Basingstoke, Hampshire RG21 2XS
and London
Companies and representatives
throughout the world

Printed in Hong Kong

British Library Cataloguing in Publication Data
Salter, R.J.
Highway design and construction. – 2nd ed.
1. Pavements – Design and construction
2. Road construction   3. Roads – Design
I. Title
625.8   TE251
ISBN 0–333–45998–9

Contents

CONTENTS

Preface

As in many other branches of civil engineering, the past decade has seen the introduction of many new techniques in the design and construction of highways. These advances have been caused by the rapid increase in traffic loading both in terms of magnitude and frequency, the need to reduce labour costs and improve output by increasing mechanisation and the desire to obtain maximum benefit from limited resources.

Drawing from recent research and development work the book reviews methods of highway design and construction. Described in detail are materials for both rigid and flexible roads, pavement thickness design, the optimisation and execution of earthworks, highway drainage, pavement construction and the maintenance of carriageway pavements.

Included are current recommendations of the Department of the Environment, The Transport and Road Research Laboratory, The Building Research Establishment, Transportation Research Board and the American Association of State Highway Officials.

The book is suitable for students on technicians courses, undergraduate and postgraduate students making a specialised study of highway engineering. Highway engineers in practice will find the current British recommendations for highway design and construction a useful source of reference.

R. J. SALTER

ix

Acknowledgements

The author wishes to thank the following who have kindly given permission for the use of copyright material.

>   The American Association of State Highway Officials
>   The American Concrete Institute
>   Aveling-Barford International
>   Blaw Know Limited
>   The Building Research Establishment
>   The Department of the Environment
>   J. A. Gaffney, B.Sc.(Eng.), C.Eng., F.I.C.E., F.I.Mun.E., F.I.H.E.,
>   Director of Engineering Services,
>   West Yorkshire Metropolitan County Council
>   Thomas Smith
>   The Transportation Research Board
>   The Transport and Road Research Laboratory
>   Quarry Management and Products
>   UMM — Greenside

Extracts from British Standards are reproduced by permission of the British Standards Institution, 2 Park Street, London W1A 2BS, from whom complete copies can be obtained.

The following material is Crown copyright and is reproduced by permission of the Controller of Her Majesty's Stationery Office

>   Standard Specification for Road and Bridge Works
>   Road Notes
>   Road Research Technical Papers
>   Transport and Road Research Laboratory Publications
>   Department of Transport Technical Memorandums.

Every effort has been made to trace all the copyright holders but if any have been inadvertently overlooked the publisher will be pleased to make the necessary arrangement arrangement at the first opportunity.

1
Highway Pavement Materials

1.1 Binders Used for Bituminous Highway Materials

1.1.1 Road Tar

Tar has been used for many years in road construction both as a binder for macadam and as a surface dressing initially on waterbound roads. Road tar is today specified in BS 76[1] by the following definition: 'tar for use in road work is prepared entirely from crude tars produced wholly or substantially as a by-product in the carbonisation of coal at above 600 °C in externally heated retorts or coke ovens'.

The British Standard specifies the essential properties of a number of viscosity grades of two types of road tar. These types differ mainly in their setting properties as controlled by the content of flux oil and its volatility. The first type, used for surface dressing, is designated as the S-series and is intended to set more rapidly than the second type, used for coated macadam and designated the C-series.

There are four grades of surface-dressing tar — S34, 38, 42 and 46 — designated according to their equi-viscous temperature, and eight grades of tar for use in coated macadam — C30, 34, 38, 42, 46, 50, 54 and 58.

In addition to specifying the equi-viscous temperature for each grade of tar BS 76 specifies the maximum water content, gives distillation yields, the softening point of the distillation residue using the ring-and-ball test, density at 20 °C and the requirements for the Beckton tray test. This later test determines the rise in viscosity as determined by the equi-viscous temperature that a film of tar undergoes during 1 h at a particular temperature and allows an assessment to be made of the hardening that will be experienced by the tar in a commercial coating plant operating at the same temperature. It is therefore a test applied to tars used for coating aggregates.

1.1.2 Bitumen

This is specified in BS 3690,[2] where bitumen is defined as a viscous liquid, or a solid, consisting essentially of hydrocarbons and their derivatives, that is soluble in carbon disulphide; it is substantially non-volatile and softens gradually when heated. It is black and brown in colour and possesses waterproofing and adhesive properties.

1

It is obtained by refinery processes from petroleum, and is also found as a natural deposit or as a component of naturally occurring asphalt, in which it is associated with mineral matter.

When the bitumen is obtained from petroleum by refinery processes the bitumen is referred to as petroleum bitumen. Where the viscosity of the bitumen is reduced by the addition of a suitable volatile diluent then the binder is referred to as cut-back bitumen.

BS 3690 gives details of the ten grades of petroleum bitumen, 15, 25, 35, 40, 50, 70, 100, 200, 300 and 450 pen, each value indicating the mid-point of the penetration or viscosity range as measured by the standard penetration test. Also specified are the softening point, the loss in weight and the drop in penetration after heating for 5 h at 163 °C, solubility in carbon disulphide or trichloro-ethylene, and ash content.

Cut-back bitumen is specified in BS 3690, which designates three grades — 50, 100 and 200 s — the mid-point of the viscosity range determined by the standard tar viscometer. Also specified are distillation yields, the penetration of the residue after distillation, solubility in carbon disulphide or tricholoroethylene and ash content.

1.1.3 Bitumen Road Emulsions

A bitumen road emulsion is specified in BS 434[3] as a liquid product in which a substantial amount of bitumen is suspended in a finely divided condition in an aqueous medium by means of one or more suitable emulsifying agents. There are two types of emulsion: anionic and cationic. In anionic emulsions the anion of the emulsifier is at the interface with the bitumen particle, which is negatively charged, and normally the aqueous phase is alkaline. In cationic emulsions the cation of the emulsifier is at the interface with the bitumen particle, which is positively charged, and normally the aqueous phase is acid.

Anionic road emulsions are classified in order of stability in the following manner

(1) *Class A1*. Labile emulsions which are used cold and are characterised by rapid breakdown on application and normally unsuitable for mixing with aggregate.

(2) *Class A2*. Semi-stable emulsions used cold and with sufficient stability to permit mixing with certain grades of aggregate before breakdown occurs.

(3) *Class A3*. Stable emulsions used cold and having sufficient mechanical and chemical stability for all purposes involving mixing with aggregate, including those containing large proportions of fines or chemically active materials such as cement or hydrated lime.

(4) *Class A4*. An emulsion specially formulated for the slurry seal process. With the addition of water they are sufficiently stable to form a free-flowing slurry with specified aggregates. They are capable of remaining stable with the laying procedure adopted and the setting time may be extended as desired. This class of emulsion is further divided into slow setting and rapid setting. The slow-setting emulsions are suitable for use in simple mixers for hand-laying, in bulk transit concrete mixers or mobile mixing machines. Rapid-setting emulsions are suitable for use only in special mobile mixing machines.

Cationic road emulsions are classified in order of stability as follows

(1) *Class K1.* A rapid-acting emulsion which is characterised by rapid deposition of binder on contact with road surfaces and aggregates followed by early resistance to rain, but which is unsuitable for mixing with aggregates. The grades with a high binder content are used hot but the other grades are used cold.

(2) *Class K2.* A medium-acting emulsion used cold in which the rate of deposition of binder is sufficiently delayed to permit mixing with certain clean coarse aggregates before breaking to form a continuous adhesive film.

(3) *Class K3.* A slow-acting emulsion used cold in which the rate of deposition of binder is sufficiently delayed to permit mixing with certain fine aggregates before breaking to form a continuous adhesive film without stripping. This group also includes cationic slurry seal emulsions, which are suitable for handling only in special mobile mixing machines.

Guidance on the choice of a suitable class of emulsion for different types of work is given in BS 434, Part 2. For normal uses table 1.1 gives the recommended emulsion types.

In general, bituminous emulsions, with the exception of type K1–70, are fluid enough to be used at normal atmospheric temperatures without the need for any further heating, and unlike hot applied binders remain fluid immediately after application. This means that care has to be taken when such emulsions are applied on steep gradients, where the emulsion may flow.

While bituminous emulsions may be applied in damp conditions, they are affected by rain or frost occurring during application; cationic emulsions tend to break more rapidly than anionic emulsions; K1–70 emulsions especially are less susceptible to rain. Hot weather may cause problems with surface dressing and premixing when emulsions are used and may require traffic to be kept off the road for several hours after the application of the emulsion.

Breaking of bituminous emulsions is indicated by the change in colour of the emulsion from brown to black and depends upon the following factors

(1) The composition of the emulsion.

(2) The rate of evaporation of the water, which depends upon wind conditions, relative humidity, atmospheric temperature, and the rate and method of application.

(3) The porosity of the surface to which the emulsion is being applied and the resulting removal of water by capillary attraction.

(4) The chemical and physical influence of the aggregate with which the aggregate comes into contact.

(5) The mechanical disturbance of the emulsion/aggregate system during laying and rolling or by the action of traffic.

Bituminous emulsions are normally supplied for small-scale use in drums, and if these are stored for a period they should be turned or inverted at least once a month and also protected against frost. When it is desired to use the emulsion the containers should be rolled to agitate the contents; this is particularly important with emulsions Class A1–40 and K1–40.

The emulsion should be applied to a clean surface. In hot weather it may be necessary to wet the road surface to prevent premature breaking of the emulsion.

Table 1.1 Recommendations for the application of emulsions

Use	Emulsion Class
coated stone	A2-57, K2, K3
concrete curing	A1-40, A1-55
grouting	A1-60, A1-55, K1-60, K1-70
mist spraying	A1-40
patching	A1-60, A1-55, K1-60
premixing	A2-50, A2-57, A3
retreading	A2-50, A3
sealing formation and sub-base	A1-60, A1-55, K1-60, K1-70
slurry sealing	A4, K3
surface dressing and sealing (cold)	A1-60, A1-55, K1-60
surface dressing and sealing (hot)	K1-70
tack coating	A1-40, K1-40

In the simplest cases the emulsion may be spread evenly and without scrubbing action by hand-brushing. Frequently small pressure-spraying machines are used, but where the area to be covered is large, specialist contractors with large-scale spraying machines are normally employed.

Bituminous emulsions have a considerable number of applications in highway construction. They may be used as the binder in surface-dressing work, for the sealing of open-textured coated macadam, for the sealing of formations and sub-bases, for retreading, and for the production of coated materials for immediate use or for storage.

1.1.4 Natural Asphalts

In the United Kingdom a natural asphalt is defined as a naturally occurring bitumen in association with fine mineral matter. The two forms of natural asphalt that are of importance in highway pavement work are rock asphalt and lake asphalt.

Natural-rock asphalt consists of a porous rock, usually limestone, naturally impregnated with bitumen, the bitumen content being about 10 per cent. Natural-rock asphalt is used for the production of compressed natural-rock asphalt and also as mastic asphalt. Suitable natural-rock asphalt is quarried in the Gard district of France and the Val de Travers in Switzerland.

In lake asphalt the mineral matter is finely divided and dispersed throughout the bitumen and the whole mass is capable of flow. The type used in the United Kingdom is Trinidad lake asphalt. In Trinidad the material is dug from the Pitch Lake, and after heating to remove the water content and straining to remove the grosser impurities it is shipped as refined lake asphalt. In this state is has the following approximate composition

Bitumen	55 per cent by mass
Mineral matter	35 per cent by mass
Organic matter, etc.	10 per cent by mass

1.2 Binder Viscosity

Bituminous binders with a very wide range of consistency are employed in highway construction. At normal temperatures they range from materials that are fluid to those that are hard and brittle. According to the situation of the highway, the traffic loading and the material type, a binder having suitable properties must be specified so that it is able to meet the following requirements

(1) be sufficiently fluid to be handled either by pumping or spraying so as to coat and wet a mineral aggregate;

(2) remain sufficiently viscous at high road temperatures so that it will not deform under heavy traffic loading;

(3) remain sufficiently flexible at low road temperatures so that the surface will not fracture and disintegrate.

An important method of ensuring that the binder will meet these requirements is the specification of a suitable viscosity range. It is defined as that property which retards flow so that, when a force is applied to a liquid, the greater the viscosity the slower will be the movement of that liquid.

The practical method used for measuring the viscosity of a binder will depend upon the nature of the binder. The major tests used are

(1) The ring-and-ball test, which measures the softening point of bitumen or the distillation residue of a road tar.

(2) The penetration test for use with semi-solid and solid bituminous materials.

(3) The use of the Standard Tar Viscometer to determine the viscosity of cut-back bitumen, road oil and tar.

(4) The use of the Equi-Viscous Temperature Viscometer to determine the temperature at which tars have equal viscosity.

1.2.1 The Ring-and-ball Test

Bituminous materials do not change from a solid to a liquid state at any given
temperature but become gradually softer and less viscous as the temperature rises.
It is for this reason that the determination of the softening point must be made by
a fixed, arbitrary and closely defined method if the results obtained are comparable.

Bitumen

The closely defined method used for bitumen is described in BS 4692.[4]

In the ring-and-ball test, samples of bitumen are prepared by pouring the bitumen,
which has been heated under specified conditions, into metal rings which serve as
moulds. Preparation of the bitumen samples must be carried out in the controlled
manner detailed in BS 4692.

The determination is usually carried out in duplicate and the apparatus is
designed to hold two discs. The apparatus is assembled with the rings, the appropriate thermometer, and ball guides in position, and the bath is filled to a height of
50 mm above the upper surface of the rings, as shown in figure 1.1, with freshly
boiled distilled water at a temperature of 5 °C when the softening point is below
80 °C, the water temperature being maintained at 5 °C for 15 min.

Using forceps, a steel ball, previously cooled to 5 °C, having a diameter of 9.53
mm and weighing 3.50 ± 0.05 g, is placed upon each sample disc contained within
a tapered brass ring with a larger internal diameter of 17.5 mm. A ball guide
previously placed over the disc assists in placing the ball in position. The bath is
then heated and the water stirred so that the temperature rises at a uniform rate
of 5 ± 0.5 °C/min until the bitumen softens and allows the ball to pass through
the ring. The rate of temperature rise should not be averaged over the test period
and any determination where the rate does not fall within the specified limits after
the first 3 min must be rejected.

For each ring and ball the temperature shown by the thermometer is taken at
the instant the sample surrounding the ball touches the bottom plate. If, however,
the difference between the values obtained in the duplicate determinations exceed
1 °C the test must be repeated.

When the softening point is expected to be above 80 °C the water is replaced
with glycerol, which is maintained at a temperature of 35 °C for 15 min before
placing a steel ball at the same temperature on to the disc.

1.2.2 Distillation Residue from Road Tar

In BS 76, Tars for Road Purposes,[1] the ring-and-ball softening point of the distillation residue of a road tar is specified.

A similar test to that previously described for bitumen is used but there are
some differences in the apparatus and in the technique employed. A detailed
specification of the method of obtaining the distillation residue and of carrying out
the ring-and-ball test is given in Appendixes D and E of BS 76. As with bitumen, a

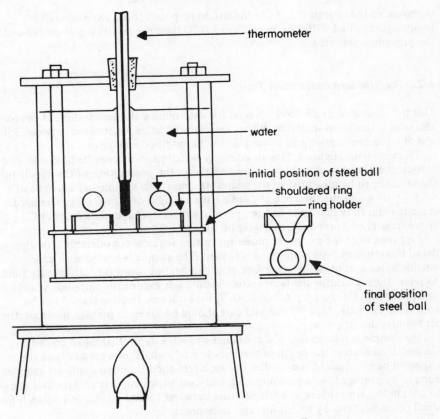

Figure 1.1 Apparatus for ring-and-ball test

sample of distillation residue is used to fill two pitch rings with residue in a standard manner.

The water used for the heating bath is cooled to at least 45 °C below the expected result of the test, but for residues of low softening point the temperature should not be below 5 °C. Sufficient of this water is poured into the beaker, shown in figure 1.1, for the final liquid level to be at least 50 mm above the top of the rings, while at the same time avoiding any aeration. The pitch rings, filled with residue, are placed into the support and then placed concentrically in the beaker; the thermometer is then placed in position. The steel balls are placed in the liquid but they are not placed in position upon the rings until 15 min has elapsed, during which time the temperature of the liquid is maintained constant.

The water is then heated so that its temperature rises at a rate of 5 °C/min, and after the first 3 min this rate of temperature rise must be maintained within ±0.5 °C over each 1 min period. The mean of the two temperatures at which the residue surrounding each steel ball first touches the lower plate of the support is then reported, to the nearest 0.2 °C, as the softening point. If the two balls fall at temperatures which differ by more than 1.0 °C then the results are discarded and the procedure repeated.

1.2.3 The Standard Penetration Test

This test described in BS 4691[5] is used for determining the penetration of semi-solid and solid bituminous materials. Where the material has a penetration between 350 and 500 the penetration can be obtained with modified apparatus.

The apparatus (figure 1.2) is an assembly which permits a needle holder to move vertically without measurable friction and allows the penetration of the needle into the bitumen to be measured to the nearest 0.1 mm. The spindle has a weight of 47.5 ± 0.05 g and the spindle and needle have a weight of 50 ± 0.05 g. The needle is made from fully hardened and tempered stainless steel and has a length of approximately 50 mm and a diameter of 1.00 to 1.02 mm.

Preparation of the sample required for testing requires considerable attention to detail if consistent results are to be obtained. The sample is heated with care, stirring as soon as possible to prevent local overheating, until it is sufficiently fluid to pour. During heating the temperature should not exceed the softening point by more than 60 °C for a tar pitch and 90 °C for bitumen. Heating should not be continued for more than 30 min and care should be taken to prevent incorporating air bubbles into the mix.

The sample is poured into the container to such a depth that when cooled to the test temperature the depth of the sample is at least 10 mm greater than the expected penetration of the needle. For each test condition two duplicate samples need to be prepared. As a precaution against dust each sample is covered and allowed to cool in the atmosphere at a temperature between 15 and 30 °C for 1 to $1\frac{1}{2}$ h for small containers and $1\frac{1}{2}$ to 2 h for large containers.

To carry out the penetration test the penetration needle is cleaned with toluene or other suitable solvent and then inserted into the penetrometer. A 50 g weight is then placed above the needle so that the total weight of the moving parts is 100 ± 0.1 g. The sample container is then placed so that the penetrometer needle may be lowered into contact with its surface, and during this time the sample is completely covered with water maintained at a constant temperature, normally 25 °C.

The needle is positioned by slowly lowering it until it just makes contact with the surface of the sample, achieved by bringing the needle tip into contact with its image reflected by the surface of the sample from a properly planned source of light. The needle holder is then released for a period which is normally 5 s and the depth of penetration in tenths of a millimetre noted.

At least three separate determinations are made at points on the surface not less than than 10 mm from the side of the container and not less than 10 mm apart. A clean needle is used for each determination and if the penetration is greater than 200 at least three needles are used, which are left in the sample until the determinations have been completed.

If the bitumen has a penetration of 350 to 500, an approximate determination may be made using a larger container for the bitumen but with a needle loading of

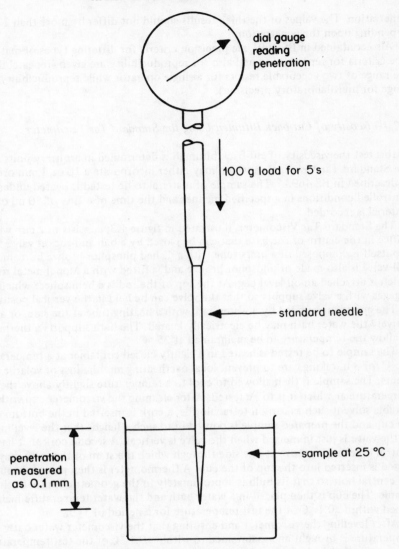

dial gauge
reading
penetration

100 g load for 5 s

standard needle

sample at 25 °C

penetration
measured
as 0.1 mm

Figure 1.2 Outline of apparatus for Standard Penetration Test

only 50 g. The approximate penetration may then be obtained by multiplying the observed value by 2. A direct measurement may be made by using a container for the bitumen that is at least 60 mm deep but of not more than 125 ml, permitting proper temperature control of the bitumen. A special needle is used with a minimum exposed length of 50 mm.

The average of three determinations to the nearest whole unit is reported as the penetration. The values of the three results should not differ by more than 2 to 8, depending upon the penetration.

Also contained in BS 4691 are precision criteria for differing types of material. The criteria for repeatability and also for reproducibility are given (repeatability is the range of two acceptable results for a single operator while reproducibility is the range for multilaboratory precision).

1.2.4 Viscosity of Cut-back Bitumen Using the Standard Tar Viscometer

In this test the viscosity of cut-back bitumen is determined in arbitrary units using the Standard Tar Viscometer, which may either incorporate a 10 or 4 mm orifice, as described in BS 4693.[6] The sample of material to be tested is heated under controlled conditions in a specified manner and the time of efflux of 50 ml of the material is recorded.

The Standard Tar Viscometer, illustrated in figure 1.3, consists of a cup with an orifice in the centre of the base that can be closed by a ball-and-socket valve. The cup itself is composed of a brass tube with a dished phosphor-bronze bottom. The ball valve is also made of phosphor-bronze and is fitted with a Monel metal rod to which is attached an oil-level peg. At the top of the rod is a hemisphere which engages with a valve support so that the valve can be held in the vertical position.

The cup is surrounded by a water bath with a heating tube at the side, or alternatively the water bath may be electrically heated. The bath supports a thermometer to allow the temperature to be maintained at 25 °C.

The sample to be tested is heated in a tightly closed container at a temperature of 60 °C for 3 h, taking care to prevent local overheating and the loss of volatile constituents. The sample is then allowed to cool to a temperature slightly above the temperature at which it is to be tested. After cleaning the viscometer cup with a suitable solvent such as carbon tetrachloride, a cork is inserted in the bottom of the cup and the prepared sample is poured in to such a height that the levelling peg on the valve is just immersed when the valve is vertical. A second cork that has a control hole and a groove at one side through which the stem of the valve may be passed is inserted into the top of the cup. A thermometer is then placed through the central hole so that its bulb is approximately in the geometric centre of the sample. The cup is then placed in a water bath and the water temperature maintained within ±0.1 °C of the test temperature for a period of $1\frac{1}{2}$ h.

After levelling the viscometer and ensuring that the viscometer water-bath temperature is brought and maintained to within ±0.1 °C of the test temperature, frequently stirring the water, the cup is placed in position in the viscometer and the corks and thermometer removed. Any excess bitumen is then removed from the cup so that its surface level is at the centre of the peg. Light mineral oil is poured into a receiver up to the 20 ml graduation mark and the receiver placed directly under the orifice of the cup. The valve is then lifted and suspended from the valve support; as the bitumen flows into the receiver a timing device is started when the liquid in the receiver reaches the 25 ml mark and is stopped when the liquid reaches the 75 ml mark.

The time of flow is noted and reported, together with the orifice size and the test temperature.

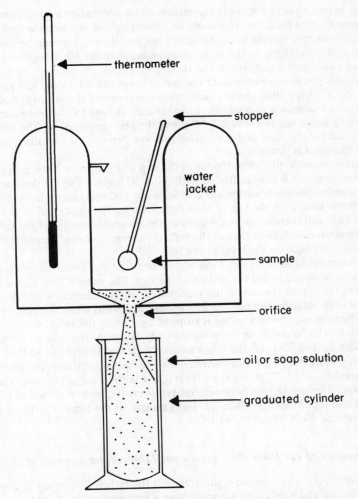

Figure 1.3 Outline of operation of Standard Tar Viscometer

1.2.5 Viscosity of Tar Using the Standard Tar Viscometer

The Standard Tar Viscometer as described in BS 76[1] may also be used, determining the viscosity of a tar in seconds, and then indirectly the equi-viscous temperature of the tar.

Once again preparation of the sample is important, and if it is received at the laboratory in a cold condition it is warmed until it is sufficiently fluid for pouring or mixing by immersing the tar container in water at not more than 30 °C higher than the expected equi-viscous temperature. As an alternative a controlled-temperature oven may be used, but care must be taken to avoid any intense direct source of heat. Should the sample be received in a hot condition, it should be cooled without undue exposure to the air to a temperature about 30 °C higher than the expected equi-viscous temperature of the tar.

After this preliminary treatment the tar is brought to a temperature approximately 20 °C higher than the test temperature and mixed thoroughly. Not less than 250 ml of the sample is poured into a beaker and allowed to cool with continuous stirring to a temperature about 0.5 °C above the test temperature. The orifice of the cup is closed by the valve and tar poured into the cup until the levelling peg on the vertical valve-rod is just immersed.

A thermometer is placed in the tar in the cup and used to stir the tar gently until the tar temperature is as specified or within 0.1 °C higher. The tar thermometer is then suspended coaxially within the cup with the 100 mm immersion mark on the thermometer level with the top of the hemisphere on the upper end of the valve so that the bulb will then be approximately at the geometric centre of the tar. When the tar temperature falls to that of the test, the thermometer is removed and the tar surface is brought to the level of the test.

A receiver containing 20 ml of mineral oil or of a 1 per cent mass/mass solution of soft soap is placed under the orifice of the cup. The valve is then opened and tar allowed to flow from the cup to the receiver; timing commences when the level of the oil or soap solution reaches the 25 ml mark and stops when it reaches the 75 ml mark. After timing, the flow of tar is stopped by closing the valve.

To obtain the equi-viscous temperature (evt) of the tar the time of efflux must lie between 33 and 75 s and the temperature of the test is adjusted so that the time of flow is within this range. For convenience a temperature that is the multiple of 5 °C nearest to or 2.5 °C above the expected evt is chosen and this gives the required efflux time. The connection between test temperature, time of flow and evt is given in BS 76 and reproduced as table 1.2. For example, if the time of efflux is 65 s at a temperature of 40 °C the evt is 41.6 °C.

1.2.6 Viscosity of Tar Using the Equi-viscous Temperature Viscometer

A direct-reading evt viscometer is illustrated in figure 1.4. Essentially it consists of a cylindrical cup and a cylinder; a viscous drag is imposed on the cylinder by the tar that is contained in the cup. Both the cylinder and the cylindrical tar-cup are made of stainless steel or heavily chromium-plated brass. The cup has an internal diameter of 22 mm while the cylinder has a diameter of 16 mm; there is 3 mm clearance between the bottom of the cylinder and the cup. The cylinder is suspended by a straight beryllium—copper alloy torsion wire 200 mm in length and 0.65 mm in diameter. At the lower end of the torsion wire is a circular flywheel of 92 mm diameter and 340 g mass; it is positioned at a suitable distance above the water bath. On the upper surface of the flywheel 45° divisions are marked and above the flywheel is a fixed pointer.

The upper end of the torsion wire is attached to the torsion head, which can be turned through 180° between two stops. This head and the tar cup are attached to a supporting pillar which can be set by levelling screws so that the main axes of the cup, cylinder torsion wire, flywheel and torsion head are co-linear and vertical. As

Table 1.2 Correction in degrees Celsius to be applied to temperatures of test to give evts[1]

Viscosity in seconds	0	1	2	3	4	5	6	7	8	9
10	− 10.4	− 9.8	− 9.2	− 8.7	− 8.2	− 7.7	− 7.3	− 6.9	− 6.5	− 6.1
20	− 5.7	− 5.4	− 5.1	− 4.8	− 4.5	− 4.3	− 4.0	− 3.8	− 3.5	− 3.3
30	− 3.1	− 2.9	− 2.7	− 2.5	− 2.3	− 2.2	− 2.0	− 1.9	− 1.7	− 1.5
40	− 1.4	− 1.2	− 1.1	− 0.9	− 0.8	− 0.6	− 0.5	− 0.4	− 0.3	− 0.1
50	0	+ 0.1	+ 0.2	+ 0.3	+ 0.5	+ 0.6	+ 0.7	+ 0.8	+ 0.9	+ 1.0
60	+ 1.1	+ 1.2	+ 1.3	+ 1.4	+ 1.5	+ 1.6	+ 1.7	+ 1.7	+ 1.8	+ 1.9
70	+ 2.0	+ 2.1	+ 2.2	+ 2.2	+ 2.3	+ 2.4	+ 2.5	+ 2.5	+ 2.6	+ 2.7
80	+ 2.8	+ 2.8	+ 2.9	+ 3.0	+ 3.0	+ 3.1	+ 3.1	+ 3.2	+ 3.3	+ 3.3
90	+ 3.4	+ 3.5	+ 3.5	+ 3.6	+ 3.6	+ 3.7	+ 3.7	+ 3.8	+ 3.9	+ 3.9
100	+ 4.0	+ 4.0	+ 4.1	+ 4.1	+ 4.2	+ 4.2	+ 4.3	+ 4.3	+ 4.4	+ 4.4
110	+ 4.5	+ 4.6	+ 4.6	+ 4.7	+ 4.7	+ 4.8	+ 4.8	+ 4.9	+ 4.9	+ 5.0
120	+ 5.0	+ 5.1	+ 5.1	+ 5.2	+ 5.2	+ 5.2	+ 5.3	+ 5.3	+ 5.4	+ 5.4
130	+ 5.5	+ 5.5	+ 5.5	+ 5.6	+ 5.6	+ 5.7	+ 5.7	+ 5.7	+ 5.8	+ 5.8
140	+ 5.9	+ 5.9	+ 6.0	+ 6.0	+ 6.0	+ 6.1	+ 6.1	+ 6.1	+ 6.2	+ 6.2

[1] NOTE. That part of the table giving corrections for tars having viscosities between 33 s and 75 s inclusive (indicated by bold type) may alone be used in calculating the evt to be reported. The remainder of the table will be useful in ranging tests.

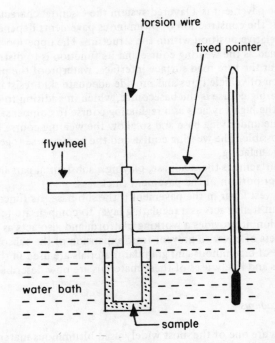

torsion wire

fixed pointer

flywheel

water bath

sample

Figure 1.4 Outline of operation of direct-reading evt viscometer

shown in figure 1.4, the tar cup and cylinder are completely immersed in the water
bath, which also has a manually operated paddle-stirrer and a water-heating device.
Before use the apparatus must be calibrated and the procedure is described in
BS 76.[1]
, To determine the evt of a tar the apparatus is set up and levelled, the tar cup is
then removed and the tar, prepared as previously described, is poured into the cup
to a standard height as indicated by the use of a gauge. Care must be taken to
prevent the tar splashing the sides of the cup during this operation.

The filled cup is then placed in position in the viscometer, the cylinder placed
within the cup and the water bath filled so that the cup and cylinder are both
immersed. The pointer above the flywheel is then set directly above one of the
graduations of the flywheel. The temperature of the water bath is then adjusted to
not less than 10 °C below the expected evt of the tar, the temperature is then
raised at a uniform rate of 1 °C/min. The water is agitated and periodically the
torsion head is turned smartly through 180°; as the tar becomes more fluid the
flywheel will gradually begin to overswing its normal position of rest. As overswing
commences the torsion head is rotated as frequently as possible, allowing the
flywheel to come to rest after each rotation. The temperature in degrees Celsius at
which an overswing of one 45° division is first attained is then the evt of the tar.

1.3 Materials Used for Flexible Pavements

Because a flexible pavement is a layered system the essential characteristics of the
materials used for the construction of bituminous pavements depend to a large
extent on their relative position within the structure. The uppermost layer of a
pavement is defined as the wearing course and its function is to distribute the high
stresses imposed at the tyre road surface interface, waterproof the pavement, resist
the abrasive action of vehicle tyres and provide adequate skid resistance.

Below the wearing course is the basecourse, which in addition to distributing the
loads carried by the highway acts as a regulating course to compensate for any
irregularities in the underlying base and so allow the wearing course to be as uniform
in thickness as possible. The wearing course and the base course together are
referred to as the surfacing.

Beneath the surfacing is the roadbase, playing a substantial part in load spreading.
It occupies a major portion of the pavement thickness.

Finally, the lowest layer in the pavement is the sub-base. Its function is partly
load spreading, but it also acts as a regulating layer to compensate for irregularities
in the soil formation; it provides a working platform and also acts as a layer to give
a required thickness of cover to prevent frost expansion of the subsoil.

A wide variety of bituminous and granular materials are used in these layers and
the characteristics and likely uses of these materials are now described.

1.3.1 Coated Macadams

Coated macadams are one of the most widely used bituminous materials in highway
construction and maintenance. They consist of aggregate that may be bound with

either tar or bitumen to form tarmacadam or bitumen macadam respectively. While different aggregate gradings and grades of binder will produce materials with widely varying properties they all have the same general characteristics.

(1) A reliance on mechanical interlock between the aggregate particles, in addition to cohesion between the particles because of the binder, to resist the stresses caused by wheel loads.

(2) The frequent use of a low-viscosity binder that is usually a cut-back bitumen or a low-viscosity penetration-grade bitumen. The use of low-viscosity binders results in low mixing and laying temperatures. Exceptions are dense bitumen and dense tarmacadam where viscous binders are used.

(3) Because of the relatively open grading of the aggregate combined with a low-viscosity binder these materials are easily compacted. Final compaction is by traffic, causing some problems in highway maintenance when the material is used for patching. Once again dense bitumen and tarmacadam are exceptions.

(4) The open grading of the aggregate results in coated macadam being pervious to water in its early life. Subsequent compaction by traffic will result in the material becoming impervious.

Coated macadams are normally specified by a 'recipe' developed by considerable field experience. Forms of coated macadam that have been in use for considerable periods are incorporated in British Standard specifications while newer materials are evaluated using provisional specifications.

As experience with coated macadams was gained, a series of British Standard specifications was issued for the different form of coated macadam, as follows.

BS 802   Tarmacadam with crushed rock or slag aggregate.
BS 1241   Tarmacadam and tar carpets (gravel aggregate).
BS 1242   Tarmacadam 'tarpaving' for footpaths, playgrounds and
             similar works.
BS 1621   Bitumen macadam with crushed rock or slag aggregate.
BS 1690   Cold asphalt.
BS 2040   Bitumen macadam with gravel aggregate.

The use of six separate stardards resulted in considerable duplication, and so as to rationalise the aggregate gradings and binder contents specified, a new British Standard based on metric units has been issued as BS 4987: Coated Macadam for Roads and other Paved Areas.[7] This British Standard contains recommendations for the composition, manufacture, testing, transporting and laying and laying of the following types of coated macadams.

Group 1. Roadbase material
    40 mm nominal-size dense roadbase macadam

Group 2. Basecourse materials
    40 mm nominal-size open-textured basecourse macadam
    20 mm nominal-size open-textured basecourse macadam
    40 mm nominal-size single course macadam
    40 mm nominal-size dense basecourse macadam
    28 mm nominal-size dense basecourse macadam
    20 mm nominal-size dense basecourse macadam

Group 3. Wearing-course materials
     14 mm nominal-size open-textured wearing-course macadam
     10 mm nominal-size open-textured wearing-course macadam
      6 mm nominal-size medium-textured wearing-course macadam
     14 mm nominal-size dense wearing-course macadam
     10 mm nominal-size dense wearing-course macadam
     Coarse cold asphalt (10 mm nominal-size medium-textured bitumen
        macadam)
     Fine cold asphalt (6 mm nominal size fine-textured bitumen macadam) and
        6 mm nominal size fine-textured tarmacadam

The selection of the appropriate material will depend upon the position of the
material within the layered pavement system (that is, whether it is a roadbase,
basecourse or wearing-course material), on the traffic which is to be carried by the
highway, the thickness of construction, the mandatory requirements to use certain
types of materials on certain categories of road and the preference of the highway
designer.

In BS 4987 the selection according to traffic category is made on the basis of
the present-day flow of commercial vehicles (goods or public service vehicles of
unladen mass exceeding 1500 kg) travelling in one direction over a daily period of
16 h. Category A traffic comprises 300 or more commercial vehicles per day while
Category B traffic is less than this flow.

The consolidated thickness of the layers of material will depend to some extent
on mandatory requirements for the wearing-course and basecourse material but will
also depend upon the required pavement thickness as given by the pavement-
thickness design process.

If the required thickness of a layer is known, this gives an indication of the
appropriate nominal size of material. The nominal size of a coated material is that
sieve size through which between 90, or 95, and 100 per cent of the aggregate will
pass. There is an obvious connection between nominal aggregate size and a suitable
layer thickness because if the layer is too thin relative to the nominal size then
adequate aggregate interlock cannot develop, while if this layer is too thick relative
to the nominal size there will be difficulties in compaction and excessive temperature gradients through the layer during the cooling period after laying. The recommended layer thicknesses for coated macadam are given in Table 1.3.

Frequently the choice of which coated material to use is governed by recommendations of the Department of Transport. In Road Note 29, *A Guide to the
Structural Design of Pavements for New Roads*,[8] the recommendations given in
table 1.4 for the use of coated macadam are made, based in this instance on the
total number of standard axles carried by the pavement during its design life.

1.3.2 Bituminous Roadbase Material

In the early days of road construction in the United Kingdom road pavements
had bases constructed from hand-placed stone. Increasing mechanisation led to the
replacement of the hand-placed stone or pitching by granular material. Full-scale
road experiments by the then Road Research Laboratory demonstrated the

Table 1.3 Recommended layer thickness for coated macadam[7]

Group	Subclause No.	Description	Nominal Size	Range of average thickness of compacted course
			mm	mm
One Roadbase material	2.1.1	Dense	40	65–105 (roadbases in excess of 100 mm thickness to be of two or more courses to provide required total thickness)
Two Basecourse materials	2.2.1	Open-textured	40	}60–80
	2.2.3	Single course	40	
	2.2.4	Dense	40	
	2.2.5	Dense	28	50–60
	2.2.2	Open-textured	20	}35–50
	2.2.6	Dense	20	
Three Wearing course materials	2.2.3	Single course	40	65–80
	2.3.1	Open-textured	14	}25–40
	2.3.4	Dense	14	
	2.3.2	Open-textured	10	}20–25
	2.3.5	Dense	10	
	2.3.3	Medium-textured	6	15–20
	2.3.6	Coarse cold asphalt (10 mm medium-textured bitumen macadam)	10	20–40
	2.3.7	Fine cold asphalt (6 mm fine-textured bitumen macadam)	6	}15–25
	2.3.7	Fine-textured tarmacadam	6	

superior load-carrying properties of bituminous roadbase materials. Subsequently a provisional specification was issued by the Road Research Laboratory and a specification for roadbase material is included in BS 4987 as 40 mm nominal size dense roadbase macadam. The aggregate has a wide range of grading with up to 46 per cent passing a 3.35 mm sieve and between 2 and 8 per cent passing a 75 μm sieve.

Binder contents for crushed rock aggregate are 3.5 ± 0.6 per cent and 4.3 ± 0.6 per cent for bitumen and tar binder respectively. Binder viscosity is 200 or 100 pen bitumen, B50 or B54 tar. This material is very similar to 40 mm nominal-size dense basecourse macadam, which has a higher binder content.

1.3.3 Basecourse Material

Coated macadam basecourses are divided into three types: open-textured macadams, single-course material and dense materials. Open-textured basecourse macadams are characterised by a low percentage of material passing a 3.35 mm sieve and the use of medium-to-low viscosity tar or bitumen binders. Single-course materials serve the function of both a base and a wearing course and are characterised by a larger

Table 1.4 Recommended coated macadam surfacings for newly constructed flexible pavements[8]

	Traffic (cumulative number of standard axles during design life)		
Over 11 millions (1)	2.5–11 millions (2)	0.5–2.5 millions (3)	Less than 0.5 million (4)
Dense bitumen macadam or dense tarmacadam (crushed rock or slag only)	Dense bitumen macadam or dense tarmacadam (see note 2)	Wearing course Minimum thickness 20 mm	Two-course (a) Wearing course – Minimum thickness 20 mm
		Dense tar surfacing	Cold asphalt
			Coated macadam (see notes 1 and 3)
		Cold asphalt (see note 3)	(b) Basecourse Coated macadam (see note 1)
		Medium-textured tarmacadam (to be surface-dressed immediately or as soon as possible (see note 3)	Single course
			Dense tar surfacing

Medium-textured tarmacadam [to be surface-dressed immediately or as soon as possible (see note 3)]

Dense bitumen macadam (see note 3)

Open-textured bitumen macadam (see note 3)

Basecourse

Dense bitumen macadam or dense tarmacadam

Single-course tarmacadam (see notes 1 and 4)

Single-course bitumen macadam (see notes 1 and 4)

Dense bitumen macadam (see note 3)

60 mm of single-course tarmacadam (to be surface-dressed immediately or as soon as possible (see note 3)

60 mm of single-course bitumen macadam (see note 3)

Dense bitumen macadam (see note 3)

Notes

(1) When gravel, other than limestone, is used, 2 per cent of Portland cement should be added to the mix and the percentage of fine aggregate reduced accordingly.

(2) Gravel tarmacadam is not recommended as a basecourse for roads designed to carry more than 2.5 million standard axles.

(3) When the wearing course is neither rolled asphalt nor dense tar surfacing and where it is not intended to apply a surface-dressing immediately to the wearing course, it is essential to seal the construction against the ingress of water by applying a surface dressing either to the roadbase or to the basecourse.

(4) Under a wearing course of rolled asphalt or dense tar surfacing the basecourse should consist of rolled asphalt to BS 594 (Clause 902) or on dense coated macadam (Clause 903 or 904).

nominal size of aggregate, a higher proportion of material passing a 3.35 mm sieve and higher binder contents than open-textured materials. Binder viscosity depends upon traffic intensity because of the wearing-course function of the material.

The dense basecourse macadams provide greater load-carrying ability by a combination of a denser mix due to the higher percentage of finer particles and a consequent higher binder content and higher-viscosity binders. The use of these high-viscosity binders makes it possible to employ dense bitumen or tarmacadam basecourses beneath wearing courses of higher-temperature materials.

1.3.4 Wearing-course Material

Because wearing-course material has to withstand the high stresses imposed at the tyre/road contact and in addition must be able to withstand the destructive action of tyres and weather it has a lower nominal size and a closer grading than basecourse and single-course material.

The effects of weather and traffic action have opposite effects on the optimum binder content. To resist the penetration of moisture the waterproofing action of a higher binder content is desirable. On the other hand the compacting action of traffic makes it desirable to reduce binder contents if slippery patches of binder on the road surface are to be avoided. For this reason differing binder contents are specified for traffic categories A and B. Since it is required to coat the aggregate with a thin film of binder the proportion of binder in a mix will depend on the grading of the aggregate. Wearing-course materials contain smaller stone particles than basecourse materials and for this reason a wearing-course material will have higher binder contents.

BS 4987[7] divides wearing-course material into open-textured and dense materials in 14 and 10 mm nominal sizes. As with basecourse material, the open-textured materials contain relatively low percentages of aggregate passing a 3.35 mm test sieve and use a relatively low-viscosity binder. The dense wearing-course materials contain up to 45 per cent of fine aggregate passing a 3.35 mm sieve and a higher-viscosity binder. Dense materials have greater load-spreading properties than open-textured materials and after some traffic action they become impervious to the passage of water; they do however require a matching dense basecourse.

1.3.5 Cold Asphalt

The division between cold- and hot-process asphalts is sometimes confusing because many cold asphalts are in fact laid warm. Nevertheless cold asphalts, even when laid warm, are placed and compacted at very much lower temperatures than are hot-process asphalts. Aggregate voids are kept to a minimum by careful grading and a lightly coated stone surface. Stability is achieved by the interlocking action of the aggregate, not by the cementing action of the binder and filler matrix as is the case with a hot-process asphalt. Cold asphalt is then similar to a coated macadam in its properties.

Cold asphalts were introduced into the United Kingdom in the 1920s and have found considerable application since that time. Because of the need to have a rough aggregate texture to give stability, a crushed blast-furnace slag is frequently used in heavily trafficked situations.

This material is now specified in BS 4987 : 1973. There are two nominal sizes, 10 and 6 mm, and tar, petroleum bitumen and cut-back bitumen may be used as a binder. The binder content is between 4.9 and 8.6 per cent for crushed-rock aggregate — usually just enough to lubricate the stone and allow the good compaction that develops aggregate interlock.

Because of the fine texture of the material it is easily laid by hand or machine, it knits together easily and is a self-healing material. As with coated macadam, fine cold asphalt obtains considerable compaction by traffic action. BS 4987 contains specifications for fine and coarse cold asphalts made with slag aggregate, crushed rocks and limestone for traffic loadings A and B.

As with other bituminous materials, binder contents increase with increasing roughness of stone surface texture and with decreasing traffic intensity.

The grade of binder depends upon the traffic category, whether the material is to be laid in summer or winter conditions, and whether the fine or cold asphalt is to be hand- or machine-laid. For heavy traffic conditions and winter laying by machine the bitumen viscosity is specified to range from 100 s to 300 pen. For the fine cold asphalt (6 mm nominal-size fine-textured bitumen macadam and tarmacadam) B42 or B46 tar may be used as the binder.

1.3.6 Rolled Asphalt

Rolled asphalts (hot process) consist of a dense mixture of sand-sized particles passing a 2.36 mm sieve, retained on a 75 μm sieve, and referred to as fine aggregate, or very fine material passing a 75 μm sieve referred to as filler, and a binder of asphaltic cement. Frequently, large-sized stone particles retained on a 2.36 mm sieve are included in the mix to give additional stability under heavy traffic flow and also to give a more economical mix.

The material is dense and impervious from the time of laying, does not undergo any appreciable compaction by traffic after laying, and when it contains a suitable stone content has great mechanical strength. In contrast to coated macadams, rolled asphalts gain their strength from the sand, filler, binder matrix and not from the interlocking action of aggregate particles. For these reasons it is frequently preferred as a surfacing material for city streets, where frequent reinstatements are necessary, and is specified as the surfacing for motorways, where great strength is necessary.

Since the first use of rolled asphalt as a road pavement material in the United Kingdom at the end of the last century, the specified mixes have undergone considerable development as traffic conditions have changed. The results of this experience have been embodied in BS 594, Part 1, Hot Rolled Asphalt for Roads and Other Paved Areas[9] and BS 594, Part 2, Specification for the Transport, Laying and Composition of Rolled Asphalt.

The binders which may be incorporated in the hot rolled asphalt mixes may be penetration-grade bitumen, lake asphalt–bitumen mixtures or pitch–bitumen mixtures. The viscosity of the penetration-grade bitumen may vary from 35 to 100 pen, lake asphalt–bitumen from 35 to 70 pen and pitch–bitumen from 50 to 70 pen.

Hot rolled àsphalt mixes may be either recipe-type mixes or design mixes based on Marshall-type tests carried out on the total mix. The composition of all rolled asphalt mixtures is given in a series of tables. Aggregate gradings are given as single curves covering all aggregate sizes from the largest down to the filler. Binder contents are specified for differing types of coarse aggregate and when a designed mix is used a minimum binder content is given. The mixes are designated by two numbers where the first figure denotes the nominal coarse aggregate content and the second the nominal size of the aggregate, where coarse aggregate is material substantially retained on the 2.36 mm test sieve.

For roadbase, basecourse and regulating-course material mixes range from one containing 50 per cent of coarse aggregate and having a 10 mm nominal size aggregate to a mix containing 60 per cent of coarse aggregate and with a 40 mm nominal size of aggregate.

For wearing courses there are two types of mix recipes. Those mixes of traditional composition with a gap-graded aggregate and where the fine aggregate is usually sand are designated by the letter F. Mixes with a coarser fine-aggregate grading, such as are associated with a crushed rock or slag, are designated by the letter C. Fine aggregate is defined as material which substantially passes a 2.36 mm sieve and can be sand or fines produced by crushing material which would have been suitable as a coarse aggregate.

When a type-F mix is specified not more than 5 per cent by mass should be retained on a 2.36 mm sieve and not more than 8 per cent by mass should pass a 75 μm sieve. For type-C mixes the relevant percentages should be 10 per cent and 17 per cent respectively.

When unfamiliar aggregates are used in the production of rolled asphalt wearing courses then it is useful to employ a laboratory design procedure to determine the appropriate binder content. The starting point in the design of a rolled asphalt wearing course is the selection of a suitable aggregate grading from the previously discussed range of recipes.

The method uses the Marshall test equipment to determine the binder content and binder type as will be used for the plant mix. The Marshall test method determines Marshall stability and flow and in addition mix density and compacted aggregate density can be calculated.

It is recommended[17] that there should be precise conformity to all the specified requirements for apparatus and procedure and if this is achieved then the resulting binder content will be reliable. The general test procedure is to mix and compact three specimens at each binder content and sufficient mixes to cover the desired range of binder contents necessary to determine the optimum, including at least nine binder contents at intervals of 0.5 per cent of total mix with at least three binder contents on each side of the optimum value.

The average value of stability, flow, mix density and compacted aggregate density for the three specimens at each binder content are then plotted against the binder content and a smooth curve drawn through the resulting point values. The optimum binder content is then the average value of the maximum value obtained from the stability, mix density and compacted aggregate density curves. The flow value at optimum binder content is also reported.

BS 594[9] gives guidance on suitable stability and flow values for rolled asphalt wearing-course material. For pavements where the design traffic is less than 1500 commercial vehicles per lane per day it is recommended that the stability should be in the range 2 to 8 kN, 1500 to 6000 commercial vehicles per lane per day in the range 4 to 8 kN and over 6000 commercial vehicles per day 6 to 10 kN. For stabilities up to 8 kN the maximum flow value should be 5 mm; where the stability is in excess of 8 kN a maximum flow value of 7 mm is permitted.

Guidance on the selection of rolled asphalt mixes is also given in BS 594. For roadbase mixtures it is recommended that one of the recipes for roadbase, basecourse and regulating-course material should be used, the nominal size of aggregate being selected with regard to the layer thickness. In normal circumstances a 50 pen binder is used although a 70 pen binder may be used in lightly trafficked situations. Basecourse mixtures are selected from the same table as roadbase mixtures and again nominal aggregate size should be related to layer thickness. Coarse-aggregate content also depends on layer thickness but in normal circumstances a 60 per cent coarse-aggregate content is usual for basecourses, with a 50 per cent coarse-aggregate content for regulating courses.

For wearing courses traditional rolled asphalts have been composed of sand fine aggregate and 50 pen binder. If crushed fines (or some harsher sands) are used a softer binder can be used. When intense traffic is to be expected then a 35 pen binder or crushed fines may be employed to give greater stability. If the rolled asphalt is to be placed in situations where the weather is normally colder and wetter than the average in the United Kingdom it is recommended that an additional 0.5 per cent of binder be used to assist in the durability of the mix.

1.3.7 Asphaltic Concrete

Asphaltic concrete differs from hot rolled asphalt (as specified in BS 594) in having a continuous-aggregate grading whereas BS 594 rolled asphalt has a gap-graded aggregate. It has found extensive use in the United States and is used today in that country for the surfacing of most major flexible highways, in contrast to the United Kingdom where rolled asphalt to BS 594 is the surfacing material used for heavily trafficked routes.

Asphaltic concrete consists of a carefully proportioned mix of continuously graded aggregate, usually with a nominal size of 20 mm ($\frac{3}{4}$ in.), mineral filler and penetration-grade bitumen. The composition of basecourses and wearing courses is somewhat similar, the major difference being the grading of the aggregate. Larger aggregate sizes are usual in basecourses because they are laid and compacted to greater thicknesses and do not need to have such dense natures because they do not have to resist traffic action.

In contrast to BS 594 asphalts, which have developed as a result of experience and where the sand/bitumen matrix has great importance, asphaltic concretes are usually designed by some mechanical laboratory-testing procedure. The selection of a suitable mix is therefore rather a trial-and-error process, but the usual starting point in the design process is to ensure that

(1) The aggregate grading chosen will give as dense a mix as possible.

(2) The maximum size of aggregate is not greater than 75 per cent of the compacted layer thickness. This is particularly important with wearing courses

because it is necessary to ensure adequate compaction to give a dense layer and also it should be remembered that layer thicknesses may vary due to constructional defects and tolerances.

Other properties, in addition to the grading, are of course essential. The aggregate should be resistant to polishing. If it is to be used for a wearing course it should have adequate impact and crushing strength and should not be attacked by frost. The criterion used for aggregates in conventional open-textured mixtures should be applied. There is also the question of aggregate shape — a rounded gravel is less likely to produce a stable material than a crushed stone and this should be remembered in aggregate selection.

When the fine aggregate is considered, that is, sand-sized particles (passing a 3.35 mm sieve, retained by a 75 μm sieve), then greater resistance to deformation is likely to be obtained if the particles are angular crushed material rather than water-worn, natural sand deposits. Nevertheless in many situations natural sands prove perfectly suitable for asphaltic concrete.

The quantity of filler in the mix will affect the stability of the material — an increase in stability will result from an increase in filler content because of a reduction in air-voids content. On the other hand, too high a filler content can lead to brittle mixes.

A binder type which produces satisfactory mixes is bitumen of 85 to 100 pen grade. In particular heavily trafficked situations a harder binder may be used but the cost of the material and laying will be increased. In colder situations a softer binder may be necessary because of laying difficulties and because of a desire to cheapen the mix. As with all bituminous materials that are mixed in heated conditions it should be remembered that the binder is considerably harder after mixing than before — a change caused by the loss of volatiles and by oxidisation.

1.3.8 Bituminous Materials in Europe

An interesting review of the use of bituminous pavement materials in Europe has been given by Chipperfield and Leonard.[10] They state that the majority of European countries use Marshall-designed asphaltic concretes for wearing courses with 18 mm maximum aggregate size. Finer gradings are favoured in the Federal Republic of Germany, Switzerland and Austria with high filler contents. It is felt that these resist better low temperatures and the ingress of water. Very fine gradings can, however, lead to smooth surfacings lacking texture and skid resistance.

Asphaltic concrete employs a continuous grading with close packing and therefore interlock of the aggregate fractions, and the binder—filler mortar largely fills the voids in the aggregate, providing a dense impermeable structure.

Another important type of surfacing material is Gussasphalt, a heavy-duty dense asphalt surfacing of the mastic asphalt type. It was developed in the Federal Republic of Germany and has largely been employed there for surfacing motorways. It has also been used to a limited extent in Austria and Switzerland.

Gussasphalt differs from conventional mastic asphalt in that it has a lower binder content, but uses a softer binder and sand as the fine aggregate component (not limestone), and includes a proportion of coarse aggregate. These factors enable the material to be machine-laid.

Gussasphalt is mixed in a normal asphalt mixer at 180 to 240 °C and then discharged into cookers with some form of heating and also a stirring mechanism, which continues the mixing process for 45 to 60 min to ensure a homogeneous

At the laying site the cookers are emptied on to the binder course and a special laying machine fitted with a heated screed is used to level the material to the required depth. After cooling, lightly coated chippings are applied to the surface, which is then rolled using a patterned roller that not only pushes the chippings into the surface but also imparts diagonal indentations.

In Scandinavia a frequently used heavy-duty surfacing is Topeka, which closely resembles hot-rolled asphalt. It is a gap-graded asphalt manufactured to a recipe specification and is used for the most heavily trafficked roads where excessive wear is anticipated. The binder is either 50/70 or 80/100 pen, depending upon traffic and climate, and the material is normally designated by stone size and content. Pre-coated chips are frequently used with Topeka to provide skid resistance.

Denmark uses an equivalent surfacing material, Asfaltbeton med Nedtromlede Skaever ABS, which is similar to hot rolled asphalt. The stone fraction can be crushed rock or gravel, with a preference for light-reflecting surfacings. It is common to replace up to 20 per cent of the stone fraction with calcined flint, and natural or synthetic aggregate of light colour is often selected for the pre-coated chippings.

Oiled gravel has been used in a number of countries but is particularly associated with Scandinavia, where it has been developed to replace water-bound gravel. The gravel is invariably of local origin and crushed to give a minimum of 50 per cent of broken material in the mix. The binders employed include fuel oil and cut-back bitumen, but the most widely used is referred to as Scandinavian road oil, which is blended to meet the Scandinavian Road Board Specification.

The cold damp gravel and the road oil, at about 90 °C, are mixed in the presence of an adhesion agent; a typical binder content would be 3.5 per cent. Mixing can be effected in a normal asphalt plant but mixers of a much simpler design are commonly used.

Oiled gravel is often manufactured in advance of laying work because it can be stockpiled without undue deterioration. Spreading can be achieved by grader, simple spreader-box or paver. Oiled gravel is normally laid to give a compacted thickness of about 40 mm. Rolling is not essential, although on high-speed roads a few passes with a pneumatic-tyred roller are used to reduce the risk of flying stones

In Europe during recent years there has been a greatly increased use of bitumen-bound mixes for roadbases. In the Federal Republic of Germany alone between 1966 and 1971 the proportion of bitumen-bound base course in Federal roads nearly doubled. In most other countries the advantages and convenience of base construction using bituminous mixtures have been recognised and exploited.

Basecourse mixtures range from asphaltic concretes to sand bitumens. In some countries, including Switzerland, basecourses are dense mixtures, while in others they are of lean high-stone-content materials that, although permeable, have good load-bearing properties. The inclusion of some rounded stone in basecourse mixtures has been accepted until recently in a number of countries. At present, however, for heavy-duty pavements, most of the aggregate has to be crushed.

The French have been active in the development of gravel-asphalts (gravel-bitumens) for roadbases. These materials can be compared with dense bitumen macadam but with a higher filler content and a 4 per cent binder content. Such mixes are designed on the basis of laboratory compaction and stability tests. They are also tested in an immersion—compression routine to ensure that they do not decrease markedly in strength if in contact with water over long periods. Gravel-asphalts of this type are also being used as overlays to existing roads.

In laying these materials the normal maximum layer thickness is approximately 200 mm. For this reason laying machines require heavy vibrating screeds. Compaction is carried out using a pneumatic-tyred roller immediately behind the finisher and the load imposed by each wheel should be greater than 2 tonnes. In addition, a vibrating roller is used to achieve the required density.

In areas without stone or gravel deposits, sand—bitumen mixtures provide good results when used as base-course materials. In Holland these have been employed for many years. They are produced in normal asphalt plants with dune sand and 50/60 pen bitumen, using a binder content of 3.5 to 4.5 per cent. Usually about 5 per cent of limestone filler is added to the mix to gain the required stability. The voids content of such mixes can be very high (up to 20 per cent). These materials have been used for basecourses or for the lower layer of basecourses for major roads and are placed on compacted sand, which normally forms the drainage layer. Compaction of hot sand mixes is carried out using a 2-tonne tandem roller because the material is very soft until it cools.

1.4 Granular Materials in Highway Pavements

Granular materials may be used in a bound or unbound form in the construction of highway pavements, either as a base in flexible road construction or as a sub-base for flexible or rigid pavements. The Specification for Road and Bridge Works issued by the Department of Transport[11] specifies two types of granular material for use in sub-bases. Type 1 material is a crushed-rock, crushed-slag, crushed-concrete or well-burnt non-plastic shale. The material is well graded as given in table 1.5, and the material passing the 425 μm BS sieve must be non-plastic. Type 2 material may be a natural-sand, gravel, crushed-rock, crushed-slag, crushed-concrete or well-burnt non-plastic shale. This material, while being well graded, has a finer particle size than Type 1 material and the material passing the 425 μm sieve must have a plasticity index of less than 6. When used as a sub-base the material must have, or be

Table 1.5 Grading of type 1 and 2 sub-base material from clauses 803 and 804 of the Department of Transport Standard Specification[11]

BS Sieve Size	Percentage by Mass Passing	
	Type 1	Type 2
75 mm	100	100
37.5 mm	85—100	85—100
10 mm	40—70	45—100
5 mm	25—45	25—85
600 μm	8—22	8—45
75 μm	0—10	0—10

considered to have, a California Bearing Ratio of at least 20 or 30 per cent, according to the traffic loading. It must also be protected from wet conditions.

Granular material may also be used as a roadbase in the form of dry-bound macadam, one of the earlier forms of roadbase construction that replaced hand-placed stones or pitching. Crushed rock or crushed slag of either 50 or 40 mm nominal size is used as the coarse aggregate, and fine aggregate is also used that all passes a 5 mm BS sieve. This fine aggregate must be kept dry until required for use. The coarse aggregate is spread first to a thickness within the range 75 to 100 mm and rolled; the fine aggregate is next spread on the top to a thickness of approximately 25 mm and vibrated into the voids between the larger particles. Because the load-spreading ability of a dry-bound roadbase will greatly depend on the lack of voids in the compacted material, maximum permitted layer thickness is relatively low, so that the fine material can fully fill the voids between the larger particles. Recommendations of the Department of Transport[11] limit the use of this material in the United Kingdom to pavements that will carry not more than 11 million standard axles during their design lives. There are also restrictions on the use of natural sands and gravels for trunks roads in the United Kingdom.

Alternatively a wet-mix macadam may be used as a roadbase, the grading having a nominal size of 37.5 mm and a closely controlled grading with up to 30 per cent of the material passing a 2.36 mm sieve. The moisture content of the wet-mix macadam is specified to be within ±0.5 per cent of the optimum as determined by the Vibrating Hammer Method, and this and the grading of the material must be carefully controlled by sampling and testing because of the loss of strength that can occur due to small variations from the specification. As with dry-bound material, placing of the roadbase should follow as soon as possible in an attempt to reduce the ingress of moisture. Wet-mix macadam is recommended by the Department of Transport[11] for use as a road base in the United Kingdom for all traffic intensities but excluding motorways and dual trunk roads.

1.5 Cement-stabilised Materials in Highway Pavements

The term 'cement-stabilised materials' describes a group of materials in which the addition of cement makes a previously unsuitable material perform in a satisfactory manner or improves the qualities of a satisfactory material. These materials are (1) soil cement, in which cement is added to a finely graded material that frequently exists as the naturally occurring subsoil, (2) cement-bound granular material using naturally occurring gravel-sand, (3) washed or processed granular material, (4) crushed rock or slag and (5) lean concrete using aggregate with a closely controlled grading.

When these materials are to be used as a sub-base the Department of Transport[11] recommends the use of soil cement and cement-bound granular material as a sub-base for all categories of highway. Lean concrete is recommended as the sub-base for all concrete pavements.

It also recommends that roadbases be constructed of soil cement only when the anticipated future traffic loading does not exceed 1.5 million standard axles and of cement-bound granular material only when the loading does not exceed 5 million

standard axles. Lean concrete, however, may be used as a roadbase for all categories
of traffic loading.

1.5.1 Soil Cement

Soil cement may be formed by the addition of cement to a wide range of materials,
including natural soils, chalk, pulverised fuel ash or other waste products such as
spent oil shale or well-burnt shale, crushed rock or slag and processed granular
material. It is recommended[11] that the material be well graded, with a coefficient
of uniformity of not less than 5, which will produce a well-closed surface after
compaction. All the material must pass a 50 mm sieve and material passing a 425 μm
sieve should not have liquid and plastic limits greater than 45 and 20 per cent
respectively. This is a practical restriction necessary because of the problems of
incorporating the cement in cohesive materials. Lime can reduce the cohesion of a
clay but normally in such circumstances an alternative form of construction would
be used.

A minimum 7-day crushing strength is specified by the Department of Transport
as an average value from five test specimens of 2.8 or 3.5 N/mm² (cylindrical,
cubical specimens respectively). Because of the possibility of obtaining very variable
results it is also specified that the coefficient of variation of crushing strength of
five successive batches of five test specimens shall not exceed 40 per cent.

Most industrial countries have large deposits of waste materials and in certain
circumstances they can be stabilised with cement to give a useful alternative to
conventional materials. Sherwood and Pocock[12] have investigated the performance
of the following types of waste material found in the United Kingdom: chalk,
pulverised fuel ash, colliery shale, spent oil shale and quarry waste.

Chalk represents 15 per cent of the major geological formations of the United
Kingdom occurring mainly in the South of England. Pulverised fuel ash is a waste
product of coal-burning power stations; approximately 8 million tons are produced
annually. Colliery shale is the main waste produce of coal mining; it consists of two
types, rock and shale, which are usually dumped on the same spoil heaps together
with small quantities of coal. They are thus very variable in composition and there
is the possibility of spontaneous combustion, burnt shales having very different
properties from unburnt shales. Spent oil shale is a similar material to colliery shale;
it is the waste product of the now extinct shale-oil industry in Scotland.

Quarry waste is an extremely variable material and only those materials containing a suitable quantity of non-plastic soil particles are considered.

None of these materials were found suitable for pavement construction unless
stabilised with cement, and the cost of the cement stabilisation must be added to
the cost of the raw material. Normally this will imply using these stabilised materials
in areas where roadstone is not readily available and where the waste material has
not to be hauled far.

The greatest disadvantage of these waste materials was found to be their frost
susceptibility together with their varied physical properties. It was found, however,
that when these materials contained sufficient cement to produce the required
compressive strength for the Department of Transport specification, none of them
were frost-susceptible.

When the minimum compressive-strength recommendations were considered, it was found that chalk required a cement content of 14 per cent to achieve the strength requirements for cubical specimens of 3.5 N/mm^2 after 7 days' curing.[13]

Pulverised fuel ash is available from power stations in two forms: (1) lagoon ash, a very variable product, particularly with regard to grading, and (2) hopper ash, which differs materially between different power stations but is reasonably consistent when obtained from one power station – this type of ash has been used extensively for cement stabilisation.

When stabilised with 10 per cent cement the ashes from differing power stations show marked variations in 7-day unconfined compressive strength owing to differences in compacted dry density and the pozzolanic activity of different ashes that allows them to react with the lime liberated by the hydration of the cement.

The results of tests on pulverised fuel ash from eight British power stations showed that when stabilised with 10 per cent of cement, five of the eight ashes would meet the 7-day strength requirements, the remaining three ashes giving strengths which were so low that at least 15 per cent of cement would be required to reach satisfactory strengths. Conversely 10 per cent of cement would be an excessive amount for the stabilisation of the ash from three of the stations.

Considerable use has been made of pulverised fuel ash for the construction of pavement sub-bases, car parks and similar areas.

Burnt colliery shale, when obtained with correct grading requirements, can be used in an unstabilised form provided it is not subject to frost attack. For material within 450 mm of the surface or for poorly graded material it is necessary to stabilise the shale with cement. The addition of 10 per cent of cement results in the minimum strength requirement being easily reached. It has been shown[14] that 5 per cent is sufficient to reduce frost susceptibility.

One difficulty which must be remembered is the presence of sulphate in the shale. Cement-stabilised shales should have a total sulphate content of more than 1 per cent by weight of sulphate.[16]

Unburnt colliery shale has not been used to any large extent in the past for roadworks because of a fear of spontaneous combustion, but its use is now permitted under conditions stipulated by the Road Research Laboratory and the Department of Transport.[15,16] Most unburnt shale is not suitable for base or sub-base construction because it is liable to soften on exposure to water; if, however, they are stabilised with approximately 7 per cent of cement a satisfactory material is likely to result.

Spent oil shale is a similar material to colliery shale. The unburnt material suffers from frost susceptibility but it has been noted that the addition of about 5 per cent reduces frost heave to acceptable limits. Quarry wastes are naturally very variable materials but, in general, materials with low silt and clay contents are likely to require least cement and be easier to mix.

1.5.2 Cement-bound Granular Material

Cement-bound granular material is normally produced from 'as dug' aggregate selected or blended to produce a continuous grading with a 37.5 mm nominal size. As with soil cement the Department of Transport specifies[11] an average 7-day crushing strength of five test specimens of 3.5 N/mm^2 for cubical specimens and a coefficient of variation of crushing strength of five successive batches of five test specimens not exceeding 25 per cent. To achieve this strength the cement content is likely to be in the range of 4 to 8 per cent, depending upon the type of aggregate which is being stabilised. This type of material is intermediate in character between soil cement and lean concrete. Because the aggregate grading limits are wider than those for lean concrete the material is cheaper. However, because the aggregate will frequently be gravel used directly from the quarry there is the possibility of considerable variation in material properties making site quality control of importance. This type of material will normally be mixed in a paddle- or pan-type mixer.

1.5.3 Lean Concrete

Lean concrete is a high-quality material which has found considerable use as a sub-base beneath concrete pavements and as a roadbase. It uses aggregates of the quality used in conventional concrete.

The use of this material as a roadbase appears to have evolved during the 1930s but received an added impetus in the late 1940s and 1950s when there were periodic shortages of cement in the United Kingdom. The reduced cement content that was possible when the material was used as a base (together with a bituminous surface) compared to a conventional concrete slab was attractive, and at the same time the difficulties of joint construction and riding surface quality were removed.

The Department of Transport specification[11] gives the recommended grading for 40 and 20 mm nominal-size material. The cement aggregate ratio will normally be between 1:15 and 1:20. Mixes richer than a 1:12 ratio should not be used but some limestone aggregates with a fine proportion of fines can become cementitious, and if the required compressive strength can be met, lower cement contents are possible. It should be remembered, however, that mixing techniques and quality control will become more important, to ensure a homogeneous material.

Concrete strength is measured in the Department of Transport Specification[11] by a cube-compression test. A testing sequence is given which is generally met if the average 28-day strength is 14 N/mm^2. A 7-day test is also given to ensure that low-strength material is detected early in the construction process. After compaction the average density is specified as not being less than 95 per cent of the theoretical dry density with zero air content.

Moisture content of the mix is selected to ensure satisfactory compaction by rolling using smooth-wheeled, rubber-tyred or vibrating rollers. If the mix is too dry the surface remains loose, while too wet a mix will result in an irregular surface with the roller picking up the material. Normally the water content is selected as the optimum for compaction and is in the region of 5 to 7 per cent by weight.

Lean-concrete sub-bases are increasingly being placed by slip-form pavers. In this case compaction is achieved by the use of vibration, and it is then necessary to increase the water content to between 7 and 11 per cent. The material is referred to as wet lean concrete and the Department of Transport specification limits its use to sub-bases.

Normal free-fall mixers may be used for the production of lean concrete and the maximum time that should elapse between mixing and compaction is recommended as 2 h. When two-layer construction is used the placing and compaction of the upper layer should follow as soon as possible after the completion of the lower layer.

References

(1) BS 76: 1974   Tars for Road Purposes
(2) BS 3690: 1982   Bitumens for Building and Civil Engineering, Part 1: Specification for Bitumens for Road Purposes

(3) BS 434: 1973   Bitumen Road Emulsions (Anionic and Cationic), Part 1: 1973   Requirements; Part 2: 1973   Recommendations for Use
(4) BS 4692: 1971   Determination of Softening Point of Bitumen (Ring and Ball)
(5) BS 4691: 1974   Determination of Penetration of Bituminous Materials
(6) BS 4693: 1971   Determination of Viscosity of Cutback Bitumen and Road Oil
(7) BS 4987: 1973   Coated Macadam for Roads and Other Paved Areas
(8) DoE, Road Research Laboratory Road Note 29, 3rd ed., *A Guide to the Structural Design of Pavements for New Roads* (HMSO, 1970)
(9) BS 594: 1985   Hot Rolled Asphalt for Roads and Other Paved Areas, Part 1: Specification for Constituent Materials and Asphalt Mixtures

(10) E. H. Chipperfield and M. J. Leonard, 'How Our European Neighbours Tackle Bitumen Road Construction', *J. Instn. highw. Engrs*, 23 (1976) 9–19
(11) Department of Transport, *Specification for Road and Bridge Works*, 5th ed. (HMSO, 1976)
(12) P. T. Sherwood and R. G. Pocock, 'The Utilization of Cement Stabilized Waste Materials in Road Construction', *Rds Rd Constr.* 47 (1969) 43–50
(13) R. G. Pocock, Transport and Road Research Laboratory Report LR 328: *The Use of Cement Stabilized Chalk in Road Construction* (Crowthorne, 1970) *A Laboratory Investigation of the Physical and Chemical Properties of Burnt Colliery Shale* (Crowthorne, 1967)
(15) J. R. Lake, Road Research Laboratory Technical Note TN 317 (revised) *Unburnt Colliery Shale – Its Possible Use as a Road Fill Material* (Crowthorne, 1968)
(16) Department of Transport, Technical Memorandum H4/74 (London, 1974)

(17) BS 598: 1985   Sampling and Examination of Bituminous Mixtures for Roads and Other Paved Areas, Part 3: Methods for Design and Physical Testing

2

The Production and Testing of Bituminous Materials

2.1 Mixing Plants for Bituminous Highway Materials

The operation of proportioning the various aggregate sizes, adding binder and mixing the whole to produce as far as possible a homogeneous mass is a relatively simple process if a soft binder is employed; quality control is not important and only a small amount of mixed material is required. All that is required is a heated tray and several men with shovels.

Production of large quantities of material with highly viscous binders to exacting specifications is a much more complex task, however, and various specialised items of plant have been evolved to meet these needs.

2.1.1 Coated-macadam Mixing Plants

Traditionally, mixing plants developed in two separate ways: one type of plant for the production of coated macadam and another for producing asphalts. Because coated macadams frequently have binders of low viscosity and contain a relatively low proportion of fine material these plants are often sited close to the aggregate source, making it necessary to haul the mixed material for considerable distances to the laying site.

In a typical coated-macadam plant a range of aggregate sizes appropriate to the grading of the material being produced is placed in storage bins that have at their lowest points devices allowing a weighed quantity of each aggregate size to be discharged onto a conveyor. A batch of aggregate is then heated in an oil-fired batch heater before being discharged into a mixer, the binder and the filler being added separately before the mixing process commences. After mixing, the coated macadam is discharged directly into road transport or else conveyed to insulated storage bins. An outline diagram of a typical plant is shown in figure 2.1.

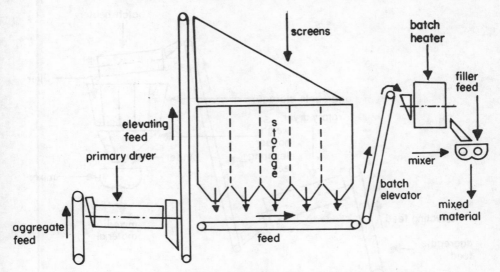

Figure 2.1 Outline of the arrangement of a coated-macadam plant

2.1.2 Asphalt Mixing Plants

Rolled asphalt is delivered to the laying site at high temperatures and for this reason it is frequently necessary for the mixing plant to be sited within a reasonable hauling distance of the laying site. For this reason asphalt mixing plants are commonly made in a form allowing them to be moved closer to the site of construction operations. Even in industrial areas where there is likely to be a reasonably constant demand for asphalt the plant may still be designed for portability.

In addition to the high mixing temperature of rolled asphalt it frequently contains 35 per cent or more of sand, which may be damp or saturated, requiring large amounts of heat to dry it and to complete the heating process. For this reason the layout of an asphalt mixing plant differs from a coated-macadam mixing plant.

As can be seen in figure 2.2 the coarse and fine aggregate is dried and heated in a continuous oil-fired rotary dryer. From the dryer the mixed aggregate is conveyed to the screens and after screening discharged into heated aggregate storage hoppers, which then feed the twin-shaft rotary mixer. The capacity of the hoppers is small compared with a coated-macadam plant, usually not containing more than the aggregate required for half an hour's production.

While a coated-macadam plant cannot be used to produce asphalt it is possible for an asphalt plant to produce coated macadams.

2.1.3 Drum-mixing Plants

A range of plants in which the binder is added to the aggregate during the drying and heating process and referred to as drum mixers is gaining increasing popularity

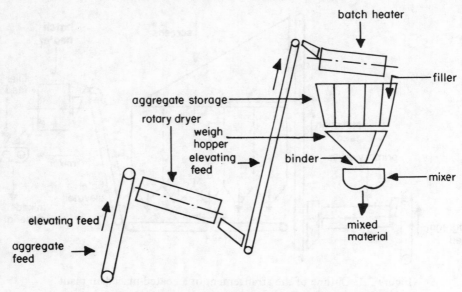

Figure 2.2 Outline of the arrangement of an asphalt plant

in the United States. There are variations between the various makes of plant but they have a basic common process that is illustrated in figure 2.3. Graded aggregates are blended by volume in a cold undried condition, together with any filler which is required, on to a belt conveyor which incorporates a belt weigher. The aggregate is then fed into a drum mixer and at some point during the drying and heating operation the hot binder is added. The binder supply is metered and the quantity of binder added is adjusted automatically according to the signal from the belt weigher. Within the drum mixer the aggregate is dried, heated and mixed with the hot binder; these operations are continuous but each of the processes merges with the other. After discharge from the drum mixer it is normally necessary to store the mixed material because of the continuous nature of the production process and the intermittent nature of the demand.

This process has many advantages in that the separate predrying and heating of the aggregate is eliminated, so that a hot-aggregate elevator, screening deck, hot-aggregate storage bins, weigh-hoppers and pugmill are not required. There is also the advantage that dust emission is greatly reduced because the aggregate is either moist or in contact with the binder throughout the greater part of the mixing process.

In an attempt to evaluate the effectiveness of the mixing process a study team from the Transport and Road Research Laboratory, the Engineering Intelligence Division of the Department of the Environment and a representative of the Asphalt and Coated Macadam Association visited the United States in 1974. Their conclusions on the operation of this type of mixer are given in *Bituminous Drum Mixing Plants in the U.S.A.*[1] and reproduced below.

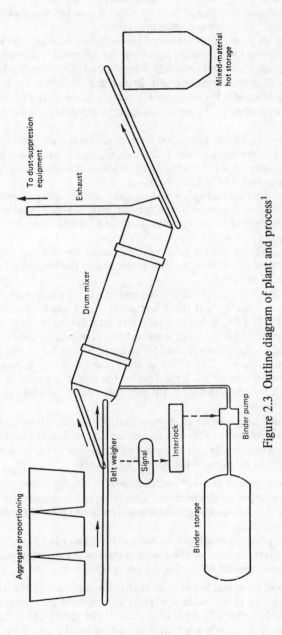

Figure 2.3 Outline diagram of plant and process[1]

(1)   Mixed materials, containing a range of aggregates and penetration-grade petroleum bitumens and produced by the drum-mixing process at temperatures similar to those used in the United Kingdom, were well coated and handled in a normal way during paving operations.

(2) The use of consistent stockpiles and accurate cold feeders to proportion the aggregates, together with the aggregate/binder interlock system on the plant, produced mixed materials that generally complied with the specification requirements for composition. Compliance with British specifications for binder content would not be maintained without more effective control of the plant operations but compliance with the requirements for aggregate grading should not be difficult to achieve.

(3) Tests on the binder recovered from drum-mixed materials showed less hardening than is found with binder from conventionally produced mixes. There was a slight possibility of some contamination and softening of the binder when heavy burner fuels were not efficiently burnt.

(4) The use of large stockpiles of aggregate with consistent moisture contents and the normal production of only one type of material made temperature control simple. This was reflected in very small variations in the temperature of the mixed materials leaving the drum.

(5) The mixing temperatures being used during the visit were rarely below 105 °C and were similar to those usually employed in the United Kingdom for the equivalent grades of bitumen.

(6) At the mixing temperatures used and at outputs well within the capability of the plants it was unlikely that there was more than 1 per cent of 'free' water in the mixture leaving the drum. No evidence was seen during the visit of the use of the relatively low mixing and laying temperatures reported in the early papers where mechanical compaction was said to be aided by the lubricating effect of 2 to 3 per cent of residual water. The effect of the presence of any substantial quantity of residual water on the behaviour of the mixed material during paving and rolling, on the subsequent long-term performance of the laid material, has not been clearly established.

(7) There was no evidence to suggest that the service life of drum-mixed material would be inferior to that of conventionally produced mixtures.

(8) Drum-mixing plants can be operated with very low emission levels provided full account is taken of the following factors

    (a) the moisture content and dustiness of the aggregate,
    (b) the output of the plant in relation to its rated capacity,
    (c) the dust-suppression equipment required under the operating conditions,
    (d) the position along the drum that the binder is added,
    (e) the temperature of the material leaving the drum in relation to the characteristics of the binder being used.

(9) There was a general impression that the economics of the drum-mixing process were attractive to the plant operators and that the purchasers of mixed materials were likely to benefit from lower costs. The capital, running and maintenance costs should be lower than for conventional plant. Also, the basic simplicity, mobility and ease of erection of the plant should lower overall costs

especially where plant has to be moved frequently and where high output is an advantage.

(10) Essentially the State specifications demanded the same quality of material from the drum-mixing plant as from conventional mixing plant. Small reductions were sometimes made in the minimum temperatures for production and laying but the usual compaction requirements were maintained. The maximum residual moisture content was generally increased to 3 per cent although in some cases lower figures of 1.0 or 1.5 per cent were specified.

(11) There is no reason why a U.K. Provisional Specification should not be issued covering all bitumen macadams prepared with penetration-grade petroleum bitumens, and rolled asphalt base and basecourse. Trials would be necessary to establish the suitability of the process for the production of

- (a) wearing-course rolled asphalt, with either bitumen or pitch/bitumen,
- (b) tarmacadams,
- (c) materials containing cut-back bitumens.

2.1.4 The Wibau Dustless Asphalt Plant

The Wibau dustless asphalt plant has been developed in Western Europe and differs from conventional plants in that the binder is mixed with the wet and cold aggregate before it is heated. An adhesive-promoting agent, 'Adhistab', is incorporated with the cold wet binder during the mixing process and the developers of the system claim that it can be stockpiled in this condition for a considerable period before it is dried and heated. The major advantage of the process is that the aggregate is either wet or coated with binder so that dust emission is reduced to negligible proportions and it is not necessary to provide expensive dust-collecting equipment.

An outline diagram of the plant is shown in figure 2.4. The cold aggregate is proportioned by volumetric feeders (1) as in a conventional coated-macadam plant and after passing over a scalping screen (2) that removes oversize material the aggregate is passed into a surge hopper (3). The aggregate is then batched into a weigh hopper (4), where the moisture content is sensed by probes and the wet-aggregate batch weight is adjusted to give the required dry-aggregate weight. If necessary, filler (5) can be batched in a separate weigh hopper before the combined aggregates are discharged into the mixer (6) with the correct proportion of binder (7).

On contact with the wet cold aggregate in the mixer the binder solidifies and becomes distributed throughout the mix in the form of small globules. At this stage the premixed material is free flowing and relatively inhomogeneous. The additive, 'Adhistab', is added either to the mixer (8a) or later when the premixed material is added to the activator (8b), which is a modified form of continuous dryer. The material may be stored for considerable periods if desired before being introduced into the activator (9), where it is dried and coated with binder and heated to the required output temperature. It is claimed that the 'Adhistab' adhesive assists both the drying and the coating process. The coated material may then be stored (10) until required.

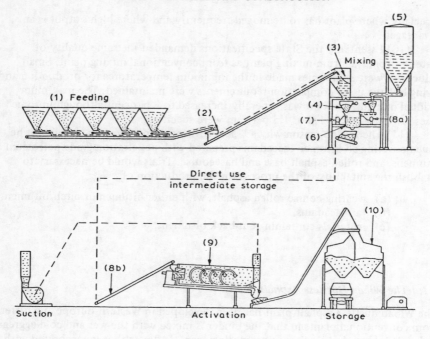

(1) Cold aggregate feed system
(2) Scalping screen
(3) Cold aggregate surge hopper
(4) Aggregate weigh hopper
    and moisture measurement
(5) Filler addition
(6) Mixer
(7) Binder addition
(8) Additive addition (a) at mixer (b) on transfer
(9) Activator
(10) Hot-mix storage

Figure 2.4 Schematic diagram of Wibau SL Plant[2]

A review of the characteristics of this type of plant may be found in a report by the Department of the Environment[2] containing details of visits made to Wibau plants in Switzerland, Denmark and France by a team from the Transport and Road Research Laboratory, the Engineering Intelligence Division of the Environment and the Asphalt and Coated Macadam Association. The conclusions from their investigation are given below.

(1) The latest Wibau SL plants do not emit a significant amount of dust and therefore justify the description 'Dustless'.

(2) The general noise level of the Wibau SL plants visited did not seem to be markedly different from conventional plants of the same output. There was also no evidence that the general level of fumes emitted was any higher than from conventional plants.

(3) A wide range of dense bitumen-coated materials has been produced by the Wibau SL process and it is expected that the following materials can be produced successfully and without difficulty

    (a)   rolled asphalts containing penetration-grade bitumen,

    (b)   dense bitumen macadams containing penetration-grade bitumens and mixed at a temperature above 120 °C,

    (c)   cold asphalt containing penetration-grade bitumen and mixed at a temperature above 120 °C.

(4) There is little evidence as to the likely future road performance of materials mixed by the SL process; most of what was seen on the visits had only been lightly trafficked for a short period of time. However, on one heavily trafficked road, lengths of dense asphaltic concrete which had been mixed by both conventional and SL plants were examined. Comparison of the condition of the sections suggest that no serious road performance problems should be encountered as a result of using material produced by the SL process.

2.1.5 The Coatmaster DFE Bituminous Coating Plant

A mixing plant that eliminates the need for expensive dust-collecting equipment has been developed by cooperation between Redland Roadstone and Underground Mining Machinery Limited. It is referred to as the Coatmaster DFE bituminous coating plant and is similar in operation to the drum-mixing plants described previously in that the process of heating, drying and mixing are combined into a single stage and the presence of water and binder eliminates the dust problem. It differs from drum-mixing plants, which are continuous in operation, in that it incorporates batch-mixing, so allowing greater control over the quality of the product.

A diagram showing the layout of the 313-type Coatmaster plant is shown in figure 2.5, where the outline method of operation of the plant can be seen. Moist graded aggregate is introduced into a weigh-hopper and is then loaded into the heat-mix drum, which can be tilted to allow the aggregate to enter. A burner directs a stream of hot air into the rotating heat-mix drum after the binder has been added. The moisture is then driven from the aggregate and at the same time the binder is incorporated into the mix. Moisture and exhaust hot air leave the stack via the expansion chamber. The mixed material is then discharged by tilting the mixer.

For the 313 model the drum capacity is 3.3 tonnes and the total cycle time for a batch will depend upon the moisture content of the aggregate. For typical dense bituminous base material where the temperature of the material leaving the mixer is 125 °C the total cycle time varies from 2 min 12 s for an initial moisture content of 2 per cent, giving an output of 90 tonne/ph, to 3 min 24 s for an initial moisture content of 6 per cent, giving an output of 58 tonnes per hour.

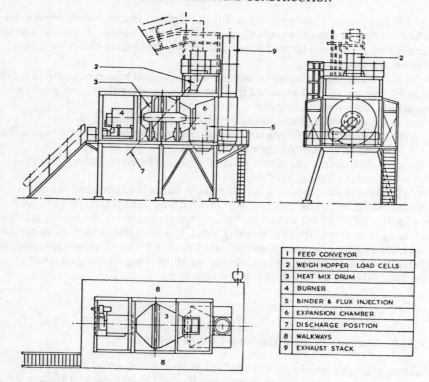

1	FEED CONVEYOR
2	WEIGH HOPPER LOAD CELLS
3	HEAT MIX DRUM
4	BURNER
5	BINDER & FLUX INJECTION
6	EXPANSION CHAMBER
7	DISCHARGE POSITION
8	WALKWAYS
9	EXHAUST STACK

Figure 2.5 Diagram showing layout of the 313 Coatmaster plant

More detailed information on the development and operation of the plant can be found in a paper by Taylor.[3]

2.2 The Sampling and Examination of Bituminous Materials

To ensure that bituminous materials are in complete compliance with the relevant specification it is necessary to determine

(1) the proportion of binder,
(2) the grading of the mineral aggregate,
(3) the nature and viscosity of the binder,
(4) the nature of the mineral aggregate.

for most practical purposes, however, (1) and (2) are determined from samples and (3) and (4) are best determined by sampling at the mixer. It should be particularly noted that (3), the nature and viscosity of the binder, is difficult to determine when the binder has to be recovered from mixed material.

2.2.1 Sampling

BS 598, Parts 1 and 2,[4] deals with the sampling and testing procedures recommended for bituminous materials used in road construction.

As with any sampling and testing process, considerable supervision and attention to detail are required, not only in the laboratory testing process but also in the sampling procedures adopted on the site. It is this latter aspect of the testing process that is most likely to be carried out in an unscientific manner and considerable attention should be given to the field procedures adopted, the training of operatives and the supervision of their work.

When sampling in the field there is a minimum mass of material that must be obtained for forwarding to the laboratory for testing. This is referred to as a bulk sample and is taken from a mass of material that the bulk sample is considered to represent. The bulk sample is composed of one or more increments, which is material taken in a single operation.

The minimum mass of a bulk sample depends upon the grading of the material being sampled: where the nominal size is larger than 20 mm the minimum mass is specified in BS 598 to be 24 kg, and where the nominal size is 20 mm or smaller (with the exception of mastic asphalt) the minimum mass is specified to be 16 kg.

The method by which these bulk samples are obtained depends upon the point in the mixing and laying process at which the sample is taken. The points at which a sample may be obtained are

(1) from a lorry load of material,
(2) during the discharge from the mixing plant,
(3) from the hopper of a paving machine,
(4) from around the augers of the paving machine,
(5) from the laid material before it is rolled.

The British Standard gives precise recommendation for the procedure to be adopted when these methods of sampling are used.

(1) When the sample is taken from a lorry load it is specified that three sample increments of material of 20 mm nominal size and smaller be taken, and four increments be taken when the nominal size of the material is greater than 20 mm. These increments should be taken from as widely spaced different positions as possible, not closer than 300 mm from the side of the lorry and from about 100 mm below the surface of the material. Special care must be taken to remove the complete surface material down to 100 mm below the surface, including any coarse material that may fall into the hole before the sample is taken. The increments taken should each have a mass of about 7 kg and should be taken using a size 2 square-mouth shovel (BS 3388, Part 1).

(2) Sampling during discharge from a mixing plant requires the use of a special sampling pan, made from mild steel in the form of a cylinder with a diameter of 240 ± 10 mm and a depth of 75 ± 5 mm. A specially designed sampling set-up is used that allows the pan to be passed transversely through the centre part of the curtain of material being discharged either directly from the mixer or from a storage hopper. The sampler is operated so that as the pan is passed through the curtain of material surcharge is not built up above the sides of the pan.

When sampling is from a batch-type mixer the sample increment is taken approximately midway through the period of discharge of the batch; three such increments are taken when the nominal size is greater than 20 mm and two increments when the nominal size is 20 mm and smaller. Similar sample increments are taken when sampling from continuous mixers, care being taken to avoid sampling the first and last material to be discharged from the mixer.

(3) If samples are taken from a paver hopper then it is important to carry out the sampling after approximately one half of a lorry load of material has been discharged into the paver. For material larger than 20 mm nominal size four sample increments are to be taken, for 20 mm and smaller material three increments are necessary. Samples should be taken at least 100 mm from the outer surface of the heap in the hopper and once again special care is taken to remove any coarse material that may fall into the hole when the surface layer is being removed. Increments are taken with a size-2 square-mouthed shovel and will have a mass of approximately 7 kg.

(4) Frequently samples are taken from around the augers of a paver using a size-2 shovel, fitted if necessary with a long handle. Two increments are to be taken from each side of the paver from any position below the augers or from the extension boxes where the material is easily available. Samples should only be taken when the augers are fully charged with material.

(5) The final method of sampling is from newly laid material that has not as yet been rolled. It is not a recommended method of sampling wearing-course material because of the disturbance to the finished surface, nor should it be used when the difference between the layer thickness and the nominal material size is less than 20 mm. Sampling trays 375 ± 25 mm square and not more than 10 mm deep are placed on the road surface and not more than 10 m apart in a direction parallel to the movement of the paver. A multi-strand wire is attached to a corner of each tray; the wire, being at least 3 m long, extends outside the area being paved and assists in retaining the tray against the forces set up by the paving machine as well as allowing the tray to be withdrawn after the paver has passed. The two increments obtained from each tray are combined to form a bulk sample.

With any sampling procedure the question of the frequency of sampling is of considerable importance, and this is particularly true in the case of highway material where large quantities of material are required. It is recommended in BS 598 that tests are required on every 100 tons of material, except where the material is found to be of good quality when a test on every 200 tons of material may be found to be adequate.

When a choice is being made between the various sampling methods the advantages of each method as given in BS 598 should be considered.

2.2.2 Sample Inspection

Upon receipt of a sample at the laboratory it should be inspected and the following points should be given special attention. When the sample has been taken after laying it should be examined to determine its average thickness and inspected to see if extraneous material is present. Where coated chippings are present they can frequently be removed after warming the sample; if this is not possible they may be identified after removal of the binder and an allowance made for their presence. Surface dressing may be more difficult or, if deeply embedded, impossible to remove and this fact should be reported. When the sample contains several layers of different material it is placed face down on a sheet of metal, warmed and the layers separated by a wide-bladed tool.

Samples taken after laying frequently contain unevenly dispersed free water. The sample should be broken up into small pieces and the sample left exposed in a thin layer on a clean hard surface in a warm laboratory.

Should the binder be found to be draining from the sample it should be collected; after any division of the sample the proportionate amount of binder should be added back to the sample.

Reduction of the sample received for testing normally requires the sample to be heated so that it can be remixed and reduced to a suitable size for testing. Heating should be carried out for the minimum time possible and not for more than 4 h. BS 598, Part 2 gives recommended temperatures for reheating samples prior to sample reduction. These temperatures vary from 60 °C for viscosities of less than 40° evt and 200 s at 40 °C, to 160 °C for materials with a penetration of less than 25 at 25 °C.

To reduce the sample to the size required for the determination of water content, binder content and aggregate grading a heated or lightly oiled riffle box may be used or quartering employed. The sample is first weighed, placed on a sheet-metal tray and thoroughly mixed before riffling or quartering. The size of the reduced sample will depend upon the nominal size of the aggregate in the material, ranging from 3000 to 5000 g for a 50 mm nominal-size material to 200 to 500 g for 3 mm nominal-size material.

Quartering is an operation which must be carried out with considerable attention to detail if accurate results are to be obtained. The sample is mixed thoroughly by heaping it into a core and then turning it over to form a new core until the core has been formed three times. When a conical heap is formed, each shovelful of the material is deposited on the apex of the core, the material that rolls down the sides is distributed as evenly as possible so that the apex of the core is not displaced. Large pieces that roll down and scatter around the base should be pushed back to the edge of the heap.

When the third core has been formed it is flattened by repeated vertical insertions of the edge of a board or shovel. The insertions are commenced at the centre and, lifting the board or shovel clear of the sample, worked progressively around the core. When finally the heap is uniform in depth and diameter the heap is quartered. One pair diagonally opposite are then shovelled into a heap and the remainder discarded. The quartering process is repeated until the amount which is to be quartered is approximately four times the mass of sample which is required for testing. After the next quartering the two portions that were previously discarded are used for a water-content determination if this is considered necessary.

From the mass of the original sample the mass remaining after quartering can be estimated, and if this is too great the mass of the original sample is reduced by one quarter. This is achieved by quartering twice, combining the remainder from the second quartering operation with the portion which was put aside from the first quartering process.

2.2.3 Determination of Water Content

Unless the binder content and aggregate grading are being obtained using the hot extractor process, which allows the water content to be determined at the same time as the binder content, it is necessary to make a separate determination of water content.

The apparatus used consists either of a brass cylinder containing gauze of 1 to 2 mm operative size (figure 2.6) or alternatively a spun copper tube with a ledge at the bottom on which rests a removable brass gauge disc. This container is held in the top two-thirds of a metal pot that is flanged and fitted with a cover as shown, using a solvent right gasket.

A graduated receiver is used that is suitable for use with solvents having a density higher than water and that has a stop-cock so that the water may be drawn off into a Crow receiver. Any suitable reflux condenser may be used, its lower end ground at an angle of approximately 45° to the axis of the condenser.

The test procedure is as follows. The portion of the sample which had been previously placed on one side for the determination of water content is divided into two portions by quartering. One is placed in a closed container and the other portion is weighed to the nearest 0.05 per cent of the mass taken and placed in a well-ventilated oven at a temperature of 100 to 120 °C for 1 h. If after further weighing the loss in mass exceeds 0.1 per cent the portion retained is weighed and transferred to a dry hot extractor pot. If the loss in mass does not exceed 0.1 per cent further action for the determination of water content is not necessary.

Sufficient trichloroethylene is added to allow refluxing to take place, the cover is placed over the condenser and heat applied to give a steady reflex action. Heating is continued until the volume of water in the receiver remains constant, so giving the mass of water in the sample.

2.2.4 Determination of the Binder Content and Aggregate Grading

Five methods of determining the binder content and aggregate grading of a bituminous road material are described in BS 598, Part 2. Provided the test procedures as given in the British Standard are strictly adhered to, the individual test procedures give comparable results. These methods are now described in outline.

Funnel Method

This is a simple if slow method of removing binder from the bituminous material when the sample does not exceed 1500 g. The solvent used to remove the binder is either trichloromethylene or dichloromethane (methylene chloride).

A filter paper, folded as shown in figure 2.7, is dried in an oven at 110 to 120 °C for not more than 60 min, cooled in a desiccator, weighed without delay and then placed in the large funnel as shown. The sample is then weighed to the nearest 0.05 per cent of the mass taken and placed in a suitable weighed beaker. A stirring rod is placed in the beaker, solvent added and a glass cover placed over the beaker to prevent evaporation of the solvent.

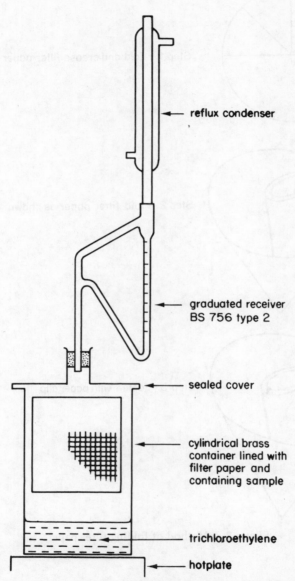

reflux condenser

graduated receiver
BS 756 type 2

sealed cover

cylindrical brass
container lined with
filter paper and
containing sample

trichloroethylene

hotplate

Figure 2.6 Apparatus for the hot extractor method and determination of water
content

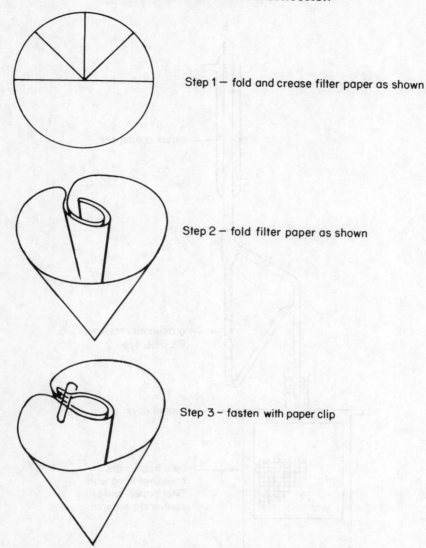

Step 1 – fold and crease filter paper as shown

Step 2 – fold filter paper as shown

Step 3 – fasten with paper clip

Figure 2.7 Method of folding filter paper

The solution in the first beaker is poured immediately into a weighed settling beaker through a 75 μm sieve protected by a larger sieve, every effort being made to transfer the material passing the 75 μm sieve. The bulk of the mineral matter in the settling beaker is allowed to remain after decanting the solution through the small funnel into the centre of the filter paper, which has just been wetted with solvent, as shown in figure 2.8.

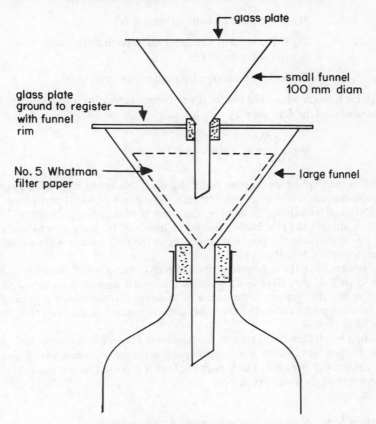

Figure 2.8 Apparatus for funnel method

Fresh solvent, which may be warm, is added to the first beaker and the sample then stirred and the process repeated until the filtrate becomes colourless.

While the sample is being washed it is desirable to maintain the level of the solution in the filter paper above the level of the bottom of the small funnel and to keep the top of the small funnel covered.

The aggregate remaining in the beakers on the sieve and on the filter paper, washed free from binder, is then placed in a well-ventilated oven at a temperature of 100 to 120 °C and dried to a constant mass; that is, the difference between successive weighings, carried out at half-hourly intervals, does not exceed 0.05 per cent.

The soluble binder content may then be calculated from

$$S = \frac{100(M_1 - M_2) - M_1 P}{M_1(100 - P)} \text{ (percentage by mass)} \qquad (2.1)$$

where M_1 is the mass of undried sample (g)

                        M_2 is the mass of insoluble material in both beakers and the filter paper (g)

                        P is the percentage by mass of water in sample.

With tar binders where the binder is not completely soluble in the solvent the total binder content B is given by

$$B = \frac{100S}{100 - T} \text{ (percentage by mass)} \qquad (2.2)$$

where T is the percentage by mass of binder insoluble in the solvent employed.

Provided decantation from the first into the second beaker is carried out immediately after stirring the sample, the amount of material passing the 75 μm sieve remaining in the first beaker should be less than 1.5 per cent of the total aggregate. If this is so the material remaining in the first beaker is graded using the general principles described in BS 812.[5]

Where necessary the aggregate is divided into coarse-grained material retained on a 3.35 or 2.36 mm sieve and fine-grained material passing these sieves. Only a portion of the fine-grained material needs be sieved. To the material passing the 75 μm sieve must be added the material from the second beaker and that retained on the filter paper.

Grading results are calculated to the nearest 0.1 per cent and reported to the nearest 1.0 per cent, except for material passing the 75 μm sieve, which is reported to the nearest 0.1 per cent. The binder content is reported to the nearest 0.1 per cent by mass of the total dry sample.

Extraction-bottle Method (Binder Content by Difference)

A sample with a mass dependent on grading is obtained by quartering. If the presence of water in the sample is suspected it is measured.

After weighing the sample to the nearest 0.05 per cent of the mass taken it is placed in a suitably sized metal container that has a wide mouth and a suitable means of closure. The solvent dichloromethane is added to the sample to give a solution of approximately 3 to 4 per cent concentration of soluble binder. The container is then closed and placed on a machine which will rotate the containers about their longitudinal axis at a speed between 10 and 30 rev/min. The time of rolling depends upon the type of bituminous material and the binder type, varying between 10 min for coated chippings and 20 min for dense tarmacadam.

After shaking is completed the contents of the container are allowed to settle for 2 min to make filtration easier. The solution is then poured through a nest of sieves, the finest of which is 75 μm, into a pressure filter fitted with a weighted Whatman No. 5 filter paper. The solution is then forced through the filter at a pressure not exceeding 200 kPa (2 bar).

The aggregate remaining in the bottle is then shaken with a further quantity of solvent, approximately equal to half the quantity of solvent originally used or about

100 ml, whichever is the smaller. Immediately after shaking, the solution is poured through the sieves into a pressure filter, illustrated in figure 2.9, taking care not to lose any mineral matter. The solution is then forced through the pressure filter. This process is repeated until no discoloration of the solvent is visible and the washings are visibly free from material in suspension. The aggregate is then placed on a nest of sieves, the container finally washed out and the washings placed into the pressure filter.

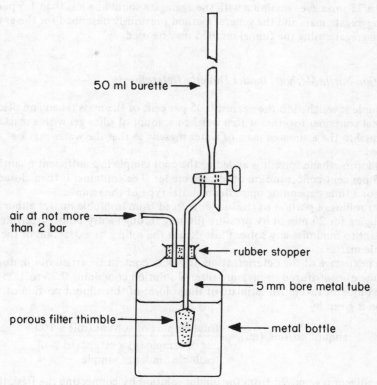

Figure 2.9 Filtering apparatus

Aggregate on the sieves is then transferred without any loss to a metal tray and then dried. The metal container is also dried and any aggregate in it transferred to the tray and the mass of the aggregate noted.

The binder content S can then be calculated from

$$S = 100 \frac{100(M_1 - M_2) - M_1 P}{M_1(100 - P)} \quad \text{(percentage by mass)} \qquad (2.3)$$

where M_1 is the mass of the undried sample (g),

M_2 is the mass of the aggregate and insoluble matter from the binder (g),

P is the percentage by mass of water in the sample, and

$$\text{total binder content } B = \frac{100S}{100 - T} \text{ (percentage by mass)} \qquad (2.4)$$

Provided the aggregate has been thoroughly washed, the proportion of material passing a 75 μm sieve remaining with the aggregate should be less than 1.5 per cent of the aggregate mass and the general method previously described for the grading of the aggregate using the funnel method may be used.

Extraction-bottle Method (Binder Directly Determined)

The sample is weighed to the nearest 0.05 per cent of the mass taken and placed in the metal container together with a weighed amount of silica gel with a mass at least equal to the estimated mass of water present so that the water may be absorbed.

Dichloromethane solvent is added to the cool sample in a sufficient quantity to give a 3 per cent concentration of soluble binder. The container is then closed and rolled for a time depending upon the material type of the sample.

After rolling, a portion of the binder is freed from insoluble matter either by centrifuging for 20 min or by pressure-filtering through a dry binder-free filter. It is important to minimise any solvent loss during the rolling or extraction of the insoluble matter.

The next stage of the determination of binder content is carried out in duplicate. A volume of centrifuged or pressure-filtered solution containing 0.75 to 1.25 g of soluble binder is taken. An estimate of the volume of this aliquot portion of solution is given by

$$\text{aliquot portion (ml)} = \frac{\text{total volume of solvent (ml) x 100}}{\substack{\text{mass of sample (g) x estimated \% of} \\ \text{soluble binder in sample}}} \qquad (2.5)$$

The solvent is removed from the binder solution by connecting the flask to recovery apparatus, illustrated in figure 2.10, immersing the flask to half its depth in boiling water and distilling off the solvent. The flask is shaken during distillation and pressure in the flask reduced below atmospheric but never below 6 kPa (60 mbar).

When the bulk of the solvent has been removed there is a reduction in pressure that causes frothing of the binder. When this takes place the procedure is as follows.

(1) For petroleum bitumen and tars of 44° evt and higher the pressure is further reduced to 20 kPa (200 mbar) in 1.5 min and maintained at this pressure for a further 3 to 5 min.

(2) For cut-back bitumens and tars below 44° evt the pressure is allowed to

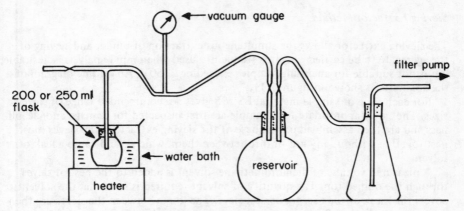

Figure 2.10 Binder recovery apparatus

increase to approximately atmospheric pressure, reduced to 60 kPa (600 mbar) in 1.5 min and further maintained at this pressure for a further 3.5 min.

At the conclusion of distillation the air within the flask is allowed to return to atmospheric pressure, the flask is dried and any solvent remaining in the flask removed by a gentle current of air. After cooling in a desiccator the flask is weighed to the nearest 0.01 g and if the recovered binder lies outside the limits of 0.75 to 1.25 g the recovery process is repeated with the volume suitably adjusted.

If the difference between the binder recovered in the two determinations is greater than 0.02 g these results are rejected and a new set of duplicate determinations have to be made.

The soluble binder content is then calculated from

$$S = \frac{10\,000zV}{vM(100 - P)} \left(1 + \frac{z}{dv}\right) \text{ (percentage by mass)} \tag{2.6}$$

where

M is the mass of undried sample (g),

z is the average mass of binder recovered from the two aliquot portions (g),

V is the total volume of solvent (m_1),

d is the relative density 15.5/15.5 °C (1.0 in the case of bitumen or 1.15 in the case of tar mixtures),

P is the percentage by mass of the water in the sample,

v is the volume of aliquot (ml).

As in the previous methods, a further correction is made for tar binder where some of the binder is not soluble in the solvent used.

The process of sieving is essentially similar to that described in the funnel method but it should be noted that the total mass includes the silica gel that was added and any of the binder which is insoluble in the solvent.

Sieving Extractor Method

The sieving extractor allows the simultaneous extraction of binder and sieving of the aggregate to be carried out. It is frequently used when rapid analysis is desirable, but is not suitable for analysing samples exceeding 3750 g. An outline diagram of the apparatus is shown in figure 2.11.

For each type of sample material BS 598 gives a recommended range of sieve sizes. The sieves appropriate for a sample are first inspected for damage and cleanliness and are then assembled on the base of the sieving extractor. The sieves must nest together without any grit or dirt between them, which could cause a leak of solvent.

A measured volume of dichloromethane solvent is added to the nest of sieves through the domed top. The quantity of solvent required is such that the solvent covers the mesh of the top or coarsest sieve. The joints between the sieves are then immediately checked for leaks and the sample, weighed to the nearest 0.05 per cent of the mass taken, introduced into the nest of sieves. Care should be taken to ensure that if the sample has been heated to assist in the sample reduction it has cooled before addition to the sieves. A weighed quantity of silica gel at least equal to the

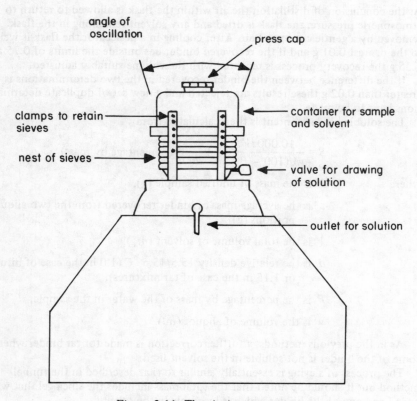

Figure 2.11 The sieving extractor

estimated mass of water in the sample is added. The orifice in the domed top is then closed with a liquid-proof cap and the shaking motion of the nest of sieves started and continued for a period varying between 10 and 20 min.

After shaking has been completed the waterproof cap is replaced by a cap that allows the entry of air without permitting the spillage of liquid. The drain cock in the sieving extractor is then opened and the solution drawn off, the process being hastened by shaking, provided the shaking process is not unduly prolonged.

A portion of the binder solution is freed from insoluble matter either by centrifuging or by the use of a pressure filter, care being taken during the extraction and centrifuging or filtration process to prevent loss of solvent by evaporation. If there is a high proportion of fine mineral matter in the binder solution that might cause prolonged filtration then centrifuging is essential.

The binder content is then determined using two aliquot portions of solvent and binder by removal of the solvent using distillation as previously described in the extraction bottle method where the binder content was directly determined.

The aggregate remaining in the sieving extractor is washed free from solution and the aggregate that passes a 75 μm sieve, using washes of about 750 ml of dichloromethane, the process being helped by briefly shaking the sieves. The sieves are taken apart, placed on trays and the aggregate dried in a warm ventilated cupboard. The aggregate remaining on the top sieve is then graded on the appropriate sieves. To make sure the aggregate remaining on the finer sieves is completely graded, each sieve is covered with a spare fine sieve and shaken over a suitable receiver; this material is then added to the next finer sieve. The material passing through the 75 μm sieve is preferably then recovered by filtering the drainings from the nest of sieves through a pressure filter, making allowance for the silica gel that was added and any insoluble binder.

As an alternative it is possible to determine the mass of material passing the 75 μm sieve by subtracting from the mass of the sample the masses of water, binder and aggregate not passing the 75 μm sieve.

Hot Extractor Method

The apparatus used in this method is the same as that employed for the determination of water content (figure 2.6).

First step in the extraction process is to line the brass-gauze cylindrical container with a No. 1 Whatman filter paper and dry both the filter paper and the container at 100 to 120 °C; they are then cooled in a desiccator and weighed. The sample reduced for testing is then placed in the container and the whole weighed to the nearest 0.05 per cent of the mass taken. The filled container is then placed in the pot and sufficient trichlorethylene added for refluxing to be subsequently possible.

The cover is then fastened in position over the sample, the receiver and condenser fitted, and heat evenly applied to the pot to give a steady reflux of 2 to 5 drops/s from the end of the condenser. After condensation, water present in the sample will enter the receiver, where it may be measured, while the solvent flows back into the container, falling on to the sample, dissolving the binder and then flowing through the filter paper into the bottom of the container, where it is once more vaporised.

Heating is continued until the extraction of the binder is considered to be complete and water ceases to collect in the receiver. The washed mineral aggregate is then removed together with the gauze container and filter paper and dried to a constant mass at a temperature of 100 to 120 °C (constant mass is the state at which the difference between successive weighings at half-hourly intervals does not exceed 0.05 per cent). When constant mass is achieved the gauze cylinder and its contents are cooled in a desiccator before weighing.

Because there may be fine material present in the binder/solvent solution at the end of the test the whole of the solution is either filtered through a Whatman No. 5 or centrifuged, and the mass of the insoluble matter determined.

Soluble binder content is then obtained from

$$S = 100 \times \frac{M_1 - (M_2 + W + M_3)}{M_1 - W} \text{ (percentage by mass)} \qquad (2.7)$$

where M_1 is the mass of the undried sample (g),

M_2 is the mass of the recovered aggregate in the gauze container,

W is the mass of the water collected in the receiver (g),

M_3 is the mass of the residue obtained on filtering or centrifuging the solution (g).

If a portion of the binder is insoluble in the solvent then a correction must be made to the soluble binder content as previously described.

To grade the aggregate it is transferred from the filter paper to a suitable metal container. The filter paper is brushed to remove as much as possible of the material adhering to it and the material placed with the remainder of the aggregate in the metal container. The filter paper is then placed back in the gauze container, weighed, and any increase in mass added to the mass of the material passing a 75 μm sieve.

Solvent is added to the aggregate in the bottle until it just covers the aggregate, the bottle is then sealed and rolled for about 5 min so as to separate the particles· of aggregate. The solvent is then poured through a 75 μm sieve, protected by a 1.18 mm sieve, particular care being taken to prevent as far as possible the transfer of coarse aggregate particles. The mass of the fine particles is then determined either by filtering through a No. 5 Whatman filter paper or by the loss in mass of the aggregate caused by the washing process.

When the sample in the container has been washed substantially free from material passing the 75 μm sieve it is transferred to the 1.18 mm sieve or to a tray, all the aggregate being removed by washing with solvent.

The washing process should ensure that the fine material remaining with the aggregate should be less than 1.5 per cent of the total aggregate and that the aggregate grading procedure previously described for the funnel method is appropriate.

2.2.5 Repeatability and Reproducibility for Binder Content and Aggregate Grading

Repeatability is the quantitative expression of the random error which is associated with a single test operator in a given laboratory obtaining successive results with the same apparatus under constant operating conditions on identical test material. It is defined in BS 598 as that difference between two such single results as would be exceeded in the long run in only one case in twenty in the normal and correct operation of the test method. Identical test material for repeatability tests is obtained by dividing a sample of twice the size required for a single test either by using a riffle box or by quartering.

Reproducibility is the quantitative expression of the random error that is associated with test operators working in different laboratories, each obtaining single results on identical test material when applying the same method. It is defined in BS 598 as that difference between two such single and independent results as would be exceeded in the long run in only one case in twenty in the normal and correct operation of the test method. Identical test material for reproducibility tests is obtained by dividing a sample of eight times the size required for analysis into two approximately equal portions, one for each laboratory, each laboratory reducing its portion to the size required for a single test either by a riffle box or by quartering.

2.2.6 Subsampling

When any bituminous material is divided by riffling or quartering there is the possibility of some distortion in the aggregate grading of the actual sample which is analysed, the amount of the distortion depending to a large extent on the care and skill of the person carrying out the sampling process. The distortion of the grading results in changes in the binder and filler contents; when duplicate specimens are being considered it is necessary to take this effect into account.

BS 598, Part 2, gives adjustments which should be made to the binder and filler contents of the finer-graded sample when duplicate analyses are made. These deductions should be made to the sample with the higher percentage of aggregate passing the 3.35 mm sieve for macadams and the lower percentage of aggregate retained on the 2.36 mm sieve for rolled asphalt. The deductions are made before the binder and filler contents of duplicate specimens are compared for repeatability and reproducibility.

The repeatability and reproducibility limits of samples taken from the same bulk sample given in BS 598 for coated macadam, rolled asphalt and mastic asphalt have been obtained by an examination of relevant information and may need to be revised in the light of further experience of the analysis methods described in the 1974 edition of BS 598.

Where it is found that systematic differences exist between the results obtained from laboratories using the same test method, it is recommended that the laboratories should cooperate to determine the cause of the difference.

References

(1) DoE, Transport and Road Research Laboratory Report 691: *Bituminous Drum Mixing Plants in the U.S.A.* (1976)

(2) DoE, Transport and Road Research Laboratory Report 533: *The Wibau
    Dustless Asphalt Plant: the Performance of European Installation* (1973)
(3) D. Taylor, 'Development of the Coatmaster DFE Bituminous Coating Plant',
    Quarry Management and Products, September 1975
(4) BS 598: Sampling and Examination of Bituminous Mixtures for Roads and
    Buildings, Pt. 1: 1974   Sampling, 1974; Pt. 2: 1974   Testing, 1974
(5) BS 812: Methods for Sampling and Testing of Mineral Aggregates, Sands and
    Fillers. Pt. 1: 1975   Sampling, Size, Shape and Classification; Pt. 2: 1975
    Physical Properties; Pt. 3: 1975   Mechanical Properties

3

Flexible Pavement Thickness Design

3.1 Introduction

The thickness design of highway pavements requires the following large number of complex factors to be considered.

(1) The magnitude and number of repetitions of the applied wheel loads and the contact area between the tyre carrying the load and the road surface.

(2) The stiffness, stability, durability, the elastic and plastic deformation and resistance to fatigue loading of the pavement layers.

(3) Volumetric changes in the subgrade due to climatic changes, the deformation of the subsoil under load and the ability of the pavement layers to reduce the stress imposed on the subsoil by the wheel loads.

(4) The severity and incidence of frost and rainfall.

While considerable progress has been made in the development of structural theory to the design of highway pavements, the complexity of the many factors involved in practical highway design has resulted in the adoption of many thickness-design methods based on experience.

3.2 Failure Criteria

In any pavement-thickness design method there must be a criterion for the terminal or failure condition of a pavement. This criteria is also of considerable importance in highway maintenance work because the maintenance engineer is interested in a pre-failure condition at which strengthening of the pavement will result in a prolonged life.

The definition of these two conditions for flexible pavements in the United Kingdom has been described by Croney.[1] Using the results from full-scale experiments on public highways in the United Kingdom, it was found that permanent deformation of approximately 20 mm in the nearside wheel tracks of a flexible pavement when measured using a 1.8 m straight edge was normally accepted as the point at which pavement reconstruction was considered necessary.

It was also noted that when the deformation had reached this level, the normally used rolled asphalt wearing courses were beginning to crack. Because of water penetration the pavement subsequently deteriorated relatively rapid. Open-textured macadams with less-viscous binders did not suffer from cracking to the same extent but once again deformation progressed rapidly once a value of 20 mm had been reached.

Defining the critical condition was found to be more difficult but it was noted that overlays were being applied on British highways when the deformation in the nearside wheel track was between 10 and 20 mm. At this deformation cracking was generally limited and confined to longitudinal cracks in the wheel paths.

Compared with assessment methods adopted elsewhere, both these conditions are easily measured by the use of a straight edge and visual inspection.

For rigid pavements in the United Kingdom the Committee on Highway Maintenance[2] has recommended that concrete pavements should be reconstructed when the following defects are seen.

(1) The total length of all transverse cracking in reinforced slabs (from hair to wide cracks) exceeds 75 m (250 ft) per 30 m (100 ft) of traffic lane. Any transverse cracking in unreinforced slabs, however fine, is an indication of failure, probably needing reconstruction.

(2) The average difference in level over the length of transverse joints exceeds 6 mm ($\frac{1}{4}$ in.) on 50 per cent of the joints per 75 m (250 ft) length of carriageway.

(3) Surface irregularity indicated by the bump integrator (r values) reaches the following values in the near-side traffic lanes: trunk and important principal roads, 180 to 200 in./mile; other principal roads and important non principal roads, 200 to 240 in./mile. The first figure for each category indicates the normal maximum acceptable r value and the second figure the permissible maximum.

An alternative concept for determining the point of failure of a pavement has been developed in the United States. This is the present serviceability index (PSI), which was first proposed by Carey and Irick.[3] The index is formulated by rating a series of pavements by a group of individuals who drive over selected pavements and rate the pavements on a scale of 0 to 5 and state whether the road is acceptable for the intended traffic. At the same time drivers are asked to state their opinions on the objective features of the pavement that influenced their rating. A rating of 5 indicates a perfect ride, 4 to 5 is described as very good, 4 to 3 described as good, 3 to 2 described as fair, 2 to 1 described as poor and 1 to 0 as very poor.

This concept was used during the American Association of State Highway Officials Road Test (AASHO) to assess and compare the performance of experimental pavements incorporated in the test track.[4] The average ratings obtained were correlated with measurements of roughness, patching and cracking to give a measure of driver satisfaction with a pavement to give equation 3.1 for flexible pavements and equation 3.2 for rigid pavements.

$$\text{PSI} = 5.03 - 1.91 \log(1 + SV) - 1.28RD^2 - 0.01\sqrt{(C+P)} \qquad (3.1)$$

$$\text{PSI} = 5.41 - 1.80 \log(1 + SV) - 0.09\sqrt{(C+P)} \qquad (3.2)$$

where   PSI is the present serviceability index based on values measured on the
                pavement surface,

             SV is the mean slope variance,

             C is the lineal feet of major cracking per 1000 ft^2 area,

             P is the bituminous patching of ft^2 per 1000 ft^2 area,

             RD is the mean rut depth in inches for both wheel tracks.

The slope variance is obtained by a device known as the AASHO slope profilometer, illustrated in outline in figure 3.1. This instrument uses an imaginary fixed
horizontal (or vertical) plane that is established approximately by means of a
relatively long wheel base. This made it necessary to assume that the angle between
the pavement and the longitudinal axis of the profilometer was equal to the angle
between the pavement and the horizontal. This was only approximately correct
but the error was small and random in nature.

At the end of the profilometer two small wheels with a wheel base of 0.75 ft
are so fixed that they are able to measure small changes in the slope of the pavement. These measurements are recorded in the form of an ink trace of slope and
longitudinal distance along the carriageway. From field testing it was observed that
the variance of the slope at points at 1 ft intervals along the pavement correlated
with subjective rating of pavement serviceability. A log transformation was used to
produce a linear relationship.

Measurement speed is 5 to 8 km/h. The slope variance is then given by

$$SV = \frac{\Sigma Y^2 - (1/n)(\Sigma Y)^2}{n - 1} \tag{3.3}$$

where Y is the difference in elevation of the two wheels,

             n is the number of readings which are taken.

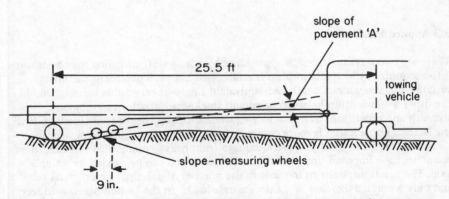

Figure 3.1 Outline of AASHO slope profilometer, which continuously measures
angle 'A'

From answers to the question 'Is this an acceptable pavement?' it was concluded that a serviceability rating of 2.5 described an acceptable pavement for the primary road system and a rating of 2.0 for the secondary road system.

A comparison between the PSI method and the British method of using rut depth has been given by Croney.[1] He states that while the PSI is a useful guide for assessing riding comfort and maintenance requirements it does not provide a very satisfactory criterion for structural performance. This is mainly because the index value is largely determined by the slope variance term. The terms involving rutting and cracking have little direct influence on the calculated value of PSI. Indirectly, of course, these terms affect riding quality and hence slope variance. This factor is also influenced, however, by the initial riding quality and by foundation movements which may themselves be independent of traffic stresses — for example, differential consolidation and compaction or swelling due to moisture migration.

In the published results of the AASHO Road Test Report,[3] Appendix F tabulates calculations of PSI made from the data obtained in three States and from measurements made during the Road Test itself. For the three States there is no apparent correlation between the rut depths measured and the PSI, although there is close agreement between the Present Serviceability Rating determined by panels of observers and the calculated values of PSI. This may well reflect inaccuracies in the determination of rut depth and the very small significance of rut depth in the calculation. The results from the AASHO Road Test show generally much larger rut depths than those observed in the three States for equivalent PSI values and for this data there is a fairly clear tendency for the PSI to decrease with increasing rut depth. In the AASHO Test a 4 ft straight-edge was used to measure rut depth and these values need to be increased by 30 per cent to give equivalence with a 6 ft straight-edge as used in the United Kingdom. The factor of 30 per cent was obtained from a study of the corresponding road-surface profiles given in the AASHO reports.

A rut depth of 15 mm (0.6 in.) corresponding to the critical condition in the British system would be equivalent to a PSI value of about 3.2, while the failure criterion of 19 mm (0.75 in.) would be equivalent to a PSI value of about 2.5. This probably provides the best basis for translation between the two systems.

3.3 Applied Loading

There are two pavement-design approaches by which traffic loading may be taken into account: in one a relationship is established between pavement thickness, variations in subgrade strength and equivalent single-wheel or axle loading, and in the other a relationship between pavement thickness, variations in subgrade strength and repetitions of a standard equivalent single-wheel or axle loading. It is the latter approach that is more common in highway pavement design.

In an attempt to limit pavement damage from heavy commercial vehicles, most countries have imposed limits on the total load which can be carried by a single axle. The result has been an increase in the number of axles per commercial vehicle and only a gradual increase in maximum axle loads. In the United States a widely accepted single-axle load is 18 000 lb (8200 kg) while in the United Kingdom maximum axle loading is limited to 10 tons for wheels at the ends of an axle and

11 tons where wheels are spaced along the axle. The effects of other vehicle loadings are normally accounted for in terms of equivalent 18 000 lb single-axle loads.

Extensive use has been made both in the United States and in the United Kingdom of the equivalency factors developed from the AASHO Road Test equations. In this method the number of repetitions of load to failure for either flexible or rigid pavements is expressed in terms of a pavement stiffness or rigidity value, load characteristics and the terminal level of serviceability selected as the pavement failure point.

For flexible pavements the rigidity is expressed in terms of the Structural Number (SN) of the pavement; for rigid pavement the thickness D is used. Vehicle characteristics are expressed by L_1, the axle code, in which $L_2 = 1$ for a single axle and $L_2 = 2$ for a tandem axle. The general equation developed from the AASHO Road Test is

$$G = \log \left(\frac{C_0 - p}{C_0 - C_1} \right) = \beta \, (\log W - \log p) \tag{3.4}$$

where

G is a function (the logarithm) of the ratio of loss of serviceability at any time to the total potential loss taken to a point where $p = 1.5$;

β is a function of design and load variables that influences the shape of the p versus W serviceability curve;

C_0 = initial serviceability for the pavement sections;

C_1 = 1.5, the cut-off serviceability level at which a section was removed from the Road Test experiment;

p = serviceability level;

W = accumulated load applications of axle load W;

P = load applications to $p = 1.5$.

It has shown[5] that for flexible pavements and single axles

$$\log \left(\frac{W_{18}}{W_x} \right) = 4.79 \log (x + 1) - 4.79 \log (18 + 1) + \frac{G}{\beta_{18}} - \frac{G}{\beta_x} \tag{3.5}$$

and for rigid pavements and for single axles

$$\log \left(\frac{W_{18}}{W_x} \right) = 4.62 \log (x + 1) - 4.62 \log (18 + 1) + \frac{G}{\beta_{18}} + \frac{G}{\beta_x} \tag{3.6}$$

here

W_{18} = the accumulated load application of the 18 000 lb single axle load to terminal serviceability desired,

W_x = the accumulated load application of the x lb single-axle load to terminal serviceability desired,

G = the function loss of serviceability for the terminal serviceability desired.

For flexible pavements

$$\beta = 0.40 + \frac{0.081(L_1 + L_2)^{3.23}}{(SN + 1)^{5.19}L_2^{3.23}} \tag{3.7}$$

For rigid pavements

$$\beta = 1 + \frac{3.63(L_1 + L_2)^{5.20}}{(D_2 + 1)^{8.46}L_2^{3.52}} \tag{3.8}$$

where L_1 is the load on one single load axle or one tandem axle set (kips); L_2 is the axle code, 1 for single, 2 for tandem axles. A further treatment of SN and D is given in section 3.9.

The computed values of the equivalence factors for varying axle loads and types are shown in tables 3.1 and 3.2 for flexible and rigid pavements. It can be seen that these factors are not significantly affected by the value of the structural number or the terminal serviceability selected.

In the United Kingdom a simplified version of the AASHO equivalence factors has been adopted for highway pavement design in Road Note 29[6] without implying acceptance of the performance data from the AASHO test, which Leigh and Croney[7] do not consider applicable to British conditions. The relative damaging power of various wheel loads, however, can be used with greater confidence.[8]

The AASHO factors are affected by the Structural Number of the pavement considered. British pavements cover a range of Structural Numbers between 2.5 and 6.0, with the majority towards the upper end of this range. Significant variations

Table 3.1[20]

Axle Load Kips	Structural Number, SN					
	1	2	3	4	5	6
2	0.0002	0.0002	0.0002	0.0002	0.0002	0.0002
4	0.002	0.003	0.002	0.002	0.002	0.002
6	0.01	0.01	0.01	0.01	0.01	0.01
8	0.03	0.04	0.04	0.03	0.03	0.03
10	0.08	0.08	0.09	0.08	0.08	0.08
12	0.16	0.18	0.19	0.18	0.17	0.17
14	0.32	0.34	0.35	0.35	0.34	0.33
16	0.59	0.60	0.61	0.61	0.60	0.60
18	1.00	1.00	1.00	1.00	1.00	1.00
20	1.61	1.59	1.56	1.55	1.57	1.60
22	2.49	2.44	2.35	2.31	2.35	2.41
24	3.71	3.62	3.43	3.33	3.40	3.51
26	5.36	5.21	4.88	4.68	4.77	4.96
28	7.54	7.31	6.78	6.42	6.52	6.83
30	10.38	10.03	9.24	8.65	8.73	9.17
32	14.00	13.51	12.37	11.46	11.48	12.17
34	18.55	17.87	16.30	14.97	14.87	15.63
36	24.20	23.30	21.16	19.28	19.02	19.93
38	31.14	29.95	27.12	24.55	24.03	25.10
40	39.57	38.02	34.34	30.92	30.04	31.25

Table 3.2[20]

Axle Load Kips	D – Slab Thickness – inches					
	6	7	8	9	1	
2	0.0002	0.0002	0.0002	0.0002	0.	0.0002
4	0.002	0.002	0.002	0.002	0.002	0.002
6	0.01	0.01	0.01	0.01	0.01	0.01
8	0.03	0.03	0.03	0.03	0.03	0.03
10	0.09	0.08	0.08	0.08	0.08	0.08
12	0.19	0.18	0.18	0.18	0.17	0.17
14	0.35	0.35	0.34	0.34	0.34	0.34
16	0.61	0.61	0.60	0.60	0.60	0.60
18	1.00	1.00	1.00	1.00	1.00	1.00
20	1.55	1.56	1.57	1.58	1.58	1.59
22	2.32	2.32	2.35	2.38	2.40	2.41
24	3.37	3.34	3.40	3.47	3.51	3.53
26	4.76	4.69	4.77	4.88	4.97	5.02
28	6.59	6.44	6.52	6.70	6.85	6.94
30	8.92	8.68	8.74	8.98	9.23	9.39
32	11.87	11.49	11.51	11.82	12.17	12.44
34	15.55	15.00	14.95	15.30	15.78	16.18
36	20.07	19.30	19.16	19.53	20.14	20.71
38	25.56	34.54	24.26	24.63	25.36	26.14
40	32.18	30.85	30.41	30.75	31.58	32.57

in damaging power from the values assumed in Road Note 29 only arise in the case of very thin pavements. These fail so rapidly under the traffic conditions prevailing on full-scale road experiments that close observations in terms of standard axles are not possible.

The values adopted in Road Note 29 for all types of flexible and rigid pavements are given in table 3.3 and it can be seen that only the effect of heavy vehicles is likely to be of significance in design. For this reason only vehicles with an unladen weight of 1.5 tonne 1530 kg (that is, all commercial vehicles with the exception of light vehicles), are considered in pavement design.

Traffic-flow measurements and predictions of commercial vehicles in the United Kingdom are normally made in terms of vehicles with only a very limited number of axle-loading measurements. For this reason it is also necessary to know the lane distribution of heavy vehicles, the distribution of axles for heavy vehicles and the typical distribution of axle loads for these vehicles.

Early observations in the United Kingdom[9] have been amended in Department of Transport Technical Memorandum H6/78 which gives the average number of axles per commercial vehicle, the number of standard 8160 kg (18 000 lb) axles per commercial axle and hence the number of standard axles per commercial vehicle, for four types of road; (these values are given in table 3.4). Latter research[10] gives more detailed information and shows that on some motorways there is a large difference in the damaging power of vehicles travelling in opposite directions, due to variations in the load being carried.

More recent observations reported by Currer[10] have allowed revised conclusions to be drawn of the way in which commercial traffic is distributed between the left-hand and overtaking lanes on motorways and trunk roads. Experience until

Table 3.3 Equivalence factors and damaging power of different axle loads[6]

Axle load		Equivalence factor
kg	(lbs)	
910	(2000)	0·0002
1810	(4000)	0·0025
2720	(6000)	0·01
3630	(8000)	0·03
4540	(10000)	0·09
5440	(12000)	0·19
6350	(14000)	0·35
7260	(16000)	0·61
8160	(18000)	1·0
9070	(20000)	1·5
9980	(22000)	2·3
10890	(24000)	3·2
11790	(26000)	4·4
12700	(28000)	5·8
13610	(30000)	7·6
14520	(32000)	9·7
15420	(34000)	12·1
16320	(36000)	15·0
17230	(38000)	18·6
18140	(40000)	22·8

1974 did not go beyond a total flow of 7000 commercial vehicles per day, but there were fairly clear indications that there would be an approximately equal distribution of commercial traffic between the lanes at a commercial vehicle flow of 10 500 vehicles per day. Because of the small night flows when most of the commercial traffic would occupy the left-hand lane, equal flows are not a practical possibility. These figures indicate that the recommendations given in the 3rd edition of Road Note 29 will give an overestimate of the number of commercial vehicles on the left-hand lane and lead to a measure of over-design.

Table 3.4 Conversion factors to obtain the equivalent number of standard axles

Type of Road	Number of Standard Axles per Commercial Vehicle
Roads designed to carry over 2000 commercial vehicles per day *in each direction* at the time of construction	2¾
Roads designed to carry between 1000 and 2000 commercial vehicles per day *in each direction* at the time of construction	2¼
Roads designed to carry between 250 and 1000 commercial vehicles per day *in each direction* at the time of construction	1¼
All other public roads	¾

3.4 Subgrade Strength and Condition

The performance of a highway pavement is influenced to a very considerable extent by the subgrade material, and because the pavement has an extensive area the properties of the subgrade are likely to vary considerably along its length. There is also a further source of variation in that an important feature of the subgrade, the moisture content at any given point, is likely to vary with time.

Because of this latter source of variability it is necessary to discuss the variation in subgrade moisture content found in practice before describing the tests that may be used to assess the pavement-supporting properties of a subgrade.

Water beneath a pavement may come from many sources: directly from rainfall by cracks in the pavement itself or by the use of pervious pavements; lateral movement of water from the pavement edges; by suction from the water table; and by seasonal movements in the water table itself.

Some highway authorities, particularly in the United States, expecting high moisture content to occur under pavements, occasionally assess the strength of the subgrade in a soaked condition. This of course results in many cases in over-design since the subgrade does not always become saturated.

In the United Kingdom the criteria for estimating the final moisture content of a subgrade have been discussed by Croney and Bulman.[11] They state that the principles of thermodynamics applied to the soil/water/air system with particular reference to road and airfield pavements enable subgrade moisture conditions to be classified in three main categories as follows.

(1) Under conditions of rainfall and evaporation such that a water-table forms in the soil within 5 m of the surface, an equilibrium moisture condition will develop under an impervious pavement. Edge effects are small unless vegetation is allowed to grow very close to the pavement boundary. The equilibrium condition will be attained by a process of drainage or by upward capillary movement, depending on the state of the soil when it is covered by the pavement. A method has been developed for estimating the equilibrium moisture condition from the sorption and compressibility characteristics of the soil and the position of the water-table.[11] This approach has also been extended to enable the equilibrium strengths of the soil foundation to be estimated for different levels of water-table.[12] A temperature climate with well-distributed rainfall combined with moderate evaporation normally leads to a shallow water-table of this type, but similar conditions may arise in coastal areas of tropical regions or in the flood plains of rivers.

(2) Where there is no water-table within 5 m of the surface but the climate is such that for several months of the year rainfall exceeds moisture loss by evapotranspiration, a relatively stable moisture condition will be achieved under an impervious surfacing by a process of moisture exchange to and from the verges. This 'equilibrium' condition, which will be subject to some cyclic variation depending on the permeability of the soil, can be related to the soil type and to a moisture index derived from the annual rainfall, evaporation rate and other meteorological factors.[13] From this approach the average moisture content and strength of the soil under a pavement can be estimated. This climatic condition will generally be represented by a hot climate and highly seasonal rainfall exceeding 250 mm per year.

(3) In dry arid climates such rainfall as there may be has no influence on the moisture condition under roads, and the moisture content of the subgrade will be close to the average value observed in the surrounding uncovered soil, of the same type.[14]

Air temperature influences evaporation rates from soil but there is no conclusive evidence that temperature gradients in soil beneath road pavements result in any significant accumulation of moisture in the subgrade, by the process of vapour migration or thermo-osmosis. Freezing of moist soil increases the suction forces present above the zero isotherm and in silty soils of medium permeability can give rise to an upward migration of water in road subgrades.[15] A high water-table (within 1 m of the formation) favours this type of moisture movement. The strength of a subgrade affected in this way falls to zero immediately after the thaw. The thickness of road construction over frost-susceptible soils should be such that the zero isotherm will not descend into the subgrade.

For the United Kingdom the subgrade condition falls into the first category and every attempt is made during the construction of the highway to ensure that the pavement is as impermeable as possible. In addition land-drains are frequently provided to prevent lateral movement of water from verges and central reservations.

To determine the supporting power of the subgrade the pavement designer has two options. If the necessary laboratory facilities are available the California Bearing Ratio (CBR) at the estimated equilibrium moisture content and density can be determined. Alternatively the designer can use the information given in table 3.5, in which the ultimate CBR value is broadly related to the soil classification and the drainage condition using the thermo-dynamic approach. In view of the rapid changes which occur along most road alignments in the United Kingdom, very detailed soil investigation is not usually worth while and a strength assessment based on soil type is generally sufficient.

3.4.1 The California Bearing Ratio Test

The supporting value of the subgrade may be made by a number of field and laboratory tests, which include the California Bearing Ratio test, the *R* value test, the plate-bearing test, the triaxial test and the Group Index method of soil classi-fication. In the United Kingdom, pavement design involves the CBR test, using soil samples either at the calculated equilibrium moisture content or at the existing moisture content found at a depth below which seasonal fluctuations occur (normally 1 m). In the United States soaking of the samples for 4 days prior to testing is usual.

Road Note 29 recommends that where the specialist equipment and experience is available the CBR may be carried out on recompacted samples in accordance with BS 1377;[16] the method of compaction used preferably being that referred to as Method 2 in section 5.1.3 of the Standard. To estimate the appropriate density condition it is suggested that a preliminary test should be carried out using the method specified in test 14 of BS 1377, but with the soil at the expected average moisture after construction. The CBR test specimen should then be compacted to a density corresponding to 95 per cent of the value obtained in the preliminary test.

Table 3.5 Estimated laboratory CBR values for British soils compacted at the natural moisture content[6]

Type of soil	Plasticity index (per cent)	CBR (per cent)	
		Depth of water-table below formation level	
		More than 600 mm	600 mm or less
Heavy clay	70	2	1*
	60	2	1·5*
	50	2·5	2
	40	3	2
Silty clay	30	5	3
Sandy clay	20	6	4
	10	7	5
Silt	—	2	1*
Sand (poorly graded)	non-plastic	20	10
Sand (well graded)	non-plastic	40	15
Well-graded sandy gravel	non-plastic	60	20

* See para. 27

For cohesive soils where the restraint effect of the CBR mould and of surcharge is small, *in situ* CBR measurements may be used for design purposes. It is important that moisture content and dry density conditions at the time of the test should approximate to those expected under the completed pavement. If it is possible the test should be carried out in a freshly exposed soil surface at a depth below which seasonal changes in moisture content are not expected.

In the laboratory the test is carried out, as specified in BS 1377, on material passing the 20 mm BS test sieve. If the test is to be made on samples containing larger particles than 20 mm the fraction retained on the 20 mm BS test sieve should be removed. If this does not exceed 25 per cent of the whole it is unnecessary to make any correction. If the percentage retained on the 20 mm BS test sieve is greater than this, it should be replaced with a similar fraction of 20 mm to 5 mm of like material.

The mass of wet soil required for one test specimen can be calculated from

$$m_1 = 23.05(100 + w)\, \rho d \tag{3.9}$$

where w is the moisture content of the soil expressed as a percentage and ρd is the dry density of the soil (Mg/m^3). To prepare the test specimen the mould shown in figure 3.2 is assembled and the base of the mould covered by a filter paper. The calculated mass of wet soil is then divided into three equal parts and each sealed in a container to prevent loss of moisture. The specimen is prepared by filling the mould, one-third at a time, and compressing each third of the sample. Finally the

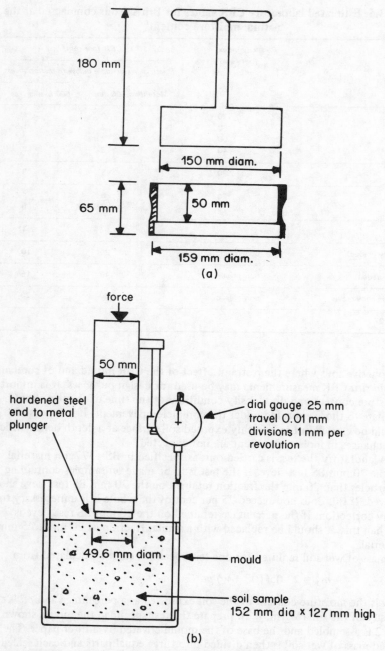

Figure 3.2 (a) Plug and collar with cylindrical mould for the determination of the California Bearing Ratio. (b) Apparatus for the California Bearing Ratio Test

whole sample is compressed until the top surface of the soil is level with the top of the collar of the mould.

If the sample is not to be tested immediately then the top plate of the mould is screwed on to prevent moisture loss. Should the air content of the compacted soil be less than 5 per cent, the specimen should not be tested for 24 h, so allowing pore pressure to be dissipated.

To obtain the CBR the mould containing the specimen is placed on the platen of the testing machine and surcharge masses, if required, are placed on the specimen. The testing plunger is then seated under a force of 50 N for a bearing ratio of up to 30 per cent or 250 N for a bearing ratio above 30 per cent; it is then made to penetrate the specimen at a uniform rate of 1 mm/min. Readings of the required force are taken at penetration intervals of 0.25 mm, the total penetration not exceeding 7.5 mm.

After the penetration test has been completed a sample of the soil of about 350 g is taken from immediately below the penetrated surface of the end of the specimen and the moisture content determined.

A graph showing force on the plunger against penetration is plotted and a smooth curve drawn through the points. The curve nomally is convex upwards as in test 1, figure 3.3. If, however, the initial portion is concave upwards, as in test 2, correction is necessary. In this case a tangent is drawn at the point of greatest slope and is projected to cut the penetration axis as indicated. The curve is then shifted to the

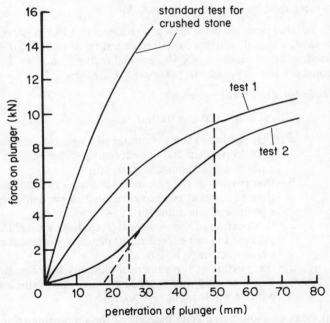

Figure 3.3 Typical California Bearing Ratio Test results

left so that the point of intersection of the tangent with the penetration axis coincides with the origin. This gives the corrected curve from which the CBR value is deduced.

The standard force penetration curve corresponding to 100 per cent CBR is also shown on figure 3.3. The forces corresponding to this curve are 11.5 kN at 2 mm penetration, 17.6 kN at 4 mm, 22.2 kN at 6 mm, 26.3 kN at 8 mm, 30.3 kN at 10 mm and 33.5 kN at 12 mm. The force, read from the smoothed curve, required to cause a given penetration expressed as a percentage of the force required to cause the same penetration on the standard curve is defined as the CBR value at that penetration. The CBR value is calculated at penetrations of 2.5 mm and 5 mm and the higher value taken.

3.4.2 Soil Classification Tests

Because of the difficulty of determining the subgrade strength under completed pavements, it has been suggested that the physical properties of soils that can easily be determined be used for classifying soils and hence assigning a bearing value to the subgrade. A system widely used for classifying soils for highway purposes is that of the Highway Research Board, American Association of State Highway Officials, or the Modified Bureau of Public Roads System.[18]

Soils are divided into two major groups: (1) granular materials containing 35 per cent or less material passing a No. 200 mesh sieve; (2) clay and silt-clay materials containing more than 35 per cent passing a No. 200 mesh sieve. The soil components recognised by this system are as follows

> Gravel, material passing a 3 in. sieve and retained on a No. 10 sieve.
> Coarse sand, material passing a No. 10 sieve and retained on a No. 40 sieve.
> Fine sand, material passing a No. 40 sieve and retained on a No. 200 sieve.
> Combined silt and clay, material passing a No. 200 sieve.

The group index for a soil is then given by

$$GI = 0.2a + 0.005ac + 0.01bd \ldots \tag{3.10}$$

where

a = that portion of the percentage passing a No. 200 sieve greater than 35 per cent and not exceeding 75 per cent, expressed as a positive whole number (0 to 40).

b = that portion of the percentage passing a No. 200 sieve greater than 15 per cent and not exceeding 55 per cent, expressed as a positive whole number (0 to 40).

c = that portion of the numerical liquid limit greater than 40 per cent but not exceeding 60 per cent, expressed as a positive whole number (0 to 20).

d = that portion of the numerical plasticity index greater than 10 per cent but not exceeding 30 per cent, expressed as a positive whole number (0 to 20).

The group index of a soil is an inverse measure of the supporting value of the subgrade. The higher the group index the lower is the soil strength. Sands and gravels are likely to have a group index approaching zero, silty or clayey gravel and sand a value between 0 and 4, silty soils a value not exceeding 12, and clayey soils a value not exceeding 20.

3.4.3 Non-repetitive Static Plate Load Tests of Soils and Flexible Pavement Components

A test which is frequently used in the United States to evaluate the supporting power of the subgrade or of pavement layers is the plate bearing test.[17]

The loading device consists of a truck or trailer or a combination of both, loaded with sufficient weight to produce the desired reaction on the surface under test. The supporting points, the wheels, must be at least 2.4 m (8 ft) from the circumference of the largest-diameter bearing plate being used.

Beneath the loading device is a hydraulic jack assembly with a spherical bearing attachment capable of applying and releasing the load in increments and equipped with an accurately calibrated gauge that will indicate the magnitude of the applied load.

The jack exerts its load on the pavement through a set of circular steel bearing plates not less than 25.4 mm (1 in.) in thickness, machined so that they can be arranged in pyramid fashion to ensure rigidity, and having diameters ranging from 152 to 762 mm (6 to 30 in.) The diameters of adjacent plates in the pyramid arrangement should not differ by more than 152 mm (6 in.)

The dial gauges are graduated in units of 0.03 mm (0.001 in.) and are capable of recording a maximum deflection of 25.4 mm (1 in.). They are mounted on a deflection beam of standard 63.5 mm ($2\frac{1}{2}$ in.) black pipe or 76 x 76 x 6 mm (3 x 3 x $\frac{1}{4}$ in.) steel angle or equivalent that is at least 5.5 m (18 ft) long and rests on supports located at least 2.4 m (10 ft) from the circumference of the bearing plate or nearest wheel or supporting leg. The whole of the deflection apparatus must be shaded from the direct rays of the sun.

To carry out the test, carefully centre a bearing plate of the selected diameter under the jack assembly. Set the remaining plates of smaller diameter concentric with, and on top of, the bearing plate. Set the bearing plate level in a thin bed of a mixture of sand and plaster of Paris, of plaster of paris alone, or of fine sand, using the least quantity of materials required for uniform bearing. To prevent loss of moisture from the subgrade during the load test, cover the exposed subgrade to a distance of 1.8 m (6 ft) from the circumference of the bearing plate with a tarpaulin or waterproof paper.

Where unconfined load tests are to be made at a depth below the surface, remove the surrounding material to provide a clearance equal to $1\frac{1}{2}$ bearing-plate diameters from the edge of the bearing plate. For confined tests the diameter of the excavated circular area must be just sufficient to accommodate the selected bearing plate.

Use a sufficient number of dial gauges, so located and fixed in position as to indicate the average deflection of the bearing plate. When using two dial gauges they should be set near each extremity of a diameter of the bearing plate, 25.4 mm (1 in.) from the circumference. When three gauges are employed they are set at an angle of 120° from each other and equidistant from the circumference of the bearing plate. Each individual set of readings shall be averaged, and this value is recorded as the average settlement reading.

After the equipment has been properly arranged, with all of the dead load (jack, plates, etc.) acting, seat the bearing plate and assembly by the quick application and release of a load sufficient to produce a deflection of not less than 0.25 mm (0.01 in.) nor more than 0.51 mm (0.02 in.) as indicated by the dials. When the dial needles come to rest following release of this load, reseat the plate by applying one half of the recorded load producing the 0.25 to 0.50 mm deflection. When the dial needles have then again come to rest, set each dial accurately at its zero mark.

Apply loads at a moderately rapid rate in uniform increments. The magnitude of each load increment should be small enough to permit the recording of a sufficient number of load/deflection points to produce an accurate load/deflection curve (not less than six). After each increment of load has been applied, allow its action to continue until a rate of deflection of not more than 0.03 mm/min (0.001 in.) has been maintained for 3 consecutive minutes. Record load and deflection readings for each load increment. Continue this procedure until the selected total deflection has been obtained, or until the load capacity of the apparatus has been reached, whichever occurs first. At this point, maintain the load until an increased deflection of not more than 0.03 mm/min for 3 consecutive minutes occurs. Record the total deflection, then release the load to that at which the dial gauges were set at zero and maintain this zero-setting load until the rate of recovery does not exceed 0.03 mm for 3 consecutive minutes. Record the deflection at the zero-setting load.

From a thermometer suspended near the bearing plate, read and record the air temperature at half-hour intervals.

From the data obtained it is then possible to plot the load for each increment against the corresponding settlement and also the recovery after full release of the load; correct, if necessary, for the zero deflection point when the dead weight of the apparatus and the seating load are considered.

The modulus k is then calculated from the slope of the load/deflection relationship; that is

$$k = \frac{dp}{d\Delta} \tag{3.11}$$

where p and Δ are load on the plate and Δ the deflection of the plate.

3.5 Thickness Design Methods

There are a considerable number of methods of pavement thickness design in use at the present time. This is to be expected since pavement design methods require some degree of correlation with pavement performance, which is itself greatly influenced by environmental conditions, so that what has proved to be an entirely satisfactory method of design and construction in one country may be totally unsuited to another. There is also the problem that definitions of failure vary considerably — a pavement which provides a suitable level of service to one population of vehicle occupants may produce many complaints from a differing population.

An interesting review of design methods for flexible pavements in Belgium, Czechoslovakia, Finland, France, the United Kingdom, the Federal Republic of

Germany, Italy, Japan, the Netherlands, Poland, Spain and Switzerland has been produced by the Permanent International Association of Road Congresses.[19]

Generally speaking, it was found that design methods could be divided into two groups.

(1) Those in which the design was based on different parameters that were used in conjunction with graphs produced from formulae (used in Czechoslovakia, the United Kingdom, Japan, Poland and Switzerland).

(2) Those in which the design was based on a restricted number of parameters and which finally produce an answer in terms of a pavement structure type (used in Finland, France, the Federal Republic of Germany and Spain).

In Belgium there are official structure types only for motorways; in Italy various design methods are used and there are structure types for motorways; in the Netherlands the Shell design method is generally used.

The pavement structure standards reported from the Federal Republic of Germany are 'Standardisierung der bituminosen Fahrbahnbefestigungen in Heisseinhan' MBV/StB7 of 1966. It contains 25 structure types for five different types of road bases for five classes of traffic. Currently these standards are being revised in an attempt to limit the initial investment by reducing total pavement thickness.

The pavement structure types of Finland give roadbase and surfacing thickness for six classes of traffic. Only unbound aggregates were reported as being used for the roadbase, while the thickness of the sub-base depends on the mechanical properties of the foundation soil.

The official French design method is given as a catalogue of pavement structure types, a choice being made according to the nature of the subsoil and the traffic intensity. Subsoils are divided into four categories and there are four traffic classes, ranging from 200 to 15 000 vehicles per day.

Total pavement thickness of bituminous pavement in Japan is calculated from

$$H = \frac{58.5 P^{0.4}}{CBR^{0.6}} \qquad (3.12)$$

where H is the total pavement thickness (sub-base, roadbase and surfacing),

P is the coefficient determined by the traffic intensity,

CBR is the California Bearing Ratio for the subsoil.

One of the Polish design methods uses a formula in which the total thickness of pavement depends upon traffic characteristics, the type and quality of the materials used, the maximum applied load, subsoil characteristics and a climatic factor.

An examination to determine whether preventive measures should be taken against frost damage is a preliminary process in pavement design in Switzerland. The thickness of sub-base is then determined from the CBR of the subsoil and the weight of applied traffic. Two design charts are used, depending upon whether the sub-base is a mixture of sand and gravel or stabilised material. Weight of applied traffic determines the depth of roadbase and surfacing in terms of a bituminous material of defined quality; equivalence factors allow the thickness of other materials to be determined.

In Czechoslovakia pavement construction is simulated by a multi-layer system. The modulus of elasticity of the foundation is deduced from the CBR value while the moduli of the different pavement layers are given in tables. The effective axle load is replaced by an equivalent load. Two criteria are used for design purposes

(1) a permissible deflection which is compared with a calculated deflection,
(2) a permissible stress in adjacent layers which is compared with a calculated stress.

There are also stipulations regarding protection from frost.

Summarising these design methods it was noted that when considering traffic loading, France and the Federal German Republic considered all traffic and also all heavy traffic as the traffic loading while the remaining ten countries reporting used standard equivalent axles usually obtained from the AASHO test.

3.6 Transport and Road Research Laboratory Report 1132: Method of Bituminous Pavement Design

TRRL Report 1132[10] revises a method of pavement design for bituminous pavements given in the 1970 edition of Road Note 29[6] and which was used as a basis of the design standards issued by the Department of Transport in 1976. These design recommendations were based on practical experience of experimental roads which had carried fewer than 10 million standard axles.

Whilst they proved generally satisfactory for roads which carried up to 40 million standard axles they were found to be unsuitable for roads which had to carry out the greatly increased present-day commercial vehicle loading. In addition the previous methods presented difficulties when new materials were being used or when reconstruction of an existing road had to be carried out.

The new design method is based upon considerably more experimental road data than the Road Note 29 method and in addition there now exists a much greater knowledge of the structural design of highway pavements. This has made it possible to develop an analytical method of design for both new and reconstructed pavements which takes into account the variability of material properties, subgrade strength and different cumulative traffic flows.

The design criteria adopted in LR 1132[10] can be summarised as follows.

(a) The vertical compressive stress or strain at formation level due to traffic loading must be limited so as to prevent excessive cumulative pavement deformation.

(b) The horizontal tensile stress or strain at the bottom of a bituminous or cement bound roadbase due to traffic loading must be limited to prevent fatigue cracking.

(c) When a pavement contains a considerable depth of bituminous material the creep of the material should be controlled to prevent rutting as a result of internal deformation.

(d) The granular sub-base should be adequate to provide an adequate construction platform.

First step in pavement design is a decision on the design life over which the pavement is subjected to traffic loading. Road Note 29 recommended a design life of 20 years for the design of a bituminous pavement. Studies by the Transport and Road Research Laboratory indicate that after taking into account construction, reconstruction costs and consequent traffic delays a design life of 20 years and an 85 per cent probability of survival provides an economic balance between a long design life and failure to achieve this life as a result of other than traffic loading.

In contrast to Road Note 29 when the end of design life was reached at the failure condition with a 20 mm rut depth, the end of the design life with the LR 1132[10] design method is the critical pavement condition where rut depth is limited to 10 mm and strengthening by overlaying is possible. Because of the difference in terminal condition in the two design methods LR 1132 gives a substantially longer life.

With a decision on design life made, it is necessary to estimate the cumulative number of equivalent standard 80 kN axles to be carried during the design life of the road. Estimated 24 hour daily commercial vehicle flows have to be converted to annual flows and an allowance made for the proportion of commercial vehicle flows travelling in the nearside traffic lane. The annual numbers of commercial vehicles are then multiplied by the estimated damaging effect of an average commercial vehicle, referred to as the vehicle damage factor, to give an estimate of the cumulative number of standard axles. In most cases it is considered to be sufficiently accurate to use the vehicle damage factor applicable at the mid-term of the design life.

It has been shown that the total number of commercial vehicles T_n using the slow lane over the design life of n years can be expressed in terms of the initial daily flow F_0 and the mean proportion P using the slow lane as

$$T_n = 365F_0 \frac{((1 + r)^n - 1)}{r} P$$

The cumulative number of commercial vehicles is converted to standard axles by multiplying the number of equivalent standard axles per commercial vehicle at the mid-term of the design life.

The vehicle damage factor D for any mid-term year is based on the 24 hour AADF of commerical vehicles for that year F. The base year is 1945 and it is the number of years t which have elapsed between 1945 and the mid-term year where

$$D = \frac{0.35}{0.93^t + 0.082} - \left(\frac{0.26}{0.92^t + 0.082}\right) \left(\frac{1.0}{3.9^{(F/1550)}}\right)$$

Table 3.6 gives details of the use of the above formula and shows the effects of year and daily flows of commerical vehicles on vehicle damage factors.

Table 3.6 Vehicle damage factors[10]

Year	Daily flow of commercial vehicles AADF			
	250	1000	2000	4000
1985	0.78	1.64	2.17	2.49
1990	0.93	1.89	2.49	2.84
1995	1.18	2.12	2.76	3.14
2000	1.22	2.31	3.00	3.40
2005	1.34	2.47	3.18	3.60
2010	1.43	2.60	3.33	3.76

3.6.1 The Subgrade

In the design of a road pavement it is required to estimate the strength and the stiffness of the subgrade for two purposes. Firstly the strength of the subgrade just before placing the capping layer or sub-base must be estimated because the capping layer or sub-base serves as a construction platform. Secondly the long-term strength and stiffness of the subgrade after disturbance during construction and when the equilibrium moisture content has become established needs to be known to determine performance under traffic loading.

Whilst the California Bearing Ratio has limitations for the characterisation of subgrade soils it has been widely used for pavement design and was adopted for use in Road Note 29. For differing soils, equilibrium suction-index CBR values depending on construction conditions, water table height and pavement thickness are recommended in LR 1132 and are given in table 3.7.

It is also necessary to estimate the stiffness modulus of the subgrade soil to allow stresses and strains in the road pavement to be calculated. The CBR value is a measure of stiffness and whilst CBR test conditions differ considerably from the stresses imposed by actual traffic loading a connection between CBR and soil stiffness is given in LR 1132; it is

$$E = 17.6 \, (CBR)^{0.64} \text{ MPa}$$

The sub-base serves two purposes, firstly it has to support construction traffic without excessive rutting and secondly it has to avoid excessive dynamic strains within the subgrade that would cause deformation. It is considered that if rutting is limited to 40 mm the sub-base can be reshaped and recompacted efficiently. Experimental investigations have demonstrated a relationship between cumulative standard axles (N) imposed on a good-quality sub-base by construction traffic and the CBR of the subgrade as follows

Table 3.7 Equilibrium suction-index CBR values[10]

TYPE OF SOIL	PLASTICITY INDEX	HIGHWATER TABLE CONSTRUCTION CONDITIONS:						LOW WATER TABLE CONSTRUCTION CONDITIONS:					
		POOR		AVERAGE		GOOD		POOR		AVERAGE		GOOD	
		THIN	THICK	THIN	THICK	THIN	THICK	THIN	THICK	THIN	THICK	THIN	THICK
HEAVY CLAY	70	1.5	2	2	2	2	2	1.5	2	2	2	2	2.5
	60	1.5	2	2	2	2	2.5	1.5	2	2	2	2	2.5
	50	1.5	2	2	2.5	2	2.5	2	2.5	2	2.5	2	2.5
	40	2	2.5	2.5	3	2.5	3	2.5	2.5	3	3	3	3.5
SILTY CLAY	30	2.5	3.5	3	4	3.5	5	3	3.5	4	4	4	6
SANDY CLAY	20	2.5	4	4	5	4.5	7	3	4	5	6	6	8
	10	1.5	3.5	3	6	3.5	7	2.5	4	4.5	7	6	>8
SILT*	–	1	1	1	1	2	2	1	1	2	2	2	2
SAND (POORLY GRADED)	–	20 (all conditions)											
SAND (WELL GRADED)	–	40 (all conditions)											
SANDY GRAVEL (WELL GRADED)	–	60 (all conditions)											

*Estimated assuming some probability of material saturating.

$$\log N_{40} = \frac{\ln (CBR)^{0.63}}{190} - 0.24$$

A graphical representation of this relationship, referred to as a modified Corps of Engineers relationship, is given in LR 3112 and is reproduced as figure 3.4.

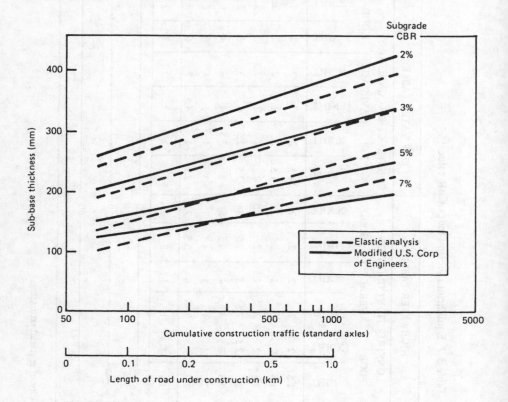

Figure 3.4   Thickness of sub-base required to carry construction traffic[10]

The second purpose of the sub-base is to limit dynamic vertical strain on the sub-base to a level which would not produce major subgrade deformation. This effect was investigated by elastic analysis using a relationship between cumulative traffic and acceptable level of subgrade strain obtained from a study of experimental roads.

An elastic analysis of sub-bases requires an adequate characterisation of the non-linear elastic response of granular materials which is particularly difficult when they are laid on relatively weak lower layers. In the approach of LR 1132 the stiffness of each successive sub-base layer which is separately compacted has been taken as three times that of the layer beneath up to an upper limit of stiffness of 150 MPa. On weak subgrades of up to 5 per cent CBR a lower sub-base layer thickness of 225 mm is assumed. The results of this analysis are shown in figure 3.4 where reasonable agreement between the two approaches can be seen. In using figure 3.4 the likely CBR value at the time of construction as shown in table 3.6 should be used.

Advice is given in LR 1132[10] that on weak subgrades of less than 5 per cent CBR, when a capping layer is not used then a sub-base greater than 225 mm is required and this should be compacted in two layers. The lower layer should be as thick as possible and preferably 225 mm thick to avoid damaging the subgrade compaction.

Capping layers of lower-quality material than Department of Transport type-1 sub-base are advantageous in that they allow the stiffness of type-1 material to be fully utilised. The use of the capping layer prevents the necessity of compacting two layers of type-1 material in thin layers. Whilst precise elastic analysis of the stresses in a sub-base and a capping layer is difficult, LR 1132[10] illustrates that the use of a 350 mm capping layer and 150 mm sub-base for sub-grades of 2–5 per cent CBR and a 600 mm capping layer and a 150 mm sub-base provides a factor of safety of at least two as regards dynamic vertical strain at formation level.

Observed performance of experimental roads is the basis of the design method and for bituminous roadbases the approach allows the use of new materials and the development of new designs. For wet-mix and lean concrete roadbases design criteria are less well established and it is more difficult to adjust the standard designs for new materials.

Rut depth and deflection measurements were made on the experimental roads and multiple regression was used to obtain the relationship between pavement life as defined by a terminal critical condition (10 mm rut depth) and also between deflection measurements and the thickness of pavement layers and the CBR of the subgrade. From the resulting equations, designs for the roadbases were developed and for roads with a bituminous roadbase figure 3.5 shows the design curves, permissible strains being shown in figure 3.6.

The results from experimental roads containing wet-mix roadbase and rolled asphalt were analysed in terms of rut depth and deflection. The resulting design curve is shown in figure 3.7. This curve is for a design CBR of 5 per cent and a sub-base thickness of 225 mm. For design CBR values of less than 5 per cent a capping layer will normally be required to carry construction traffic. At 2 per cent CBR, both at the time of construction and at design equilibrium conditions, an extra 15 mm of bituminous surfacing and the same extra thickness of wet-mix are required in addition to the extra thickness of sub-base required for construction traffic. If the CBR is greater than 5 per cent the reductions in design thicknesses are insignificant with a sub-base of appropriately reduced thickness.

Lean concrete roadbases suffer from shrinkage cracks which occur early in the life of the pavement, normally at about 4 m transverse materials. For lightly trafficked roads, cumulative traffic less than 20 msa, it may be considered desirable to allow this cracking to proceed slowly under the combined effects of traffic and temperature and then finally to reconstruct the pavement completely. For more heavily trafficked roads the removal of the roadbase may result in excessive traffic delays and it may be considered desirable to design for a longer but indeterminate life. Observations of the performance of experimental roads

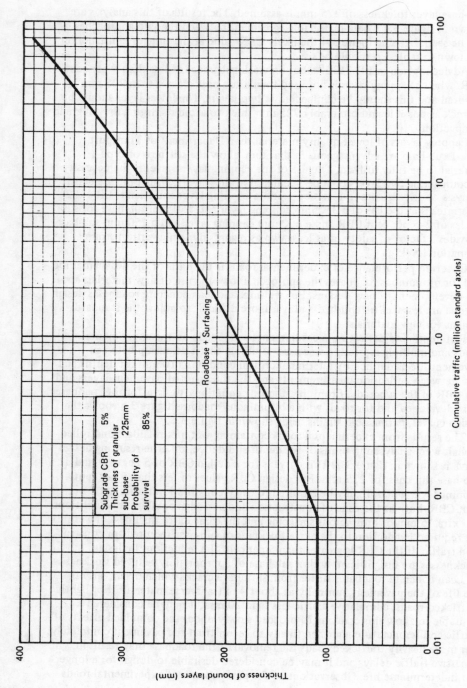

Figure 3.5 Design curve for roads with bituminous roadbase[10]

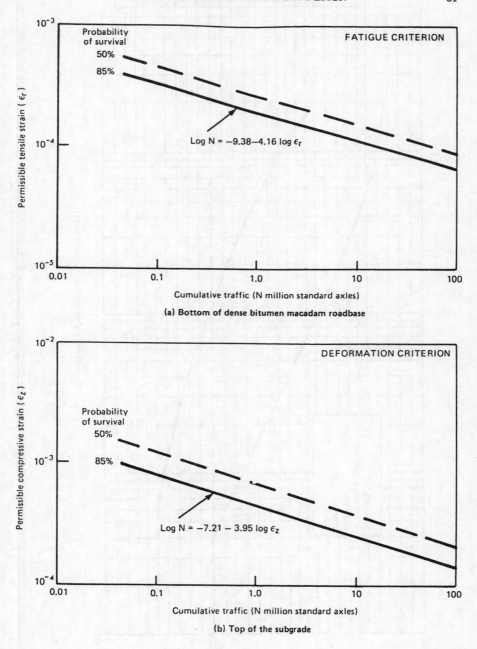

Figure 3.6 Permissible strains induced by a standard 40 kN wheel load at a pavement temperature of $20°C$[10]

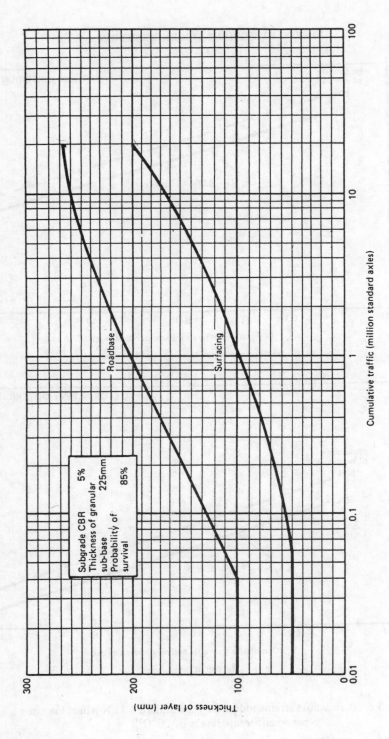

Figure 3.7 Design curves for roads with wet-mix roadbase[10]

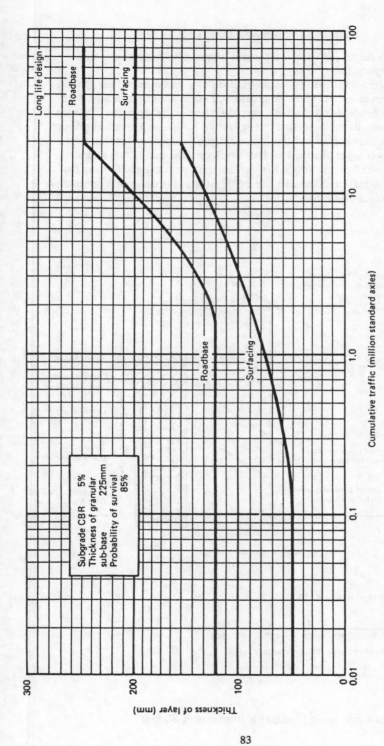

Figure 3.8 Design curves for roads with lean concrete roadbase[10]

have led to design curves for both shorter and longer life design which are incorporated in figure 3.8.

On heavily trafficked roads the reconstruction of a pavement which requires the removal and replacement of the roadbase will normally result in high delay costs. As a consequence it is desirable to avoid fatigue cracking in the roadbase which would require its replacement. In the United Kingdom a pavement design has been used which makes use of the higher fatigue or cracking resistance of a 125 mm thick lower layer of rolled asphalt roadbase. The use of this design ensures that at the end of the design life deformation or rutting will bring the pavement into a critical condition. Figure 3.9 illustrates the design for cumulative traffic flows in excess of 80 msa.

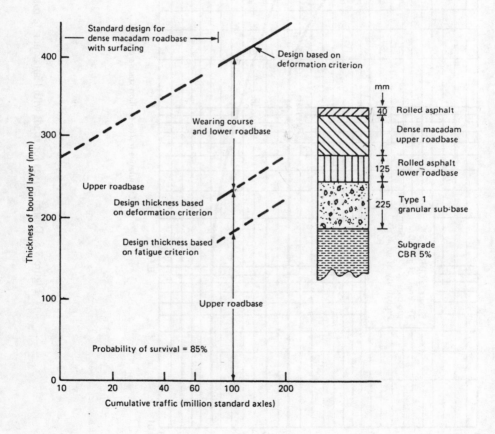

Figure 3.9 Design for traffic in excess of 80 msa[10]

The design curves given in LR 1132[10] may be adapted for different situations by the use of equivalences for bituminous and unbound granular material, for the effect of binder viscosity in dense bitumen macadam and also for changes in modulus of roadbase macadam.

Multi-layer elastic analysis has been used to obtain the equivalence between bituminous and unbound granular material. LR 1132 states that 10 mm of dense roadbase macadam is equivalent to about 30 mm of type-1 sub-base material and 20 mm of wet-mix. The equivalence with wet-mix is less certain and it is recommended that it be used with caution. In addition LR 1132[10] states that the effect of an increase in binder viscosity from 100 pen to 50 pen has been shown to have no significant effect on the laboratory fatigue or deformation characteristics but increases the stiffness modulus of the material. Critical strains in a highway pavement are also considerably influenced by the modulus of the roadbase. Further details of the adaptation of the standard design curves are given in LR 1132[10].

3.7 The Road Note 29 Method of Design for Residential Roads

For new roads to be constructed in residential areas it is not possible to estimate future commercial traffic from existing traffic volumes. Road Note 29 gives an indication of the commercial vehicles to be expected at the date of construction; these are given in table 3.8. The cumulative numbers of commercial vehicles passing over these residential roads for any given design life may then be estimated from figure 3.4.

The recommendations given in table 3.8 were based on limited information that was available at the time for lightly trafficked roads. Currer[10] gives details of further observations of commercial traffic flows made in the Bracknell Development Area. A difficulty is the classification of residential estate roads but Currer states that certain broad subdivisions may be made. All estates are likely to have one or two main entrance/exit roads normally carrying some through-traffic. Within the estate there will be some link roads connecting and serving different areas of the estate. These areas will have interconnected residential roads frequently having cul-de-sacs running off them. Shipping and other central services are normally located on the link roads. Table 3.9 gives details of the observations obtained and compares them with the recommended Road Note 29 values. It can be seen that for some of the roads Road Note 29 will somewhat overestimate the commercial traffic flow, but not to an extent where changes in the Road Note recommendations are necessary.

Table 3.8 Commercial traffic flows recommended for use in the design of roads in residential and associated developments when more accurate assessments are not available[6]

Type of road	Estimated traffic flow of commercial vehicles per day (in each direction) at the time of construction
1 Cul-de-sacs and minor residential roads	10
2 Through roads and roads carrying regular bus routes involving up to 25 public service vehicles per day **in each direction**	75
3 Major through roads carrying regular bus routes involving 25–50 public service vehicles per day **in each direction**	175
4 Main shopping centre of a large development carrying goods deliveries and main through roads carrying more than 50 public service vehicles per day **in each direction**	350

Table 3.9 Comparison of observed traffic flow on housing-estate roads with the classification system used in Road Note 29[10]

Type of road	Vehicles per day (in each direction) Commercial	P.S.V.	Road Note 29 description	Vehicles per day (in each direction) Commercial	P.S.V.
Main entrance/ exit road	200	65	Main through road carrying more than 50 P.S.V. per day	350	>50
Main link road 1.	135	35	Major through roads carrying 25-50 P.S.V. per day	175	25-50
2.	70	40			
Subsidiary link road	25	10	Through roads carrying regular bus routes with up to 25 P.S.V. per day	75	0-25
Estate roads 1.	10	0			
2.	2	0			
3.	15	0	Minor roads and culs-de-sac	10	0
Culs-de-sac 1.	3	0			
2.	4	0			
3.	1	0			

3.8 The AASHO Interim Guide for Design of Pavement Structures

Following completion of the AASHO Road Test the American Association of State Highway Officials in 1962 issued an interim design guide. Following an experimental period of use this guide was reissued without amendment in 1972, but with additional material, as the AASHO interim guide for design of pavement structures.[20]

The limitations of the design guide are stated as follows.

(1) An empirical soil-support scale with values from 1 to 10 has been developed. Point 3 on the scale represents the silty clay roadbed soils on the AASHO Road Test and is a firm and valid point. Point 10 represents a crushed-rock base such as was used on the Road Test and is a reasonably valid point. All the other points on the scale were assumed from experience and checked by theoretical computation. This soil-support value must be correlated with the soil test used by the pavement design organisation.

(2) The pavement design method produced a structural number which must be converted to an actual thickness of surfacing, base and sub-base layers by the use of layer coefficients which represent the actual strengths of the materials being used. Coefficients for asphaltic concrete surfacing, crushed-stone base and sandy-gravel sub-base used in the Road Test have been developed for the specific designs, constructional standards, environmental conditions and traffic exposure represented by the test. Careful consideration should be given to the values assigned to the coefficients in differing circumstances.

(3) A regional factor is included in the design procedure and this provides an adjustment for local environmental and other conditions. The design guide gives details of how the regional factor may be determined but consideration should be given to the possibility that the factor may not account for particularly severe local conditions.

(4) A basic traffic-analysis period must be selected for pavement-design purposes and this must not be confused with pavement life, which is affected by other factors in addition to traffic.

3.9 The AASHO Interim Flexible Pavement Design Procedure

The design procedure is presented in the form of nomographs, figures 3.10 and 3.11, for ease in the solution of the design equations. These design equations were developed on the basis of the following assumptions.

(1) That the basic equations derived from the Road Test are a valid representation of the relationship between loss in serviceability, traffic and pavement thickness. In these equations the loss of serviceability is expressed in terms of reduction in serviceability index; traffic is converted to equivalent 8160 kg (18 000 lb) single-axle load applications and pavement thickness is represented by a structural number.

(2) That the basic derived equations for a single type of subsoil may be extended to apply to any other type of subsoil using the soil-support scale.

(3) That the basic equations developed after testing by repeated applications of uniform traffic loads may be extended to mixed traffic by the use of equivalent 8160 kg (18 000 lb) axles loads.

(4) That the basic equations developed for a single environmental condition may be extended to other environmental conditions by the use of a regional factor.

(5) That the basic equations developed for the surfacing, base and sub-base materials used in the Road Test may be extended to other materials by the use of layer coefficients.

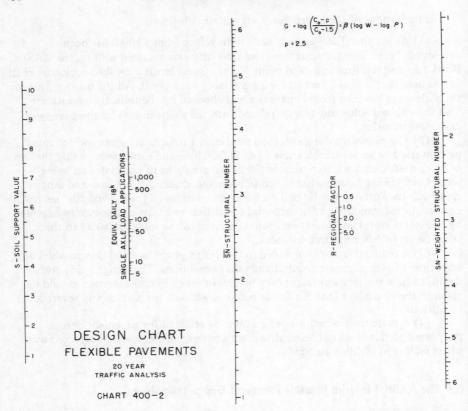

$$G = \log\left(\frac{C_0 - \rho}{C_0 - 1.5}\right) = \beta\,(\log W - \log\,\rho)$$

$$\rho = 2.5$$

DESIGN CHART

FLEXIBLE PAVEMENTS

20 YEAR
TRAFFIC ANALYSIS

CHART 400-2

Figure 3.10 Design chart for flexible pavements, 20-year traffic analysis period[20]

(6) That the basic equations developed by accelerated loading over a 2-year period may be extended to apply to traffic loading over an extended period of time.

(7) That during the construction of pavements for which the design guide is used a high quality of construction will be obtained.

3.9.1 The Soil Support Value

The basic equations developed from the Road Test are valid only for the A-6 type of soil acquired from adjacent borrow pits. The soil was placed in 100 mm layers and compacted to an average AASHO T-99 density of 97.7 per cent. As previously stated, this soil was assigned a value of 3.0 and to obtain a second point on the scale a substantial depth of crushed-rock base was given a value of 10.0. This latter value was used because observations at the Road Test indicated that approximately 110 mm of surfacing on a substantial thickness of crushed-rock base would carry

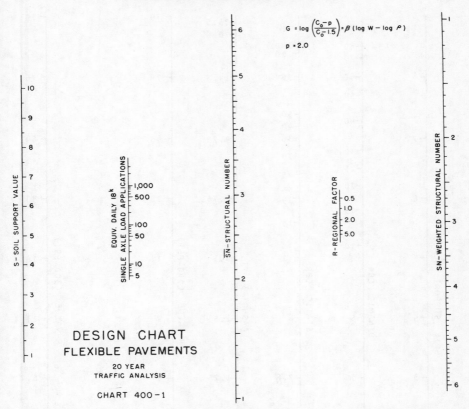

Figure 3.11 Design chart for flexible pavements, 20-year traffic analysis period[20]

approximately 1000 standard-axle applications per day for a 20-year period without the serviceability index falling below 2.0. A linear scale between points 3.0 and 10.0 was then assumed and the scale was also extended downward linearly. A check on the assumption of linearity of the soil-support scale has been made using layered elastic theory.

Because the soil-support value has no defined relationship to existing test procedures it is necessary for each authority using the design guide to establish the relationship between soil-support value and a conventional soil strength test. The Utah State Department of Highways has carried out a soil testing programme and has derived the relationships given in figure 3.12.

3.9.2 Regional Factor

Because the Road Test was carried out at one situation with a particular climatic and environmental condition a regional factor has been included in the design

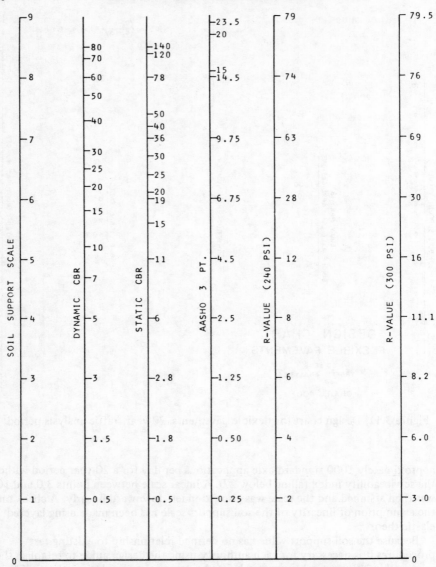

Figure 3.12 Soil support value and soil support strength test relationships as developed by the Utah State Department of Highways[20]

procedure for the design of pavements in other situations. The damaging effect of traffic at the Road Test was generally considered to be greatest during the period of spring thaw and least when the subsoil was relatively dry. At the test site the regional factor was calculated to vary between 0.1 and 4.8, with an annual value of

1.0. The lower values apply to the situation where the subsoil was relatively dry or solidly frozen and the higher values to periods during the spring thaw.

The interim design guide points out that at the date of its publication there was no exact way in which the regional factor could be calculated but that it could be estimated by analysing the duration of certain conditions during a typical year using the following guide values

Subgrade frozen to a depth of 125 mm or more	0.2 to 1.0
Subgrade dry, summer and autumn	0.3 to 1.5
Subgrade wet, spring thaw	4.0 to 5.0

These values should be seen in the context of the conditions at the test site, where the average mean summer temperature is 21 °C and the average mean winter temperature is −2 °C. The average annual precipitation is approximately 876 mm and the average annual frost penetration is 635 mm. At the site the soil usually remains frozen during the winter with alternate thawing and freezing of the immediate surface.

A survey of 50 of the United States[21] has shown that one or more of the following factors were currently being used to assign a regional factor: topography, similarity to Road Test location, rainfall, frost penetration, temperature, groundwater table, subgrade type, engineering judgement, type of highway and subsurface drainage.

The interim design guide suggests that in addition to these factors consideration needs to be given to the number of annual freeze—thaw cycles and the existence of steep gradients with large volumes of heavy-truck traffic of areas of concentrated turning or stopping movements. For the United States the regional factor should not exceed about 4.0 or be less than 0.5.

3.9.3 Structural Number

The solution of the design equations is in the form of a structural number (SN) which is an abstract number expressing the structural strength of the pavement required for a given combination of soil support value, traffic loading, terminal serviceability index and regional factor. The structural number for the whole pavement is represented by the general equation

$$SN = a_1 D_1 + a_2 D_2 + a_3 D_3 \qquad (3.13)$$

where a, a_2, a_3 are layer coefficients representative of surface, base and sub-base courses and D_1, D_2, D_3 are the actual thicknesses in inches of surface, base and sub-base courses.

3.9.4 Layer Coefficients

As stated above, a layer coefficient converts the structural number to actual pavement thickness and is a measure of the relative ability of the material to function as a structural component of the pavement.

During the Road Test, average values of layer coefficients were determined for the materials employed and these are

Asphaltic concrete wearing course	0.44
Crushed-stone base	0.14
Sandy gravel sub-base	0.11

In addition, several States have developed coefficients and a selection of the values are given below

High-stability plant-mix bituminous surfacing	0.30 to 0.44
Untreated crushed-stone roadbase	0.10 to 0.14
Cement-stabilised-soil roadbase	0.20
Bituminous roadbase material	0.30 to 0.34

3.9.5 Traffic Loading

The design guide uses as input to the design equations the total repetition of standard 8160 kg (18 000 lb) single-axle loads that occur during the traffic-analysis period. Many users of the design guide predict the future axle repetitions in various load classes. To do this with any accuracy it is not only necessary to have details of the existing axle-load spectrum but also to be able to predict future heavy-vehicle growth.

Frequently traffic loads are predicted for both directions of travel and a directional distribution must be assumed — usually 50 per cent in each direction. Distribution of traffic between lanes is usually made in the United States on a very conservative basis, with from 80 to 100 per cent of the one-direction traffic used for the design of each lane when there is a total of four lanes in both directions. When there are six or more lanes in both directions then from 60 to 80 per cent of the one-direction traffic is assigned to one or more of the outer lanes and lesser values to each of the inner lanes.

With the predicted axle-load repetitions known they are converted to standard axles, using the equivalence factors given in tables 3.1 and 3.2.

3.9.6 Use of the Flexible Design Chart

The solutions of the design equations for flexible pavements for terminal serviceability values of 2.5 and 2.0 are given as design charts reproduced as figures 3.11 and 3.12. Each chart requires two applications of a straight edge for each solution. First the soil-support value of the subgrade and the total equivalent standard axle loading are used to obtain the unweighted structural number. This latter value is then used with the regional factor to obtain the weighted structural number. Suitable designs are then those whose material types and thicknesses satisfy the general equation

$$SN = a_1 D_1 + a_2 D_2 + a_3 D_3$$

Minimum thicknesses of 50 mm are specified for wearing courses; 100 mm for roadbases and sub-bases.

3.10 Pavement Design for Bitumen-surfaced Roads in Tropical and Subtropical Countries

The Transport and Road Research Laboratory of the Department of the Environment give recommendations for the structural design of bitumen-surfaced roads in tropical and subtropical countries.[22] This Note gives recommendations for the design of roads that are required to carry up to an average of 1500 heavy vehicles per day for a design life of 10 to 15 years. Roads such as these are likely to be non-urban roads in developing countries.

As with other methods of pavement design, the major steps in design are

(1) Estimating the traffic, and its axle-load distribution, that the road will carry during its design life.

(2) Assessing the strength of the subgrade beneath the completed pavement.

(3) After consideration of (1) and (2), selecting the correct combination of materials and layer thicknesses that will produce an economical pavement with minimum maintenance.

3.10.1 Traffic Loading

Following the approach of Road Note 29, only goods and public service vehicles with an unladen weight greater than 1500 kg are considered for traffic loading. For roads that are to be improved, a traffic count can be used as a basis for estimating traffic flows during the life of the proposed pavement. For projected highways, land use/traffic planning techniques can be used. In some circumstances it may be necessary to carry out field observations to determine the axle-load spectrum. Consideration should be given to the directional distribution of axle loading because frequently trucks are heavily loaded when travelling towards a port but empty on the return trip. Specialised industrial development may also generate heavy traffic loads. Once the existing axle loading is measured or estimated then there is the additional difficulty of predicting growth rates even for the shorter design lives of 10 to 15 years recommended for developing countries. Some guidance may be obtained from past trends of traffic growth, numbers of registered vehicles or from the consumption of motor fuel. A suggested alternative is that the growth in traffic may be between one and two times the Gross National/Domestic Product.

The uncertainties regarding traffic growth are one reason for using a shorter design life, but an additional factor is that the traffic growth rate may be high so that it is likely to be uneconomic to build a road for the very much higher traffic flows expected in some 20 years' time.

As with the Road Note 29 method of design, the equivalent damaging effect of axle loads are estimated from the AASHO Road Test. For roads in developing countries Road Note 31 recommends a terminal serviceability of 2.0 and the equivalence factors appropriate for a pavement structural number of 3 or less. These values are given in table 3.10.

A decision needs to be made as to the distribution of traffic between lanes and it is recommended that on dual carriageway roads and on single carriageway roads with more than two lanes the slow lanes should be considered to carry all the commercial vehicles because observations indicate that commercial vehicles do not transfer from the slow lane until the flow exceeds 2000 commercial vehicles per day in each direction.

Where as an economy measure a single-lane bituminous road is constructed, the one-direction traffic loading should be multiplied by a factor of 4 to allow for the channelling effect which occurs.

3.10.2 Strengths of the Subgrade

The soil strengths test used to assess the supporting powers of the subgrade in the Road Note 31 method of design is the California Bearing Ratio Test. During the

Table 3.10 Factors for converting numbers of axles to the equivalent number of standard 8200 kg (18 000 lb) axles[22]

Axle load		Equivalence factor
kg	lb	
910	2 000	0.0002
1 810	4 000	0.0025
2 720	6 000	0.01
3 630	8 000	0.04
4 540	10 000	0.08
5 440	12 000	0.2
6 350	14 000	0.3
7 260	16 000	0.6
8 160	18 000	1.0
9 070	20 000	1.6
9 980	22 000	2.4
10 890	24 000	3.6
11 790	26 000	5.2
12 700	28 000	7.2
13 610	30 000	9.9
14 520	32 000	13.3
15 430	34 000	17.6
16 320	36 000	22.9
17 230	38 000	29.4
18 140	40 000	37.3
19 070	42 000	47
19 980	44 000	58
20 880	46 000	72
21 790	48 000	87

NOTE: The factors given are those derived from Liddle[11] for flexible pavements of the type designed on the basis of Fig. 3.

highway-location stage of the project due consideration will have been given to aligning the highway over those areas where the subgrade is strongest, subject to all the other constraints on the design. The density of the soil is a function of the compaction applied to the subgrade and of the moisture content during construction.

When designing a pavement, an estimate should be made of the strength of the subgrade at the moisture content equal to the wettest condition when the road is in service. This will depend upon the local climate and the depth of the ground-water table below the road surface. Road Note 31 states that under impermeable pavements in the tropics subgrade moisture conditions can be classified into three main categories.

(1) Subgrades where the water-table is sufficiently close to the ground surface to control the subgrade moisture content. The type of subgrade soil governs the depth below the road surface at which a water-table becomes the dominant influence on the subgrade moisture content. In non-plastic soils the water-table will dominate the subgrade moisture content when it rises to within 0.9 m (3 ft) of the road surface, in sandy clays (P1 < 20 per cent) the water-table will dominate when it rises to within 3 m (10 ft) of the road surface, and in heavy clays (P1 < 40 per cent) the water-table will dominate when it rises to within 7 m (23 ft) of the road surface. In addition to areas where the water-table is maintained by rainfall, this category includes coastal strips and flood planes where the water-table is maintained by the sea, by a lake, or by a river.

(2) Subgrades with deep water-tables and where rainfall is sufficient to produce significant seasonal changes in moisture conditions under the road. These conditions occur when rainfall exceeds evapotranspiration for at least two months of the year. The rainfall in such areas is usually greater than 250 mm (10 in.) per year and is often seasonal.

(3) Subgrades in areas with no permanent water-table near the ground surface and where the climate is arid throughout the year. Such areas have an annual rainfall of 250 mm (10 in.) or less.

Road Note 31 gives the following advice on estimating the subgrade moisture content.

Category (1) Where a water-table exists close to the ground surface the ultimate moisture content in the subgrade under a sealed pavement can be estimated from a knowledge of the depth of the watertable and the relation between suction and moisture for the subgrade soil.[23] The test apparatus required for determining this relationship is described in Road Note 31, but such apparatus is not normally available to road designers. As an alternative the ultimate subgrade moisture content can be determined by measuring the moisture content in subgrades below existing pavements in similar situations at the time of the year when the water-table is at its highest level. These pavements should be greater than 3 m (10 ft) wide and more than 2 years old. Allowance can be made for different soil types by virtue of the fact that the ratio of subgrade moisture content to plastic limit is the same for different subgrade soils when the water-table and climatic conditions are similar.

Where there are no existing pavements in similar situations available for

comparison, an estimate of the minimum subgrade CBR value can be obtained
from table 2.12. This table shows the estimated minimum CBR values for six types
of subgrade soil for various depths of water-table, assuming that the subgrade is
compacted to not less than 95 per cent of the maximum dry density attainable in
the British Standard Compaction test, 2.5 kg (5.5 lb) rammer method.[16] The CBR
values quoted are minimum values and should be used only in conjunction with the
design chart given in Road Note 31 and reproduced as figure 3.13.

Category (2) When the water-table is not near the ground surface the subgrade
moisture condition under an impermeable pavement will depend on the balance
between the water entering the subgrade through the shoulders and at the edges of
the pavement during wet weather and the moisture leaving the ground by
evapotranspiration when the weather is dry.[24] Where the average annual rainfall is
greater than 250 mm (10 in.) a year, the ultimate moisture condition for design

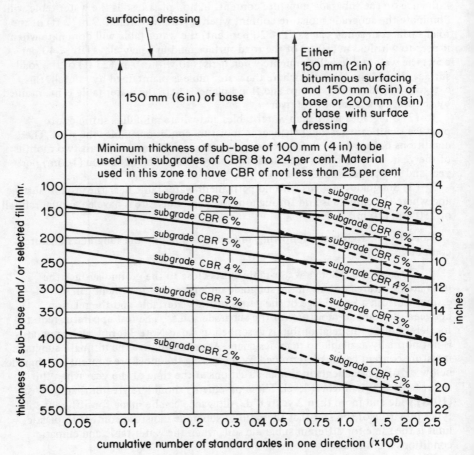

Figure 3.13 Design chart for flexible pavements[22]

purposes can be taken as the optimum moisture content given by the British
Standard Compaction test, 2.5 kg (5.5 lb) rammer method.[16]

If the equipment for carrying out laboratory compaction and CBR tests is not
available, an estimate of the subgrade CBR can be obtained from table 3.11.

When deciding on the depth of the water-table in Category (1) or Category (2)
subgrades, the possibility of the existence of local perched water-tables should be
borne in mind and the effects of seasonal flooding (where this occurs) should not
be overlooked.

Category (3) In regions where the climate is arid throughout most of the year
[annual rainfall 250 mm (10 in.) or less], the ultimate moisture content of the
subgrade will be virtually the same as that of the uncovered soil at the same depth.
This is the moisture content that should be used for design purposes. Again, if the
equipment for carrying out laboratory compaction and CBR tests is not available,
table 3.9 can be used to give a conservative estimate of the subgrade CBR.

The methods of estimating the subgrade moisture content outlined above are
based on the assumption that the road pavement is virtually impermeable. If

**Table 3.11 Estimated minimum subgrade CBR values under paved roads for
subgrades compacted to 95 per cent of British Standard maximum dry density[22]**

Depth of water-table* from formation level	Minimum CBR (per cent)					
	Non-plastic sand	Sandy clay PI = 10	Sandy clay PI = 20	Silty clay PI = 30	Heavy clay PI ⩾ 40	Silt
0.6m (2 ft)	8	5	4	3	2	1
1.0m (3.3 ft)	25	6	5	4	3	2
1.5m (4.9 ft)	25	8	6	5	3	
2.0m (6.5 ft)	25	8	7	5	3	
2.5m (8.2 ft)	25	8	8	6	4	See
3.0m (9.8 ft)	25	25	8	7	4	Note
3.5m (11.5 ft)	25	25	8	8	4	5
5.0m (16.4 ft)	25	25	8	8	5	
7.0m (23 ft) or more	25	25	8	8	7	

* The highest seasonal level attained by the water-table should be taken.

NOTES:

1. Since the values given in Table 2 are estimated minimum CBR values, wherever possible the CBR should be measured by laboratory testing at the appropriate moisture content.

2. Table 2 is to be used only in conjunction with the design chart given in Fig. 3.

3. With structured clays, such as the red coffee soils of East Africa, laboratory CBR tests should be undertaken whenever possible. Soils of this type can be identified by the fact that their plasticity, as indicated by the Atterberg limits, tends to increase when the soil is worked and its structure is broken down[15]. If CBR tests cannot be undertaken, an approximate estimate of the effective subgrade CBR for this soil type will be obtained by using the values quoted in Table 2 for sandy clays (PI = 20 per cent).

4. Table 2 cannot be used for soils containing appreciable amounts of mica or organic matter. Such soils can usually be identified visually.

5. Laboratory CBR tests are required for pure silt subgrades with water-tables deeper than 1.0m (3.3ft).

permeable base and sub-base materials are used, rain-water shed from the road surface can easily penetrate to the subgrade and may saturate it. In such cases the strength of subgrades with moisture conditions in Category (1) and Category (2) areas should be assessed on the basis of saturated CBR samples. Subgrades with moisture conditions in Category (3) are unlikely to become saturated when covered by a permeable base and sub-base and the subgrade moisture content in such situations can still be taken as being the same as that of the uncovered soil at the same depth.

Road Note 31 also gives guidance on determining the subgrade strength once the ultimate subgrade moisture content has been estimated. It recommends that subgrades should be compacted during construction to a relative density of at least 95 per cent of the maximum dry density achieved by the British Standard Compaction test. This will increase the subgrade bearing-strength and reduce permeability and subsequent compaction by traffic.

Samples of the subgrade soil at the estimated subgrade moisture content are compacted in CBR moulds to the specified density and the CBR value determined. This value is then used to determine the required pavement thickness using figure 3.13. Road Note 31 points out that with cohesionless sands, the rammer method tends to overestimate the optimum moisture content and underestimate the dry density achieved by normal field equipment. The vibrating-hammer method is more appropriate for cohesionless sands. If the reliability of the results of the CBR test is in doubt, the values given in table 2.12 may be adopted.

If samples of cohesive soils are compacted at moisture contents equal to or greater than the optimum moisture content, they should be left sealed for 24 h before being penetrated so that excess pore-water pressures induced during compaction are dissipated.

Alternatively, a more complete picture of the relationship between density, moisture content and CBR for the subgrade soil can be obtained by compacting the soil at several moisture contents and at least two levels of compaction, measuring the CBR of each sample. The design CBR is then obtained by interpolation. This method is preferable since it enables an estimate to be made of the subgrade CBR at different densities and thus indicates the value of achieving the specified density in the subgrade.

If saturated subgrade conditions are anticipated because of the use of permeable base and sub-base materials in areas with more than 250 mm (10 in.) annual rainfall, the compacted samples for the CBR test should be saturated by immersion in water for 4 days before being tested. In all other cases when CBR is determined by direct measurement, the CBR samples should not be immersed since this results in over-design.

In situ CBR measurements of subgrade soils are not recommended because of the difficulty of ensuring that the moisture and density conditions at the time of test are representative of those expected under the completed pavement.

3.10.3 Determination of Pavement Thickness

With an estimate of design CBR and traffic loading in terms of repetition of standard axles during the design-life, the thickness of pavement can be obtained from figure 3.13 which gives the sub-base thickness required. This design chart has been developed on the assumption that a standard base thickness of 150 mm (6 in.), with a variable sub-base thickness to allow for variations in subgrade strength, is the most economic design for a flexible pavement that will carry up to 0.5 million standard axles in one direction over a design life of ten years or more. An adequate surfacing can be provided by a double surface dressing.

If it is desired initially to construct a pavement that will carry a cumulative loading of up to 2.5 million standard axles in one direction Road Note 31 recommends either a 150 mm (6 in.) base with a 50 mm (2 in.) bituminous surfacing or a 200 mm (8 in.) base with a double surface dressing. In general, for roads that will carry not more than about 300 commercial vehicles per day (in both directions) at the time of construction, the most economical solution will be to choose the double surface dressing on the 150 mm (6 in.) base initially and to add the 50 mm (2 in.) bituminous surfacing some years later.

When using figure 3.13 it should be noted that if the CBR of the subgrade is 25 per cent or more, a sub-base is not required. When subgrade CBR is 8 to 24 per cent inclusive then a minimum practicable sub-base of 100 mm (4 in.) should be provided. Caution is required if the subgrade is subject to swelling due to seasonal changes in moisture content and some guidance is given in Kassif and Wiseman[25] and Chen[26].

Road Note 31 states that the sub-base material, which is expected to be normally or naturally occurring gravel or gravel—sand—clay, should have a CBR of 25 per cent or more at the density and moisture content expected in the field. However, if good sub-base material is scarce, the quality of the material used beneath the top 100 mm (4 in.) layer of the sub-base can be relaxed, provided it has a CBR of at least 8 per cent when tested at the worst moisture condition likely to occur.

A field density of 100 per cent of the maximum dry density given by the British Standard Compaction test, 2.5 kg (5.5 lb) rammer method,[16] should be readily achieved in the sub-base, so that material which has a CBR of 25 per cent at this density and at the optimum moisture content given by the test will be satisfactory under impermeable bases except when the water-table is less than 1.0 m (3.3 ft) below formation level the sub-base material must be capable of maintaining a CBR of 25 per cent when saturated. This can be checked by immersing compacted samples of the sub-base material in water for 4 days before carrying out the CBR test.

Care must be taken to ensure that the material used in the shoulders has sufficient wet strength to support the occasional vehicle running on it without excessive rutting. Usually the minimum quality of material that will be satisfactory for the shoulders will meet the specification for a sub-base, but when the road is heavily trafficked it may be necessary to use base-quality material in the shoulder.

Regular maintenance of the shoulders will prevent water ponding on them and the consequent damage to the edges of the pavement, thereby prolonging the life of the pavement.

The base may be constructed from crushed stone or gravel, or bitumen-bound or cemented materials. Except for dense bitumen-bound materials, the differences in the load-spreading properties of these materials are too small to warrant any difference in thickness when the nominal base thickness is only 150 mm (6 in.). When dense bitumen-bound material is used the nominal thickness of the base may be reduced to 125 mm (5 in.).[27]

A permeable base material is defined in Road Note 31 as a crushed stone or gravel, or open-textured macadam with less than 15 per cent of material finer than the 75 μm sieve (permeability $> 10^{-5}$ cm/s). Dense bitumen-bound materials, stabilised soil with only very fine cracks, and crushed stone or gravel with more than 15 per cent of material finer than 75 μm sieve are defined as impermeable (permeability $< 10^{-5}$ cm/s).

3.11 Structural Design of Flexible Highway Pavements

The increasing application of computers to the solution of engineering problems has materially assisted the structural design of pavements using well-known programs such as BISTRO and the extended program BISAR developed by Shell and CHEVRON developed by the Chevron Oil Company. Programs such as these require inputs of material properties, traffic loading and environmental conditions before they can be used to predict stresses in the pavement layers.

Deterioration of a pavement is usually observed to take the form of rutting in the nearside wheel track associated with cracking in the wheel track. In the structural design of pavements the calculation of the accumulation of permanent strain which results in rutting is a complex process and at the present time its development is limited by minimising the vertical strain on the subgrade. The development of cracking is limited by minimising the maximum tensile strain which occurs close to the bottom of the bituminous pavement layers. Because pavement failure occurs as a result of fatigue effects there is an obvious relationship between strain and the number of repetitions of that strain before excessive deformation or cracking occurs.

Bituminous materials have a wide range of characteristics ranging from low-strength open-textured macadams to high-strength asphalts, and as with other engineering materials a modulus is used to characterise the black-top materials. Because of their viscous nature the term stiffness modulus is used to measure the relationship between stress and strain instead of the term modulus of elasticity as with purely elastic materials.

In the laboratory the repetitive loading may be applied to the specimen either in constant-stress or constant-strain mode. The constant-stress mode is useful for predicting fatigue life in bituminous layers with thicknesses greater than approximately 150 mm whilst the constant-strain mode is used when predicting the life of thin layers. Because of the slower rate of crack propagation with the constant-strain mode of testing, longer fatigue lives are obtained.

It has been shown that tensile strain is the prime determinant of fatigue life and that a linear relationship exists between the logarithm of fatigue life and the logarithm of strain, initial in the case of stress-controlled tests.

Whilst controlled stress and strain tests are useful experimental tools, the practical highway engineer is more likely to be aware of such physical properties of the mix as binder type and content. For a given bituminous mix the relationship between tensile strain and number of load applications to failure depends on the volume of binder in the mix and the initial Ring and Ball softening point of the binder.

An alternative presentation of the relationship between strain and repetitions to failure requires a knowledge of the stiffness modulus of the mix.

The stiffness modulus of a mix may be determined by noting the relationship between stress and strain but, because of the viscous nature of bituminous materials, the time of loading and the temperature of the material must be considered.

Laboratory testing to determine stiffness is suitable for research purposes but the designer of a highway pavement requires a method of assessing mix stiffness based on the composition and properties of the mix.

The Shell pavement design method[28] used a method of determining mix stiffness which is suitable for practical pavement design purposes. In this method it is necessary to know the percentage volumes of the bituminous binder and the mineral aggregate in the mix together with an estimate of the stiffness of the binder.

The stiffness of the binder varies with loading time and temperature, exhibiting elastic behaviour at low temperatures and short loading times, viscous behaviour at long loading times and high temperatures and visco-elastic response in between. The elastic high stiffness end of the range is of interest in the structural analysis of pavements and this stiffness is frequently termed dynamic stiffness. Van der Poel[29] developed a nomograph for determining bitumen stiffness which requires the following data

(1) temperature (T) (°C)
(2) softening point (SP_r) from the Ring and Ball test (°C) of the recovered binder
(3) loading time (t) (seconds)
(4) penetration index (PI_r) which is a measure of temperature susceptibility. Alternatively, Brown[30] gives the relationship

$$S_b = 1.157 + 10^{-7} t^{-0.368} 2.718^{-PI_r} (SP_r - T)^5$$

The penetration index can be calculated from

$$\frac{1951 - 500 \log P_r - 20 SP_r}{50 \log P_r - SP_r - 120.1}$$

Where P_r is the penetration of the recovered binder (very approximately 0.65 × initial penetration).

In the classification of traffic loading a practical difficulty occurs in that vehicles have a wide range of loads which are transmitted to the pavement through many differing axle arrangements. To overcome this problem a standard 18 000 lbs (8160 kg) axle load has been adopted; this is frequently stated to be composed of two dual 20 kN wheels each with a contact stress of 6×10^5 N/m² (87 lb/in²) and a radius of contact of 105 mm. The relative pavement-damaging effect of different axle loadings varies with environmental conditions, pavement thickness and wheel arrangement but generally damaging effect is approximately related to the fourth power of the axle load.

The three major environmental effects which must be considered in pavement thickness design are frost, rainfall and temperature. Frost heave effects are usually reduced or eliminated by ensuring that frost-susceptible material is not within the depth of frost penetration for a particular locality. Currently in the United Kingdom this depth is stated to be 450 mm.

The major effect of rainfall is a reduction in the bearing capacity of the subgrade as a result of increased moisture content. In regions of substantial rainfall this effect is reduced by impervious pavements, waterproof layers at subgrade level and surface water drainage works. A subsidiary effect is the increased hardening of binders in open-textured mixes.

Variations in ambient temperature have a considerable effect on bituminous materials and if any pavement design method is to have universal application then a correction factor must be introduced for temperature variations. The Shell pavement design method uses a weighted mean annual air temperature which is related to the temperature within the pavement and the effect of that temperature upon the stiffness modulus of the bituminous mix and consequently on the permissible strain in the pavement.

An important aspect of the determination of mix stiffness and the number of repetitions of strains to failure in the laboratory is that laboratory testing conditions are different from conditions on the highway. The state of stress within the pavement differs from the simple stress conditions of most laboratory testing procedures and, in addition, on the highway the loading history differs from the uniform cyclic loading applied in laboratory conditions.

Until the results of further research become available various correction factors have been proposed. Brown et al.[31] have suggested a factor of 100 derived from a comparison of highway performance in the United Kingdom and the theoretical analysis of these pavements. In the Shell design method[28] a correction is made for random pulse loading with rest periods, and also for the random spectrum of strain values arising from different loads and the lateral distribution of loads.

Work carried out at the Transport and Road Research Laboratory by Raithby and Sterling has shown that rest periods of the order of 1 s increased the number of cycles to failure by a factor of up to 25, when compared with the life under continuous sinusoidal cyclic loading. The preparation of samples in the laboratory for testing is also different from compaction in full-scale road construction. For this reason specimens for laboratory testing are now taken from either an actual highway pavement or from a section of trial or experimental construction.

Previously it has been explained how the relative damaging effect of varying axle loads may be expressed in terms of the standard axle load with a standard contact area and tyre pressure. Using one of the stress analysis programs, it is possible to calculate the critical stresses and strains within the pavement if the stiffnesses of the pavement layers, the strength of the subgrade and the weighted mean annual average temperatures are known. With the critical strains known it is possible to estimate the number of repetitions of these strains to failure and make a comparison with the estimated number of repetitions of the strains during the design life obtained from the estimated cumulative number of standard axles during the design life of the pavement. Pavement thickness or pavement material properties may then be varied until a balance is obtained between number of strain repetitions to failure and the repetitions of axle loading.

Practically, these design methods are presented in graphical form so that convenient determinations of pavement thickness may be made.

References

(1) D. Croney, 'Failure Criteria for Flexible Pavements', *Proc. Third Int. Conf. Structural Design of Asphalt Pavements*, University of Michigan, 1972

(2) Committee on Highway Maintenance, *Report of the Committee on Highway Maintenance* (HMSO, 1970)

(3) A.A.S.H.O. Road Test, Report 5 (Pavement Research), *Spec. Rep. Highw. Res. Bd, Wash.*, 61E (1962)

(4) W. N. Carey and P. E. Irick, 'The Pavement Serviceability Performance Concept', *Highw. Res. Bull.*, 250 (1960)

(5) G. Langsner, S. Huff Talbot and J. Liddle Wallace, 'Use of Road Test Findings by A.A.S.H.O. Design Committee', *Spec. Rep. Highw. Res. Bd, Wash.*, 73 (1962)

(6) DoE, Road Research Laboratory Road Note 29, 3rd ed., *A Guide to the Structural Design of Pavements for New Roads* (HMSO, 1970)

(7) J. V. Leigh and D. Croney, 'The Current Design Procedure for Flexible Pavements in Britain', *Proc. Third Int. Conf. Structural Design of Asphalt Pavements*, University of Michigan, 1972, vol. I

8) N. W. Lister, DoE, Transport and Road Research Laboratory Report 375, *Deflection Criteria for Flexible Pavements and the Design of Overlays* (Crowthorne, 1972)

(9) E. W. Currer and P. D. Thompson, 'The Classification of Traffic for Pavement Design Purposes', *Proc. Third Int. Conf. Structural Design of Asphalt Pavements*, University of Michigan, 1972, vol. I.

(10) W. D. Powell, J. F. Potter, H. C. Mayhew and M. E. Nunn, Transport and Road Research Laboratory Report 1132, *The Structural Design of Bituminous Roads* (Crowthorne, 1984)

(11) D. Croney and J. N. Bulman, 'The Influence of Climate Factors on the Structural Design of Flexible Pavements', *Proc. Third Int. Conf. Structural Design of Asphalt Pavements*, University of Michigan, 1972, vol. I

(12) D. Croney, J. D. Coleman and W. P. M. Black, 'Movement and Distribution of Water in Soil in Relation to Highway Design and Performance', *Spec. Rep. Highw. Res. Bd, Wash.*, 40 (1958) 226–52

(13) W. P. M. Black, 'A Method of Estimating the California Bearing Ratio of Cohesive Soils from Plasticity Data', *Geotechnique, Lond.*, 12 (1962) 271–82

(14) K. Russam and J. D. Coleman, 'The Effect of Climatic Factors on Subgrade Moisture Conditions', *Geotechnique, Lond.*, 11 (1961) 22–8

(15) K. Russam, 'The Distribution of Moisture in Soils at Overseas Airfields', *Tech. Paper Rd Res. Lab.*, no. 58 (1962)

(16) BS 1377: 1975   Methods of Test for Soils for Civil Engineering Purposes

(17) American Society for Testing Materials, Standard Test Method D1196-64, Americal National Standard Institute

(18) D. J. Steel, Discussion on 'Application of the Classifications and Group Index in Estimating Desirable Sub-base and Total Thickness', *Proc. Highw. Res. Bd*, 25 (1945) 388

(19) Permanent International Association of Road Congresses, Report to XVth

Congress, Mexico City, 1975, from the Technical Committee on Flexible Pavements

(20) American Association of State Highway Officials, *A.A.S.H.O. Interim Guide for Design of Pavement Structures* (Washington, 1972)

(21) B. F. McCullough, C. J. Van Til and R. G. Hicks, 'Evaluation of A.A.S.H.O. Interim Guides for Design of Pavement Structures', *NCHRP Report*, 128 (1972)

(22) DoE, Road Research Laboratory Road Note 31, 3rd ed., *A Guide to the Structural Design of Bitumen-surfaced Roads in Tropical and Sub-tropical Countries* (HMSO, 1977)

(23) K. Russam and D. Croney, 'The Moisture Conditions beneath Ten Overseas Airfields', *Conference on Civil Engineering Problems Overseas*, London, 13–17 June 1960 (Institution of Civil Engineers, London, 1960)

(24) M. P. O'Reilly, K. Russam and F. H. P. Williams, *Pavement Design in the Tropics: Investigation of Subgrade Conditions under Roads in East Africa*, Ministry of Transport, Road Research Technical Paper, no. 80 (HMSO, 1968)

(25) G. M. Livneh Kassif and G. Wiseman, *Pavements on Expansive Clays* (Jerusalem, Academic Press, 1969)

(26) F. H. Chen. 'Foundations on Expansive Soils', *Development in Geotechnical Engineering*, vol. 12 (Elsevier, Amsterdam, 1975)

(27) J. N. Bulman and H. R. Smith, Transport and Road Research Laboratory Report LR 507, *A Full Scale Pavement Design Experiment in Malaysia – Construction and First Four Years' Performance* (Crowthorne, 1972)

(28) *Shell Pavement Design Manual* (London, Shell International Petroleum Company, 1978)

(29) C. Van der Poel, 'A General System describing the Visco-Elastic Properties of Bitumens and its Relation to Routine Test Data', *J. App. Chem.*, 4 (1954) 221-236

(30) S. F. Brown, *An Introduction to the Analytical Design of Bituminous Pavements* (University of Nottingham, 1980)

(31) S. F. Brown, A. F. Stock and P. S. Pell, 'The Structural Design of Asphalt Pavements by Computer', *The Highway Engineer*, March 1980, 2-22

4

Design of Concrete Pavements

4.1 Introduction

Concrete pavements are constructed in a variety of forms by several different construction methods. They may be reinforced or unreinforced; if reinforced the steel may take the form of individual bars or welded mesh. The slabs may contain several different types of joint or they may be unjointed or continuous. Construction may be carried out by the conventional side-form process using a concreting train with many differing units, or one of several forms of slip-form paver may be employed operating with a minimum of additional equipment.

All these forms of concrete pavement are composed of a pavement slab that is the major load-spreading component. If reinforcement is included it is placed nearer to the upper face of the slab, the minimum amount of cover depending upon slab thickness. If joints are incorporated in the slab then the transverse joints placed across the slab at right angles to the traffic flow may be either expansion, contraction or warping joints. Longitudinal joints are also normally used where the width of the slab exceeds a single traffic lane.

The pavement slab is usually supported by a sub-base frequently of granular or cement-bound material. This element of the pavement structure assists in distributing the wheel load to the subgrade, frequently ensures an adequate depth of material to prevent frost penetration and provides a working base for construction plant.

Between the pavement slab and the sub-base is a separation membrane, usually of thermoplastic sheeting. Its function is to reduce the restraint of the sub-base upon slab movement and also to prevent moisture movement between the slab and the sub-base during the early life of the pavement.

4.2 Pavement Concrete

Requirements for the concrete for pavements for roads constructed in the United Kingdom for the Department of Transport are contained in their Specification for Road and Bridge Works.[1]

The cement used for pavements must be ordinary Portland cement or Portland blast-furnace cement, rapid-hardening cements being excluded to prevent them being used to achieve the required 28-day strength with minimum cement content. A minimum cement content is given as 280 kg/m^3 of concrete.

Maximum aggregate size is 40 mm and it is specified as naturally occurring material that complies with BS 882[2] or crushed air-cooled blast-furnace slag with a bulk density not less than 1100 kg/m^2 and complying with BS 1047,[3] the grading to comply with table 1 of this British Standard. The flakiness index of the coarse aggregate must not exceed 35 (see section 8.11.3), while fine aggregate containing more than 25 per cent calcium carbonate by mass in either the fraction retained or passing a 600 μm BS sieve cannot be used in the top 50 mm of the slab. If the coarse aggregate is limestone it may be used in the top 50 mm of the pavement provided the Accelerated Wear Test result is less than 53. A choice of aggregate size is allowed provided the workability of the concrete is suitable for the plant being used and provided suitable surface regularity is obtained. Large aggregates make joint forming and the insertion of dowel bars difficult and should not be used in two-layer construction when the top layer is only 50 mm thick.

Concrete strength is specified by the use of the Indirect Tensile Strength Test of BS 1881.[4] This change from the previously specified cube-crushing test has been made because the Indirect Tensile Strength Test indicates more readily the influence of aggregates on tensile strength, tensile cracking being a frequent mode of failure of concrete pavement slabs. The required quality of concrete is achieved when the average value of any four consecutive results of tests at the age of 28 days is not less than 2.3 N/mm^2. This means that not more than 1 per cent of all test results that may be expected from an infinite population with a standard deviation of 0.4 N/m^2 will fall below a characteristic strength of 1.8 N/mm^2.

Workability of concrete is specified by the Compacting Factor Test[4] when the concrete is being laid by machine and by the Slump Test[4] if hand laying is to take place using concrete with any average slump of 40 mm or greater. The workability should be such that full compaction is achieved by the plant used, without excessive flow of the concrete.

4.3 Air-entrained Concrete

Air-entrained agents have found considerable application in concrete road construction, where their use has been found substantially to reduce frost damage and also the destructive action of de-icing salts on the concrete carriageway. While air entrainment has been extensively used for many years abroad, particularly in the United States, it is only recently that it has become obligatory to use air-entrained concrete for the upper surface layer (50 mm) of the concrete roads in the United Kingdom.

In many regions where frost damage is not a problem, air entrainment is used because of the improvement of workability and the reduction in segregation, bleeding and shrinkage of concrete that are possible.

The use of air-entrainment produces discrete cavities in the cement paste and these are not filled with water even in saturated concrete. During the initial stages of freezing these cavities are available to relieve the hydraulic pressure which develops in the capillaries of the concrete and as the freezing process develops the growth of microscopic bodies of ice is limited.

Bubbles of air entrained in the concrete should be as small as possible and have been found to vary in diameter from 0.05 to 1.25 mm. The spacing between air bubbles is important and it has been stated that this should be less than 0.25 mm and possibly as low as 0.05 mm. As the volume of air entrained is specified in the United Kingdom to be 4.5 ± 1.5 per cent by volume of the concrete mix, this will result in a very large number of minute air bubbles distributed throughout the mix. Air-entrained concrete should not, however, be confused with light-weight concrete, in which a reduction in density is obtained by the use of large air content and large air bubbles.

The almost innumerable materials which act as air-entraining agents may be classified into the following groups.

(1) Natural wood resins.
(2) Animal or vegetable fats and oils.
(3) Various wetting agents.
(4) Water-soluble soaps of resin acids and animal and vegetable fatty acids.
(5) Many miscellaneous materials, such as hydrogen peroxide and aluminium powder.

There are two methods by which the air-entraining agent may be added to the concrete; in the first method the agent is incorporated into the cement and in the second the agent is added as a separate component of the mix.

When air-entraining cements are used little adjustment can be made to the air content of the mix unless the cement content is varied. On the other hand, if the required air content can be provided there is less chance of random fluctuations in the air content.

If an air-entraining agent is used, it is possible easily to adjust the final air content in the concrete by varying the proportion of added agent. Disadvantages are that there is a greater chance of variations in the resulting air content and there is also the complexity of another ingredient to be proportioned at the mixer.

For work carried out to the specifications of the Department of Transport the following recommendations are included in the Standard Specification for Road and Bridge Works.[1] It is recommended that the ratio of free water to cement for surface dry aggregate be determined by strength requirements, with a maximum value of 0.55 by weight. It is recommended that the total quantity of air in the concrete be within 4.5 ± 1,5 per cent by volume of the mix. Detailed requirements are also given for the testing procedure and the remedial action to be carried out if adjustment of the air content is found to be necessary.

It is recommended that the air-entraining agent should be added at the mixer in solution in a portion of the mixing water. The distribution mechanism must ensure that the amount dispensed does not vary by more than 5 per cent from the quantities required and also ensure even disposition throughout the mix. A recommended form of the apparatus is shown in figure 4.1.

While there are many advantages in the use of air entrainment there is also the serious disadvantage that the inclusion of air in a content mix, by intention or otherwise, results in a loss in strength. For this reason it is important to be able to measure air contents accurately. Methods of measurement may be divided into two techniques; direct methods and indirect methods.

Direct methods find the greatest practical application and of these methods the

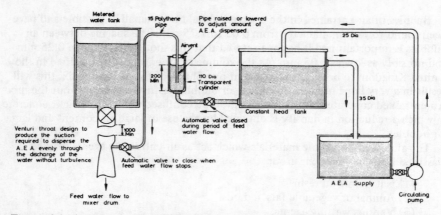

Figure 4.1 Automatic air-entraining agent dispenser. All dimensions are in milli-metres[1]

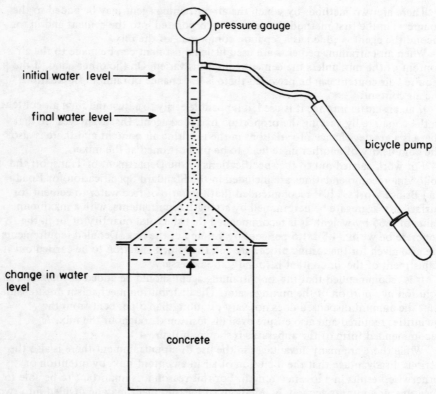

Figure 4.2 Illustration of the pressure method for determining air content of a concrete mix

pressure method is most popular. With the pressure method the volume of air is measured indirectly by the change in volume it undergoes when subjected to a known pressure. The decrease in volume of the air is measured by the decrease in volume of a known volume of concrete. The apparatus is illustrated in outline in figure 4.2.

To use the apparatus, concrete is compacted in the apparatus in a standard manner. When the vessel is full the concrete is screeded off and a thin circular metal plate placed on top of the concrete to prevent water eroding the surface. The top section is then clamped down and filled with water to the top mark on the scale. Air pressure is applied with a bicycle pump to 11 MN/m^2 (16 lb/in.^{2}). The pressure then drops slowly and when a value of 10 MN/m^2 (15 lb/in.^{2}) is reached the air content is read directly.

Another method in which the air content is measured directly uses a rolling cylinder. A certain volume of concrete is placed in a cylinder, which is then filled with water and sealed. The cylinder is rolled backwards and forwards. The concrete becomes suspended in the water and air collects at the top of the cylinder. Next a liquid, preferably an alcohol in order to reduce the foaming, is poured into the cylinder from a measuring glass. The volume of the liquid poured into the cylinder is a measure of the air content of the concrete. The method is illustrated in figure 4.3.

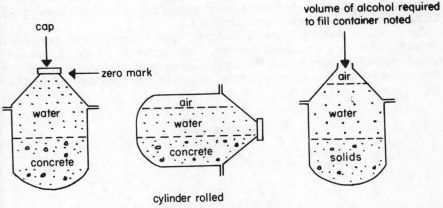

Figure 4.3 Illustration of the rolling method for determining air concrete of a concrete mix

The measurement of air content may be made indirectly by compacting concrete in a standard cylinder of known volume and weight. The volume and weight of the concrete are known and the air content can be found by comparing the weight of air-entrained concrete with the theoretical weight of the same volume of concrete free from air, calculated from the known proportions and densities of the constituents.

4.4 The Mix Design of Pavement Concrete

Design of concrete mixes for highway pavements constructed in the United Kingdom may be carried out according to a method originated by the Building Research Establishment, the Transport and Road Research Laboratory and the Cement and Concrete Association.[5]

Strength tests on cubes or cylinders indicate that concrete test results from a given mix have a normal distribution of values as shown in figure 4.4. It can be seen that many samples will have a strength greater than the target mean strength and many others a strength less than the target strength. It is these low-strength values, due to variations in mix proportions from batch to batch, which require the use of a lower value known as the characteristic strength. This value is fixed by taking into account the range of the variation or standard deviation of concrete strength and the permitted percentage of samples which may have a strength less than the characteristic strength. If less than 40 indirect tensile-test results are available, a standard deviation of 0.6 N/mm^2 is used; if more than 40 test results are known, a value of 0.3 N/mm^2 is recommended. For pavement-quality concrete the percentage of samples with less than the characteristic strength is specified to be 1 per cent. From the characteristics of the normal distribution the margin (see figure 4.4) is 2.33 times the standard deviation.

The next step in the design process is the selection of the approximate indirect-tensile strength of a mix made with a free-water/cement ratio of 0.5 according to the specified age, the type of cement and the aggregate to be used. For pavement-quality concrete these values are given in table 4.1.

This approximate strength value is plotted on figure 4.5 and a curve drawn from this point parallel to the printed curves until it intercepts a horizontal line passing through the ordinate representing the target mean strength. The corresponding value for the ratio of free water to cement can then be read from the abscissa. This

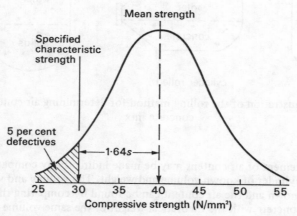

Figure 4.4 Normal distribution of concrete strengths[5] (Crown copyright, Building Research Establishment)

Table 4.1 Approximate indirect tensile strengths with ordinary Portland cement and a free-water content of 0.5 (Crown copyright, Building Research Establishment)[5]

Type of coarse aggregate	Indirect-tensile strengths (N/mm²) Age (days)			
	3	7	28	91
Uncrushed	1·7	2·2	2·8	3·3
Crushed	2·2	2·9	3·6	4·2

1 N/mm² = 1 MN/m² = 1 MPa

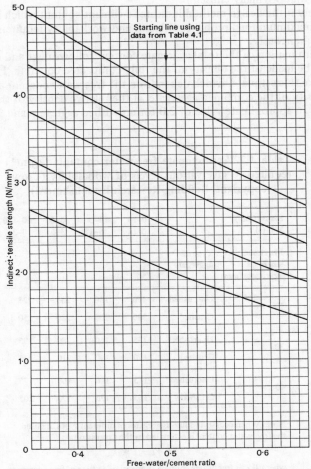

Figure 4.5 Relationship between indirect-tensile strength and free-water/cement ratio[5] (Crown copyright, Building Research Establishment)

is compared with the maximum permitted ratio of free water to cement of 0.55 and the lower value taken.

The next stage in the process is to determine the free-water content from table 4.2, depending upon the type and maximum size of aggregate to give a concrete of the specified slump or V-B time.

With the free-water content and the free-water/cement ratio determined the cement content in kg/m³ can be determined and this should be checked against the minimum cement content for pavement concrete of 280 kg/m³. If the determined cement content is less than 280 kg/m³ then either the free-water/cement ratio may be less than originally determined or else the free-water content may be greater than the value given by table 4.2. In the first alternative the mean strength will be greater than the target mean strength or with the second alternative the workability will be higher than that originally chosen.

Conversely if the design method indicates a cement content which is greater than a specified maximum then probably strength and workability requirements cannot be met simultaneously.

The determination of the total aggregate content follows next and requires an estimate to be made of the density of the fully compacted concrete. Figure 4.6 is used to make this estimate, which depends on the free-water content and the relative density of the combined aggregate. If the relative density of the aggregate is unknown an approximate value of 2.0 for uncrushed aggregate and 2.7 for

Table 4.2 Approximate free-water contents (kg/m³) required to give various levels of workability (Crown copyright, Building Research Establishment)

Slump (mm) V-B (s)		0–10 >12	10–30 6–12	30–60 3–6	60–180 0–3
Maximum size of aggregate (mm)	Type of aggregate				
10	Uncrushed	150	180	205	225
	Crushed	180	205	230	250
20	Uncrushed	135	160	180	195
	Crushed	170	190	210	225
40	Uncrushed	115	140	160	175
	Crushed	155	175	190	205

Note: When coarse and fine aggregates of different types are used, the free-water content is estimated by the expression

$$\tfrac{2}{3} W_f + \tfrac{1}{3} W_c$$

where W_f = free-water content appropriate to type of fine aggregate
and W_c = free-water content appropriate to type of coarse aggregate.

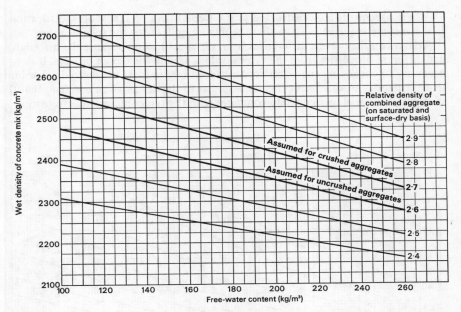

Figure 4.6 Estimated wet density of fully compacted concrete[5] (Crown copyright, Building Research Establishment)

crushed aggregate can be used. The total aggregate content (saturated and surface dry) is obtained from

$$D - W_C - W_{FW} \qquad (4.1)$$

where D is the wet density of the concrete (kg/m³),

W_C is the cement content (kg/m³),

W_{FW} is the free-water content (kg/m³).

The next step is to determine the fine aggregate or sand content — that is, the material passing a 5 mm sieve. The proportion of fine aggregate will depend upon the the maximum size of the aggregate, the workability level, the grading zone of the fine aggregate as defined in BS 882,[2] the free-water/cement ratio and the use to which the concrete is to be placed. Use of an aggregate proportion within the bands given in figure 4.7, however, will give a suitable indication for first trial mixes.

With the proportion of coarse aggregate calculated from a knowledge of the proportion of fine aggregate it is possible to subdivide the coarse aggregate if single size 10 mm, 20 mm and 40 mm materials are used. The following proportions are suggested

1:2   for combination of 10 and 20 mm material,
1:1.5:3 for combination of 10, 20 and 40 mm material.

Where pavements are constructed to the Department of Transport specification, trial mixes are required to show that the mix complies with the specification.

Trial mixes may reveal differences from the specification because the materials had different properties from the typical values used in the design process. It is necessary to check that the water content specified produces the desired workability, that the density of the fresh concrete is similar to the design value used and that the strength of the trial-mix concrete compares with the target mean strength. Any

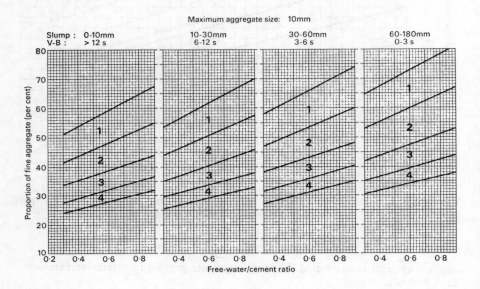

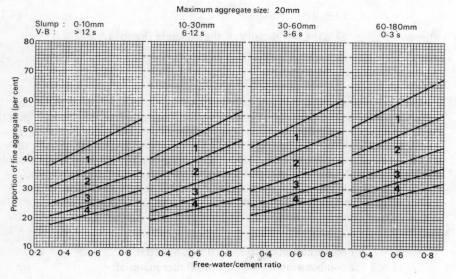

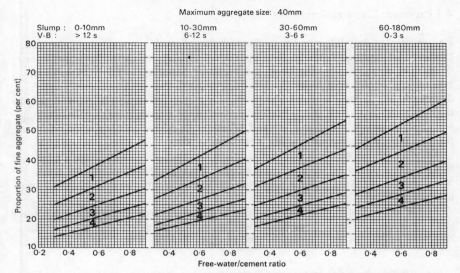

Figure 4.7 Recommended proportions of fine aggregate for BS 882 grading zones 1, 2, 3 and 4[5] (Crown copyright, Building Research Establishment)

major departure from these guide lines will require modification or redesign of the mix.

Any concrete used within the top 50 mm of the slab is normally specified in the United Kingdom to contain an air-entraining agent which will produce an average air content of 4.5 ± 1 per cent. The deliberate inclusion of air requires a modification of the mix design process. It is usually assumed that there will be a loss of 4 per cent in indirect tensile strength for each 1 per cent by volume of air entrained in the mix. This requires the target mean strength to be modified by a suitable amount. There is also an effect on workability and it is recommended that in table 4.2 for any given workability and aggregate type the next lower water content in the table be used. It may also be possible to reduce the fine aggregate content by up to 5 per cent and this will also allow a small reduction in the water content.

Table 4.3 Sub-base thickness

CBR % of Sub-soil	Sub-base Thickness (mm)
≤ 2	130*
over 2 – 4	180
4 – 6	130
6 – 15	80
> 15	0

* plus 280 mm thick capping layer

4.5 Pavement Slab Reinforcement

Reinforcement may take the form of prefabricated mesh, or in slip-form construction bar-mat reinforcement. In the Department of Transport specifications the use of reinforcement is optional, the choice normally being left to the contractor on economic grounds. Except for the most lightly trafficked highways there is no difference in the required thickness of slab for reinforced or unreinforced construction. The function of the reinforcement is to limit the size of the surface cracking so that aggregate interlock is preserved; where the steel reinforcement does not perform this function joint spacing is reduced.

Because reinforcement has a crack-control function, it is placed close to the upper surface of the slab. Department of Transport specifications require cover over the steel of 60 ± 10 mm in slabs not less than 150 mm thick and 50 ± 10 mm in thinner slabs.

The amount of steel reinforcement for roads constructed in the United Kingdom to Department of Transport specifications varies according to the imposed loading. Required weights of steel reinforcement are given in table 4.4.

4.6 Joints in Concrete Roads

Joints are provided in a pavement slab to allow for the movement caused by variations both in slab temperature and moisture content, and in the initial change in slab length due to shrinkage. When there is a rise in slab temperature or when the slab absorbs water the concrete will expand; with a drop in temperature or a loss of water the concrete will contract. Expansion and contraction joints are provided to allow movement to take place.

If the upper surface of a slab is cooled − at night for example − it will contract, causing the ends to curl upwards. This movement is resisted by the slab's own weight and a tensile stress is induced in the surface of the slab. The induced stress can be relieved by providing frequent warping joints which allow a small amount of angular rotation to occur. A form of warping joint is used to limit the maximum width of continuous slabs to 4.65 m.

4.6.1 Expansion Joints

Either gaps or (as in highway work) strips of compressible material, known as filler boards, must be provided between the ends of slabs to allow expansion to take place.

The expansion-joint assembly is positioned ahead of the concreting operations and the filler board provides a convenient end-form for the two slabs which meet at the joint. Since the ends of the slab must be vertical, to prevent one slab riding up over another, it follows that the filler board must be set vertically, and supported so that no deformation can take place during concreting.

Since a gap has been provided between two slabs, a load-transfer system is incorporated into the joint assembly so that a load on the surface of one slab is carried

Table 4.4 Concrete pavements[1]

Slab Thickness (mm) for CBR of Subgrade of: %			Millions of Standard Axles (msa)		Minimum Reinforcement (reinforced slabs only)	
2 or less	Over 2 and up to 15	Over 15	From (incl)	Up to	Mesh (kg/m²)	Bar (mm²/m width of slab)
305	280	255	60 and above		5.3	620
290	265	240	40	60	4.9	570
270	245	220	20	40	4.34*	500
250	225	200	11	20	3.9	450
235	210	185	5	11	3.41*	390
215	190	165	2.5†	5	3.1	340

Sub-base thickness (mm) ‡ for subgrade CBR %				All values of msa	Sub-base to Specification Group C
over 3–4	over 4–6	over 6–15	over 15		
180	130	80	0		

Dowel Bar Dimensions (mm)

Slab thickness	Expansion joints		Contraction joints		
	Dia	Length	Dia	Length of prepositioned bars	Length of bars vibrated into plastic concrete
240 and over	32	750	25	650	400
190 to 239	25	650	20	550	400

* Denotes Standard Mesh Reinforcement. Other mesh reinforcement quoted, assumes transverse wires of 5 mm diameter at 400 mm centres. Alternative mesh or bar reinforcement may be used by the Contractor provided it is not less than the appropriate minimum weight for each type of road, which shall be quoted in the Contract.

† Below 2.5 msa the thickness for construction shall be taken from the graph (Fig. 11) of Road Note 29 (Third edition).

‡ If the sub-grade is frost susceptible the sub-base thickness must be increased so that the full pavement thickness is 450 mm.

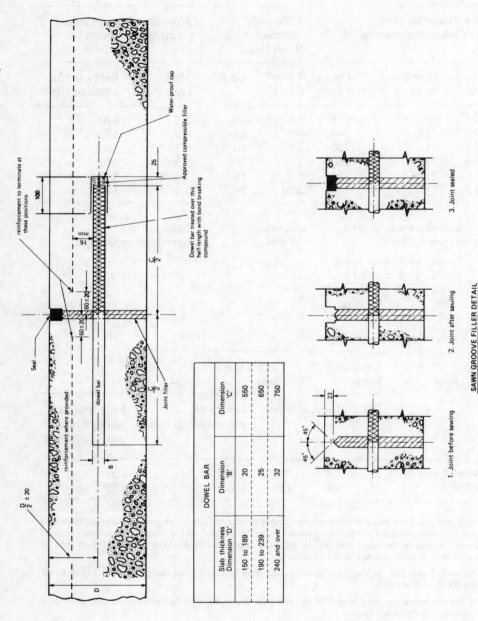

DOWEL BAR		
Slab thickness Dimension 'D'	Dimension 'B'	Dimension 'C'
150 to 189	20	550
190 to 239	25	650
240 and over	32	750

SAWN GROOVE FILLER DETAIL

1. Joint before sawing

2. Joint after sawing

3. Joint sealed

Figure 4.8 A typical expansion joint (reproduced from Technical Memo H1/72)

by both, thus ensuring that there is no relative vertical movement between the ends of the slabs at the joint.

Although dowel bars should prevent relative vertical movements between slabs, they should not prevent longitudinal movements. Therefore dowel bars must be set parallel to both the surface of the slab and the centre-line of the road. One end of each bar should be painted with a bond-preventing agent so that it does not act as reinforcement, tying the slabs together. The debonding agent specified by the Department of Transport consists of 66 per cent of 200 pen bitumen blended hot with 14 per cent light creosote oil, and 20 per cent solvent naphtha is added when cold.

The free ends of dowel bars in an expansion-joint assembly are fitted with dowel caps as shown in figure 4.8, so that a space is formed at the end of each bar, into which the bar can move when the slabs expand. An expansion joint permits contraction movements also, and provides a release for warping stresses. Required dowel-bar dimensions for work to Department of Transport recommendation are given in figure 4.8.

Many engineers believe that the initial curing contraction of the concrete that takes place during the early life of the slab in the United Kingdom provides sufficient freedom for subsequent expansion and is sufficient to prevent the development of excessive compressive stress. A compromise between the traditional viewpoint, which requires frequent expansion joints, and those who feel they are unnecessary has been reached in the recommendations of the Department of Transport, which allow expansion joints to be omitted for slabs constructed between 21 April and 21 October.

4.6.2 Contraction Joints

A contraction joint can be formed conveniently by reducing the slab section at the joint position and allowing tensile stresses in the slab to crack the concrete at this point as shown in figure 4.9. Because the crack has been induced in this way there will be a certain amount of granular interlocking of the aggregate at the joint that will assist in the transfer of loading across the joint. A load-transfer system, however, is still required, but it is possible to use a dowel bar with a slightly smaller diameter than is required with expansion joints.

The dowels are set in the same way as those in an expansion joint, but in this case it is not necessary to use a dowel cap, because when the slab contracts the free end of the dowel will leave a gap, into which it can move when the slab returns to its original length. Although a contraction joint provides release for warping stresses, it cannot, of course, accommodate an expansion movement greater than the space created during contraction.

In the past, dowel bars have normally been placed in position using prefabricated supports, the whole assembly, dowel bars and supporting cage, being placed in position on the sub-base and adequately supported so that they maintained their alignment during the placing and compaction of the concrete. During recent years dowel bars have been vibrated into position through the compacted concrete with acceptable tolerances, and the considerable saving in dowel-bar length, as given in

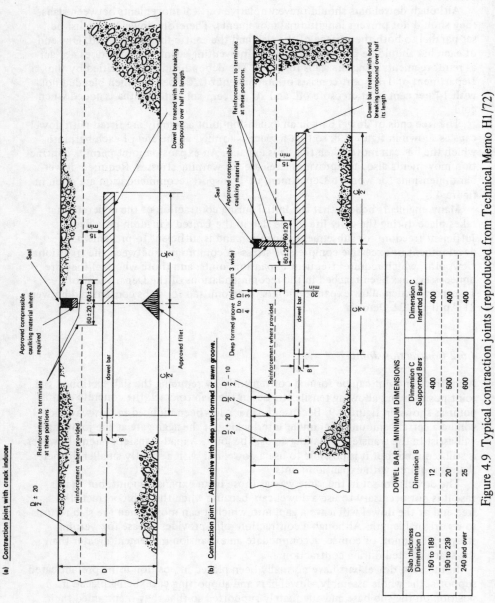

Figure 4.9 Typical contraction joints (reproduced from Technical Memo H1/72)

table 4.5, together with the elimination of supporting steel reduce construction costs.

The groove in the upper surface of the slab may either be formed by wet-forming techniques or by sawing. These techniques are discussed in section 7.5.3.

4.6.3 Warping Joints

A warping joint is designed to restrict horizontal movement to the small amount necessary for crack opening without permitting a loss of aggregate interlock. The Department of Transport specification requires steel tie-bar reinforcement of 12 mm bars to a transverse spacing of 180 to 360 mm, depending upon slab thickness; a wet-formed groove with or without a crack inducer may be used. The central 200 mm length of the tie bar is painted with a debonding agent.

Warping joints may be substituted for contraction joints in unreinforced concrete slabs provided not more than three warping joints are used in succession. This may not take place if mechanically vibrated dowel bars are placed, and on balance it appears that there is little to be gained by this substitution.

An outline diagram of a warping joint is shown in figure 4.10.

4.7 Joint Spacing

Spacing of transverse joints is governed by the length of slab that can be expected not to form unacceptable cracks during the design life; it is influenced by the amount of steel reinforcement that is provided in the slab. Details of the recommended spacing for construction in the United Kingdom are given in section 4.10.

As discussed in section 4.6.1, expansion joints may be omitted when construction is to take place during the summer months.

The joint in reinforced concrete slabs depends on the quantity of longitudinal reinforcement actually placed in the concrete. The quantity of steel depends upon slab thickness, which in turn varies with traffic loading. Section 4.10 discusses these relationships.

Longitudinal joints are provided at the edge of each traffic lane except when reinforced three-lane carriageways are constructed in two slab widths. If a hardstrip adjoins the carriageway then the width is limited to 4.8 m. This width limitation is based on the fact that the major portion of the reinforcement is in the longitudinal direction with only a small proportion in the transverse direction, so that the slab can be considered to be unreinforced transversely.

4.8 Effect of Subgrade Strength

The effect of subgrade strength on pavement thickness in British practice is not as great with rigid pavements as with flexible pavements, and for concrete carriageways three broad subgrade classes are defined as

Weak: all subgrades with a CBR of 2 per cent or less.

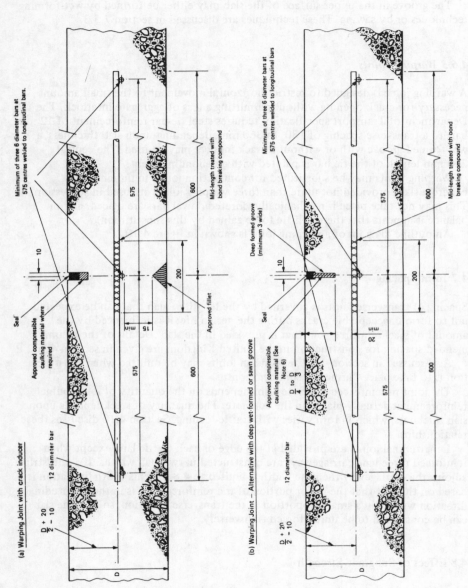

Figure 4.10 A typical warping joint for unreinforced slabs (reproduced from Technical Memo H1/72)

Normal: subgrades other than weak or very stable.

Very stable: all subgrades with a CBR of 15 per cent or more, including undisturbed road foundations.

Most concrete pavements require a sub-base to be placed beneath the slab, exceptions being (1) when the existing subgrade is a gravel or sand which can be compacted to produce a high-density material with a good running surface and which is at the same time frost-resistant, or (2) when the pavement is being constructed over sound rock, although in this case a regulating course may be required. Chalk also makes a suitable sub-base if it is not trafficked in wet conditions and if the danger of frost-expansion is slight.

As well as the more obvious functions of increasing pavement strength by giving more uniform and smooth support to the slab, increasing the thickness of cover over a frost-susceptible subgrade and reducing the danger of mud-pumping through faulty joints and cracks, a sub-base has a construction function. It must serve as a platform on which construction plant may operate without causing damage to a weak subgrade.

If the CBR of the subgrade is 2 per cent or less then a capping layer of well-graded granular natural sand, gravel, crushed rock or similar material, and a thickness of 280 mm together with a sub-base 130 mm thick is recommended. For other subgrade strengths, details of sub-base thickness are given in table 4.3. Additional material may be required if heavy loads are imposed by the mixed-concrete haul-trucks.

4.9 Waterproof or Separation Membrane

It is necessary to provide a slip-layer between the concrete slab and the sub-base and this should also retain the water in the concrete for hydration. This is usually provided by polythene or a similar flexible thermo-plastic sheeting placed in position shortly before concreting. If the membrane is laid an appreciable time before concreting or if warping joints are used in unreinforced construction then thicker plastic (125 μm) is required. In other circumstances 65 μm thick sheeting may be used.

The use of bituminous coatings is not recommended as a separating membrane because of the frictional restraint between the slab and the sub-base, which could lead to severe cracking.

4.10 The Road Note 29 Method of Design, Rigid Pavements

Concrete pavements have to withstand stresses from the following causes.

(1) The early hardening and curing of the slab, causing plastic cracking. This is controlled by contraction joints and the use of curing membranes, which reduce the rate of water loss from the slab.

(2) Temperature effects that cause (1) superficial expansion and contraction of the slab (stresses due to the restraint of this movement are controlled by contraction and expansion joints); (2) warping stresses created by differences in

temperature between the top and bottom of the slab (differential expansion causes slab-curling effects that are resisted by the weight of the slab).

(3) Wheel-load stresses. Slabs do not fail because a single application of a wheel-load creates a stress greater than the modulus of rupture of the concrete but by repeated loading by vehicles. It has been estimated that a stress of 60 per cent of the ultimate stress will cause failure after approximately 5000 applications. Where the stress is less than 50 per cent of the ultimate stress, however, fatigue failure is not normally considered.

While it is possible to calculate stresses in the slab due to these causes and compare the resulting stress with the same stress in the concrete, the relationship of this comparison with actual performance of the concrete pavement is uncertain. For this reason the design of concrete pavements in the United Kingdom is based upon an empirical approach using results from roads in service.

The effect of subgrade strength is not as great with rigid pavements as with flexible pavements and three broad subgrade classes are defined as weak, normal and very stable, as described in section 4.8.

Every attempt should be made to prevent the water table from rising to within 600 mm of the formation level. This may be achieved by subsoil drainage or by raising the level of the pavement on an embankment. Water proofing of the subgrade or sub-base during construction by sealing is also recommended.

Every concrete road normally is provided with a sub-base and the standard thickness of sub-base for differing subgrade strength is given in table 4.3. Where construction traffic runs over the sub-base then additional thickness of sub-base is required, but this is the responsibility of the contractor.

As with flexible pavements there should be no frost-susceptible material within 450 mm of the road surface. On lightly trafficked highways (that is, roads designed to carry less than 2 million standard axles) this thickness may be relaxed where local experience indicates this may be possible. Any required additional thickness is obtained by increasing the thickness of the sub-base.

The thickness of either reinforced or unreinforced slabs depends on the subgrade type and on the cumulative number of standard axles carried by the pavement during its life. The thickness of pavement is given by a design chart in Road Note 29,[6] which is reproduced in figure 4.11. Thicknesses should be rounded upwards to the nearest 10 mm. The Standard Specification for Road and Bridge Works issued by the Department of the Environment[7] classified the load-carrying capacity of various rigid pavement types and this information is reproduced as table 4.4.

On residential highways where unreinforced concrete pavements are used and heavy construction traffic is likely (construction traffic for 100 or more houses) the pavement thickness should be increased. An increased pavement thickness is necessary where the highway has to carry construction traffic for large factory-development schemes.

These design thicknesses are based on pavement-quality concrete whose strength is assessed using the indirect tensile test, the average of any four test consecutive results at the age of 28 days being specified to be not less than 2.3 N/mm^2.

For reinforced slabs the minimum weight of reinforcement varies according to the cumulative standard axles carried by the slab during its design life. Cover to the reinforcement should be 60 ± 10 mm, except in the case of slabs less than

150 mm thick where 50 ± 10 mm of cover should be provided. Minimum weights of reinforcement are given in figure 4.12, which is reproduced from Road Note 29

Joint spacing in reinforced slabs depends upon the actual weight of reinforcement used and not on the minimum amounts indicated by figure 4.12. The actual amount of reinforcement is shown in figure 4.13, which is reproduced from Road Note 29 to give the joint spacing.

Every third joint must be an expansion joint and the remainder are contraction joints, unless construction takes place during the summer months (21 April to 21 October), when expansion joints may be omitted provided the pavement is isolated from fixed structures by means of flexible construction. If limestone aggregate is used for the slab then the maximum joint spacing may be increased by 20 per cent. Tied warping joints may be used in place of contraction joints but not more than three such warping joints may be provided in succession.

Longitudinal joints are to be provided so as to limit slab width to 4.65 m unless extra transverse reinforcement is placed in the slab, unless a hardshoulder adjoins a slab when the maximum value is 4.8 m.

The maximum spacing of expansion joints for non-reinforced slabs is recommended as 60 m for slabs of 200 mm or greater thickness and 40 m for slabs of lesser thickness with intermediate contraction joints at 5 m intervals. If limestone aggregate is used it is recommended that the maximum expansion joint spacing be 72 and 48 m respectively with intermediate contraction joints at 6 m intervals.

As with reinforced concrete slabs, expansion joints may be replaced with contraction joints for summer construction. Tied warping joints may replace the contraction joints but not more than three warping joints may be used in succession.

4.11 The AASHO Interim Rigid-pavement Design Procedure

The design guide[8] points out the limitations of the rigid-pavement design procedure, as follows.

(1) The design-chart scales for working stress (f_t) in concrete and modulus of subgrade reaction (k) are derived from the Spangler modification of the Westergaard theory of stress distribution in rigid slabs. Further research will be required to establish fully the applicability of the Spangler equation.

(2) There is no adjustment in the AASHO Road Test rigid-pavement equation for an environmental or regional factor, because it was not possible to measure the effect of variations in climatic conditions over the two-year life of the pavement at the Road Test site.

(3) As with the design of flexible pavements, the traffic repetitions used in the development of the design equations were experienced over only a two-year period, but the traffic-analysis period that must be selected for design purposes is considerably longer than this.

(4) Two major overall assumptions have been made in the development of these design procedures, as follows

(a)   That the adequacy of the design will be established by soils and materials surveys and laboratory studies.

Concrete slabs

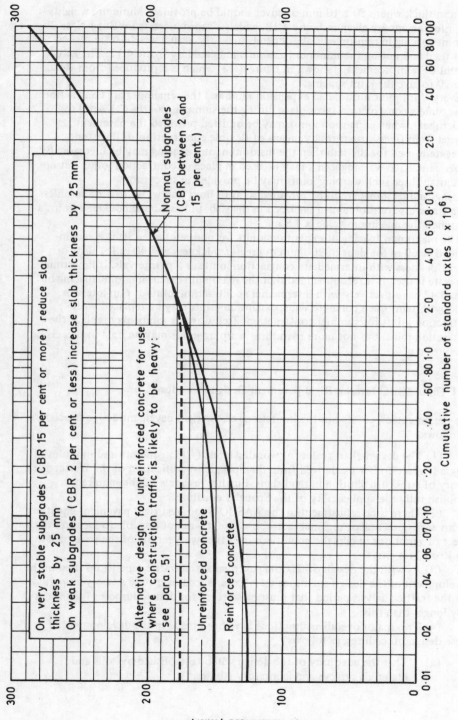

Figure 4.11 Concrete slab thickness[6]

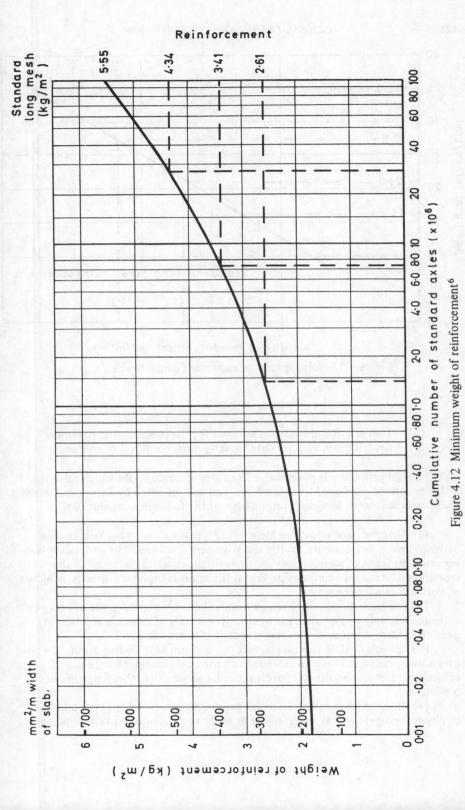

Figure 4.12 Minimum weight of reinforcement[6]

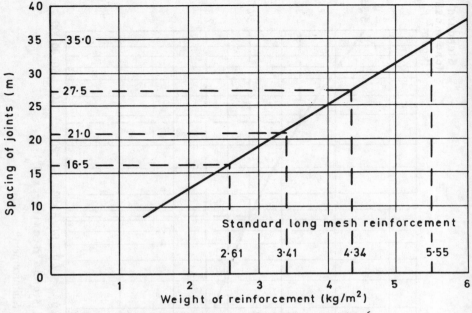

Figure 4.13 Joint spacing in reinforced concrete slabs[6]

(b)   That the design strengths assumed for the subgrade and pavement structure will be achieved through proper construction methods.

The design procedure is presented in the form of nomographs which solve the design equations developed from the Road Test and modified by theoretical analysis. These equations were developed on the basis of the following assumptions.

(1) That the basic equations are a valid representation of the relationship between loss in serviceability, traffic and pavement thickness. The first factor is expressed in terms of serviceability index, traffic is expressed in terms of the repetition of standard axles, and pavement thickness is expressed directly in inches of Portland cement concrete.

(2) The basic equations obtained from a single type of subgrade soil may be extended to apply to any subgrade by means of a scale of subgrade reaction (k) developed for this purpose. This test is described in section 3.4.3.

(3) As with flexible pavements, that the uniform axle loading during the test over a two-year period may be extended to varied axle loadings by the use of equivalence factors and that the loading may be applied over the design life of the pavement.

(4) That the basic equations developed for a concrete of one type and level of physical properties may be extended to apply to slabs of other types and levels

of physical properties by means of a scale of working stress in concrete (f_t) developed for this purpose.

(5) That uniform and high-quality construction will be obtained, particularly with respect to density, gradation and quality of materials and smoothness of the pavement surface, both transversely and longitudinally.

4.11.1 Concrete Properties and Slab Details

The average flexural strength for the concrete on the Road Test was approximately 600 lb/in.^{2} at 28 days. If the concrete strength differs from this value then the working stress (f_t) is taken as 0.75 x the modulus of rupture at 28 days determined using third-point loading (AASHO Designation T-97). A static modulus of elasticity of (4 200 000 lb/in.^{2}) was the average value for the concrete at the test.

The design guide states that expansion joints are not necessary except adjacent to structures; at these situations a 20 to 25 mm width is considered adequate. Contraction joints may be sawn in the hardened concrete or formed by plastic inserts. The joint is stated to have a depth of approximately one-quarter of the slab depth and adequate load transfer provided. Longitudinal joints are used to prevent irregular cracks and may be formed by keyed butt-joints or mechanically formed or sawn grooves.

Load transfer devices of conventional round steel dowel, details of dowel diameter, length and spacing are given in table 4.5.

Table 4.5 Load-transfer dowel details as given by the AASHO Interim Design Guide[8]

Pavement Thickness in.	Dowel Diameter in.	Dowel Length in.	Dowel Spacing in.
6	¾	18	12
7	1	18	12
8	1	18	12
9	1¼	18	12
10	1¼	18	12

4.11.2 Reinforcement

The purpose of distributing steel reinforcement in a reinforced-concrete pavement is not to prevent cracking but to preserve aggregate interlock at the cracks forming in the slab. If the steel balances the resistance to contraction due to friction between the slab and the sub-base then the cross-sectional area of steel (A_s) required per unit width of scale is

$$A_s = \frac{FLw}{2f_s} \qquad (4.2)$$

where A_s is the cross-sectional area of steel per unit width of slab,

F is the coefficient of friction between slab and subgrade,

L is the distance between free transverse joints or between free longitudinal edges,

w is the mass of the pavement per unit area,

f_s is the allowable working stress in the steel.

The solution of this equation is given graphical form in figure 4.14.

4.11.3 Slab Thickness

The thickness of the slab is determined for a given working stress (f_t) and modulus of subgrade reaction (k) by the use of either of the design charts given in figures 4.15 and 4.16 for terminal serviceability of 2.5 and 2.0 respectively.

Use is made of the design charts by drawing a line from the estimated traffic loading on the left-hand scale through the applicable value of working stress (f_t) on the second scale to intersect the pivot scale. From this point of intersection a line is drawn to the applicable value of modulus of subgrade reaction. The intersection of this line with the second scale from the right is the required thickness of slab.

4.12 Continuously Reinforced Concrete Pavements

In normally reinforced concrete pavements the function of the steel is to resist the tensile stresses that develop at the transverse cracks forming in a slab, and so preserve aggregate interlock. The amount of longitudinal steel required to perform this function is considered to be in the region of 0.3 per cent of the cross-sectional area of the slab.

Extensive experience in the United States, in Europe and to a lesser extent in the United Kingdom has demonstrated that if the percentage of steel is increased still further the steel will limit the formation of cracks as well as preserve aggregate interlock and so allow the elimination of all joints except where the pavement abuts against fixed structures. Experience has also shown that continuously reinforced slabs can be laid to a reduced thickness compared with unreinforced and normally reinforced slabs.

Continuously reinforced slabs were first constructed in the United States in the late 1930s and Gregory, Burks and Pink[9] reported that in the early 1970s the annual rate of construction of CRCP (continuously reinforced concrete pavement) in the United States was the equivalent of 4000 km of equivalent two-lane highway

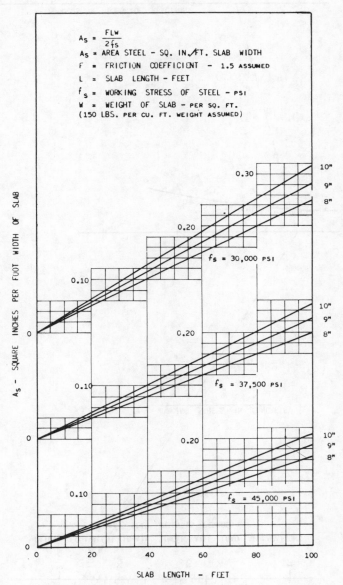

Figure 4.14 Distribution steel requirements, jointed rigid pavements[8]

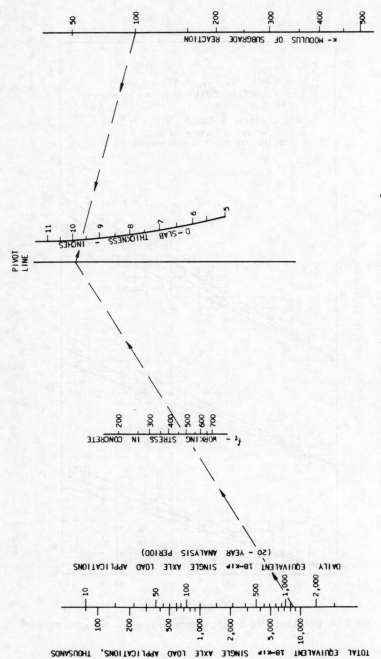

Figure 4.15 Design chart for rigid pavements, $p_t = 2.0$.[8]

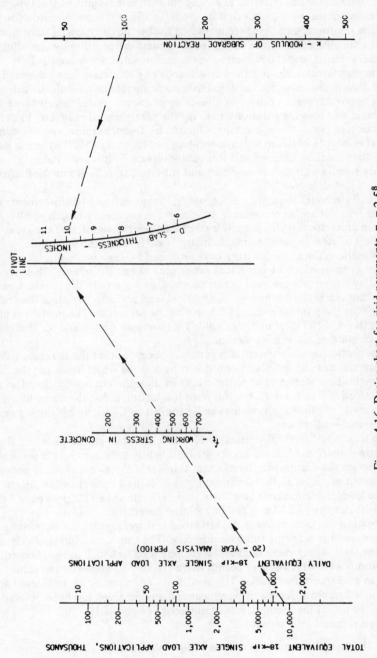

Figure 4.16 Design chart for rigid pavements, $p_t = 2.5$[8]

per year. Belgium is also reported as having considerable lengths of this type of pavement in service, with claims that its use is justified on economic grounds, the cost of the reinforcement being compensated for by the omission of transverse joints, the simplification of the pavement construction operation by the elimination of transverse joints, and the reduction in the maintenance work required.

The factors which influence the performance of CRCP have been discussed by Gregory.[8] As in the more conventional forms of concrete pavement, the sub-base plays an important role in providing a working platform, providing resistance against frost attack, and forming a uniform base for the placement of concrete. In contrast to unreinforced slabs, where cracking is limited by frequent joints and the minimum frictional resistance between slab and sub-base is desired, in CRCP slabs it is desirable that the slabs crack at uniform and frequent intervals. This is achieved by a uniformly rough interface between slab and sub-base, and the elimination of the waterproof sliding layer.

In CRCP concrete, strength, crack spacing, the quantity of reinforcement, and frictional restraint are all connected. An increase in concrete strength results in an increase in crack spacing, for a given level of frictional restraint, and the greater is the amount of steel required to maintain aggregate interlock at the joints.

The American Concrete Institute have proposed a design procedure[10] for CRCP which has been developed from actual experience of test pavements. Theories modified by experience are used in this procedure to compute the required pavement thickness and the amount of longitudinal steel and also to design the end-anchorages or the jointing means at the end of the pavement. The method is partially based on the AASHO interim design guide for pavement design and for this reason it must be considered a tentative method.

As has previously been stated, it is generally accepted that the concrete slab must resist stresses and deflections produced by applied wheel loads and the function of the longitudinal steel is to keep the cracks in the concrete tightly closed so that there is effective load transfer. On this basis it is assumed that the same design methods used for jointed pavements can be applied to CRRP by assigning a very high degree of load transfer.

When tensile and flexural stresses develop in a slab then cracks form and the stresses are redistributed. If the cracks are held tightly together there is some shear transfer across the cracks, but the moment transfer is somewhat reduced because the cracks act as hinges so that deflection may become a critical design criteria. Extensive load/deflection tests have shown the deflection of an 200 mm (8 in.) CRCP to be no greater than a 250 mm (10 in.) jointed pavement.

Rigid-pavement failures in the AASHO road test were greatly influenced by deflections and the resulting sub-base pumping. The empirical expressions developed from these tests reflect these facts and were extended to CRCP design. Subsequently modifications were developed to permit more versatility in materials and some latitude in load transfer at cracks. This modified design procedure has served as a design procedure for this type of pavement and a nomograph has been developed to facilitate the use of the method; it is reproduced as figure 4.17.

The terms used in the report are

A_s the cross-sectional area of longitudinal steel (in.^{2})
A_c the cross-sectional area of pavement being designed (in.^{2})

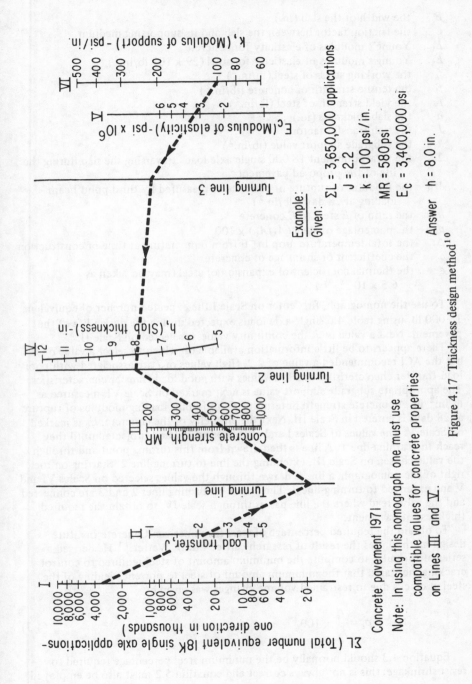

Figure 4.17 Thickness design method[10]

Example:

Given:

ΣL = 3,650,000 applications
J = 2.2
k = 100 psi/in.
MR = 580 psi
E_c = 3,400,000 psi

Answer h = 8.0 in.

Concrete pavement 1971

Note: In using this nomograph one must use
compatible values for concrete properties
on Lines III and V.

B the width of the slab (in.)
C the friction factor between the slab and its supporting medium
E_c Young's modulus of elasticity for concrete
E_s Young's modulus of elasticity for steel (29×10^6 lb/in.^{2})
f_s the working stress of steel (lb/in.^{2})
f_t' the tensile strength of concrete (lb/in.^{2})
f_y the yield strength of steel (lb/in.^{2})
h the slab thickness (in.)
J the slab transfer factor
k the subgrade support value (lb/in.^{2})
ΣL the total equivalent 18 000 single-axle loads traversing the slab during the life of the proposed pavement
M_R the modulus of rupture of concrete as measured by third-point beam loading at 28 days (lb/in.^{2})
n the ratio of E steel to E concrete
p_s the percentage of steel (A_s/A_c) x 100
Δt the total temperature drop in $^\circ$F from temperature at time of construction
δ the coefficient of shrinkage of concrete
ϵ the thermal coefficient of expansion of steel (may be taken as $6.5 \times 10^{-5}/^\circ\text{F}$)

To use the nomograph, first enter on Scale I the expected number of equivalent 18 000 lb, using table 4.6 single-axle loads expected during the design life of the pavement. Next a value of J, the continuity value, is selected on Scale II.

There appears to be little information available on which to select a value of J but the ACI recommended a value of 2.2. High values of J are associated with poor load-transfer characteristics and low values with good load-transfer characteristics. The appropriate subgrade support value is next marked on Scale VI, measured as lb/in.^{2}/in. A concrete strength in terms of a third-point loading modulus of rupture at 28 days is entered in Scale III. Next the elasticity of the concrete, E_c is marked on Scale V. The values of Scales I and II are connected and projected until they reach the turning-line 1. A line is then drawn from this turning point and through the value chosen on Scale III, extending the line to turning-line 2. Starting on the right of the nomograph, a line is drawn through the values selected on Scales VI and V and extended to turning-line 3. The points on turning-lines 2 and 3 are connected and the value read where the line passes through scale IV, to obtain the required thickness of pavement.

To obtain the required percentage of steel the American Concrete Institute design method uses the result of research carried out by Vetter.[11] He derived a series of formulae to compute the minimum amount of steel required to control cracking; he stated that the minimum amount of steel to prevent yielding of the steel at cracks due to restrained volume changes was given by

$$p_s = \frac{f_t'}{f_y} \times 100 \qquad\qquad (4.3)$$

Equation 4.3 should normally be the minimum steel percentage required to resist shrinkage; this is not always correct and equation 5.2 must also be employed

Table 4.6 18 KIP axle equivalency factors[9] (Values from Table 11f, p. A—59,
'Guide for Forecasting Traffic on the Interstate System', Highway Planning
Program Manual, Transmittal 86, V. 4, Chapter VII, Appendix A, Jan. 1969.)

Single Axles		Tandem Axle Groups	
Weight, lb	Factor	Weight, lb	Factor
1 000	0.00003	10 000	0.0126
2 000	0.00020	11 000	0.0182
3 000	0.00076	12 000	0.0256
4 000	0.00214	13 000	0.0353
5 000	0.00497	14 000	0.0475
6 000	0.0101	15 000	0.0629
7 000	0.0188	16 000	0.0818
8 000	0.0324	17 000	0.105
9 000	0.0526	18 000	0.133
10 000	0.0817	19 000	0.166
11 000	0.122	20 000	0.206
12 000	0.176	21 000	0.253
13 000	0.248	22 000	0.308
14 000	0.341	23 000	0.371
15 000	0.458	24 000	0.444
16 000	0.604	25 000	0.527
17 000	0.783	26 000	0.622
18 000	1.00	27 000	0.729
19 000	1.26	28 000	0.850
20 000	1.57	29 000	0.986
21 000	1.93	30 000	1.137
22 000	2.34	31 000	1.305
23 000	2.82	32 000	1.49
24 000	3.36	33 000	1.70
25 000	3.98	34 000	1.92
26 000	4.67	35 000	2.16
27 000	5.43	36 000	2.43
28 000	6.29	37 000	2.72
29 000	7.24	38 000	3.03
30 000	8.28	39 000	3.37
31 000	9.43	40 000	3.74
32 000	10.70	41 000	4.13
33 000	12.09	42 000	4.55
34 000	13.62	43 000	5.00
35 000	15.29	44 000	5.48
36 000	17.12	45 000	5.99
37 000	19.12	46 000	6.53
38 000	21.31	47 000	7.11
39 000	23.69	48 000	7.73
40 000	26.29	49 000	8.38
41 000	29.12	50 000	9.07
42 000	32.20	51 000	9.81
43 000	35.53	52 000	10.59
44 000	39.15	53 000	11.41
45 000	43.07	54 000	12.29
46 000	47.30	55 000	13.22
47 000	51.87	56 000	14.20
48 000	56.79	57 000	15.24
49 000	62.09	58 000	16.33
50 000	67.78	59 000	17.50
		60 000	18.72
		61 000	20.02
		62 000	21.39
		63 000	22.83
		64 000	24.35
		65 000	25.96
		66 000	27.65
		67 000	29.43
		68 000	31.30
		69 000	33.27
		70 000	35.34

Note: Multiply number of axles in each weight group by factor (second
column). Sum these products to obtain ΣL.

to determine the minimum value.

$$p_s = \left(\frac{f_t'}{f_y + \delta E_s - nf_t'} \right) 100 \qquad (4.4)$$

The minimum amount of steel to control restrained volume changes due to temperature changes was found to be

$$p_s = \left(\frac{f_t'}{f_y - nf_t'} \right) 100 \qquad (4.5)$$

The value given by equation 4.5 must be compared with that obtained from equation 4.6.

$$p_s = \left[\frac{f_t'}{2(f_y - \Delta T \epsilon E_s)} \right] 100 \qquad (4.6)$$

and the larger of the two values used.

When considering the effect of both shrinkage and temperature, Vetter noted that the amount of steel required to control cracking due to shrinkage and temperature will always be less than the amount required to control either shrinkage or temperature alone. This conclusion was developed from the fact that each of the equations for temperature and shrinkage was based on the condition that the concrete between cracks was just at the point of breaking. If additional stress were introduced, the concrete would crack again and break into shorter lengths in which the concrete again would have its full tensile capacity. Normally it is found that equation 4.5 will govern the steel design.

As well as omitting some climatological factors Vetters formulae do not take into account the friction factor C between the slab and the subgrade. If C is approximately 1.5 then it is not necessary to correct equation 4.5. If, however, it is believed that C varies appreciably from 1.5 then equation 4.5 should take the revised form

$$p_s = \left(\frac{f_t'}{f_y - nf_t'} \right) (1.3 - 0.2C)100 \qquad (4.7)$$

The design method suggests that the tensile strength of the concrete f_t' should be obtained from the correction between f_t' and M_R, which it is suggested be taken as $0.4M_R$ and a factor of a safety of 1.3 applied to p_s. In equations 4.3 to 4.7 the yield strength f_y rather than the allowable stress f_s is used, the ratio of the two values is generally 2 to 3. Having established the required percentage of longitudinal steel, the longitudinal steel area may be calculated.

The American Concrete Institute design method considers that in CRC pavements the function of transverse reinforcement is

(1) To maintain the specified spacing of the longitudinal steel.

(2) To serve as tie bars across the longitudinal joints in place of conventional tie bars.

(3) To maintain aggregate interlock across any chance longitudinal cracks which form.

(4) To assist in supporting the longitudinal steel above the sub-base when preset reinforcement is used.

When longitudinal steel is embedded in the concrete by mechanical means which ensures accurate placement of the steel and when the bars are employed then transverse reinforcement is not required. In the United States a considerable length of CRP has been constructed without transverse reinforcement.

Experience gained in CRP construction in the United States has led to the following recommendations for steel-reinforcement details. The steel may consist of deformed welded-wire fabric. It is recommended that longitudinal steel should have a minimum yield strength of 60 000 lb/in.[2]. Lower-strength steel results in a closer bar spacing and greater handling and fixing charges. Spacing of the longitudinal steel should not exceed 8 in. and have a minimum spacing of not less than 4 in., or 3 in. when the concrete is placed in two courses. Lap splices of individual bars or prefabricated mats may be located in the same transverse section or they may be staggered. If not more than one-third of the longitudinal steel is lapped within any 3 ft length of pavement the length of the lap should be 25 times the bar diameter with a minimum-length lap of 16 in. When the laps are in the same transverse section the lap length should be 30 diameters with a minimum length of 18 in.

An analysis of this design method carried out by the Transport and Road Research Laboratory[9] has indicated that it does not offer any savings in slab thickness for the two heavier classes of traffic — indeed it indicates thicker slabs than are currently employed for jointed slabs. A reduction in slab thickness is only appreciable for light traffic on poor soils.

A more economical design method is that recommended by the Continuously Reinforced Pavement Group,[12] who recommend a pavement thickness of from 70 to 80 per cent of the thickness of jointed concrete pavements.

For highways constructed in the United Kingdom with continuously reinforced concrete pavements it is recommended that first of all they should be designed in accordance with the method given in Road Note 29 (see section 4.10). For roads designed to carry a total loading of 11 million standard axles or more a reduction of 30 mm can be made in slab thickness; the associated steel area is then 0.6 per cent. Economically it is to be expected that the initial cost of CRCP in the United Kingdom will be greater than that of conventional jointed pavements as the cost of the additional steel is greater than the saving in concrete, joints and sliding layer. Savings in maintenance are likely to offset the increase however. A further advantage of the elimination of joints is that the slab can be overlaid at a future date with a bituminous layer without the danger of reflection cracking occurring at the joints.

4.13 Continuously Reinforced Slabs with Bituminous Surfacing

A frequent form of construction in heavily trafficked city streets is a continuously reinforced concrete slab with a bituminous surfacing. Such a pavement will give good service even when ground conditions are poor due to the nature of the soil or frequent excavations for services.

Recommendations for the design of this type of pavement are given in Road Note 29.[6] Design curves give slab thickness for varying cumulative repetitions of standard axle loadings for the three subgrade types — weak, normal or very stable — as defined for other types of concrete pavements in British practice. Minimum slab thickness for a cumulative loading of 2.5 million standard axles is 190, 160 and 130 mm for the three subgrade types. Maximum thickness is 290, 270 and 240 mm.

Reinforcement for this type of slab is recommended as either long mesh which is not lighter than 5.5 kg/m^2 or longitudinal deformed bar with a cross-sectional area not less than 650 mm^2 per metre width of road. As with other forms of continuously reinforced slab, the relatively heavy reinforcement is required because of the absence of transverse joints.

Bituminous surfacing will normally have a thickness of at least 90 mm and be a basecourse and a wearing course of rolled asphalt or dense bitumen macadam.

References

(1) Department of Transport, *Specification for Road and Bridge Works* (HMSO, (1976)
(2) BS 882: 1965 Coarse and Fine Aggregates from Natural Sources
(3) BS 1047: 1952 Air Cooled Blast Furnace Slag Coarse Aggregate for Concrete
(4) BS 1881: 1970 Methods of Testing Concrete
(5) DoE, *Design of Normal Concrete Mixes.* (HMSO, 1975)
(6) DoE, Road Research Laboratory Road Note 29, 3rd ed.: *A Guide to the Structural Design of Pavements for New Roads* (HMSO, 1970)
(7) DoE, *Notes for Guidance on the Specification for Road and Bridge Works* (HMSO, 1976)
(8) American Association of State Highway Officials, *A.A.S.H.O. Interim Guide for Design of Pavement Structures* (Washington, 1972)
(9) J. M. Gregory, A. E. Burks and V. A. Pink, Transport and Road Research Laboratory Report 612. *Continuously Reinforced Concrete Pavements: a Report of the Study Group.* (Crowthorne, 1974)
(10) American Concrete Institute, 'A Design Procedure for Continuously Reinforced Concrete Pavements for Highways', *J. Am. Conc. Inst.* 69 (1972) 309–19
(11) C. P. Vetter, 'Stresses in Reinforced Concrete Due to Volume Changes', *Trans. Am. Soc. Civil Enginrs.* 98 (1933) 1039–80.
(12) Continuously Reinforced Pavement Group, *Design and Construction of Continuously Reinforced Concrete Pavement* (Chicago, 1968)

5

Drainage

5.1 Introduction

The importance of adequate drainage was realised by Roman road builders, but after the decline of the Roman Empire the standard of highway construction in Europe declined and planned drainage became almost non-existent. With the advent of industrialisation increasing attention was paid to the removal of surface water and the lowering of the water-table beneath the pavement. In the United Kingdom the pioneer road-building of Telford and Macadam laid stress on the incorporation of a camber or crown into the road so that surface water could be quickly removed. Increasing urban development made open ditches inappropriate and led to the increasing use of road gulleys connected to road sewers as the means of removing surface water. Improvements in the quality of road materials have resulted in impervious pavements, making the problem of sub-soil usually greatest in the cuttings, where cut-off drainage is required.

5.2 Surface-water Drainage Works

Before construction of the pavement layers is carried out it is necessary to complete all underground pipe and cable crossings. Where this is not possible, ducts are normally placed in advance and their positions carefully recorded.

All road drainage works, surface-water sewers and associated manholes are completed and the gullies excavated for and placed in position. Road gullies are frequently of clayware, sometimes of high-strength polypropylene or a similar plastic material. Frequently they are 375 mm in internal diameter, have a maximum internal depth of 900 mm and are fitted with a 150 mm outlet. It is advisable for the gully to be fitted with a rodding eye in case the connection between gully and sewer becomes blocked by road debris. A typical arrangement of such a gully is shown in figure 5.1. The 150 mm connection from gully to sewer is then surrounded with 150 mm of concrete where it is close to the formation level.

Finally the gully frame and grating is set on two or three courses of engineering bricks so that its upper surface is at the finished road-surface level. Backfilling of the trenches for gully connections is an important operation which should be

141

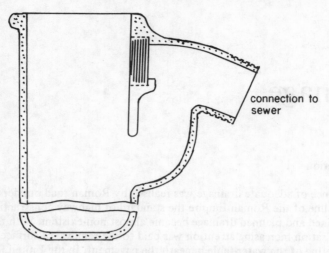

Figure 5.1 A typical street gully with rodding eye

closely supervised to ensure that material is replaced in layers not exceeding 150 mm in thickness, each layer being well compacted by hand or mechanical ramming. Inadequate compaction of gully-trench backfilling can frequently result in serious settlement after the road has been completed.

When constructing major roads there is the obvious difference in scale between the major road and the residential road. Taking rural motorways as an example of major road construction, the most obvious differences are the use of hard shoulders at the outer edges of the dual carriageways and also of a central reservation. There is also a greater emphasis on the lowering of the level of ground-water table by the use of French drains in the central reservation and cut-off French drains at the outer edges of the hard shoulders. Details of a typical motorway slip-road pavement cross-section are given in figure 5.2.

In major road construction in rural areas there will be few drainage connections beneath the carriageways so that the major drainage works will be the placing of the French drains. These are used to remove surface water and to maintain a lowered water-table. Surface water flows only infrequently and, provided the drain is not blocked or surcharged, ground-water levels will not be adversely affected by the two functions.

Pipes that may be used for French drains include open-jointed concrete and clayware pipes and perforated pipes of concrete, pitch fibre or asbestos cement. Filter material will usually be open-textured material of 37.5 mm nominal size and only 0 to 5 per cent passing a 10 mm sieve. Over a period of time the filter material will need to be renewed as it becomes blocked with fine material carried from the road surface.

The width of trench that has to be backfilled is usually limited to the outside diameter of the pipe plus 300 mm when trenches are not deeper than 1.5 m below finished level. For deeper trenches the trench width is the outside diameter plus

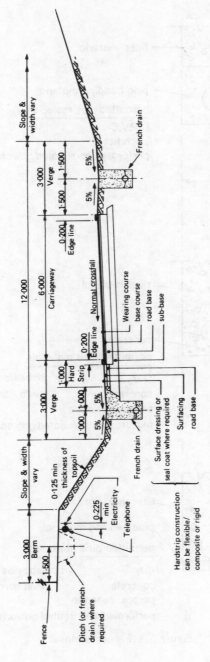

Figure 5.2 Typical cross-section of rural motorway slip roads (DoE)

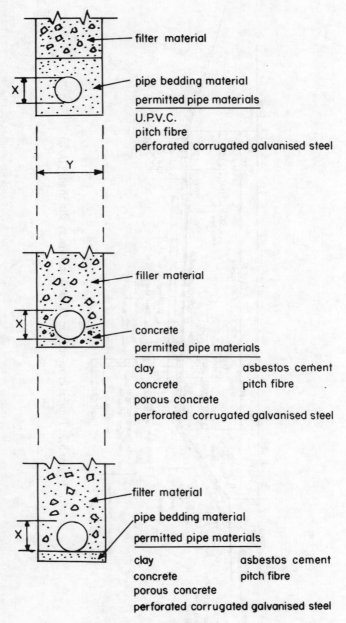

Figure 5.3 French drains

450 mm. Typical details of French drains as used in British motorways are given in figure 5.3.

5.3 The Spacing of Road Gullies

The spacing of road gullies along the channel of the highway is frequently carried out by the designer using past knowledge of arrangements which have proved satisfactory. The factors that must be taken into account are (1) carriageway width and crossfall, which determine the area draining to each gully per unit length of road, (2) the longitudinal fall of the highway, which will frequently limit the gully spacing if water is not to spread out into the carriageway and (3) the anticipated capacity of the gully grating.

Often a 'rule of thumb' design has been used, with gullies being placed at 50 yd intervals. A more sensible consideration of the factors involved is by the use of a formula[1] giving the design spacing in yards as $(1000S)/W$, where S is the longitudinal gradient of the highway expressed as a percentage and W is the width of the drained area in feet. For housing-estate roads the recommended[2] area draining to a gully has been given as 240 yd^2.

In the design of road-gully spacing it is necessary to consider the following factors: rainfall intensity, the permitted width of water encroachment on to the carriageway, physical roadway features, and the efficiency of the gully grating in actually allowing water flow in the channel to enter the gully pot.

Calculation of the rainfall intensity normally requires a knowledge of the duration and the return period of the storm. For the high rainfall intensities that are likely to produce critical conditions in the gully-spacing problem the relationship between the factors given by Holland[3] is used for highways in the United Kingdom. If 50 mm/h rainfall intensity is taken as the critical condition (and at rainfall intensities greater than this most drivers would experience difficulties of vision), it can be shown from the work of Holland that such an intensity would have a duration of 5 min in an average year while once in 5 years the storm might be expected to last for 14 min.

When calculating the maximum encroachment of water that can be permitted on to the carriageway, then account must be taken of the crossfall of the road, its longitudinal gradient and the hydraulic roughness of the road surface. In their approach to the design of gully spacing the Transport and Road Research Laboratory[4] considered three maximum widths of water in the channel of 500 mm, 750 mm and 1 m, the actual width to be selected for design purposes according to the situation. On a high-speed road where the consequences of water encroaching on to the carriageway may be serious, or where pedestrians are likely to experience difficulties, a width of 500 mm is considered appropriate. In other circumstances, on low-speed rural roads, a width of 1 m may be considered suitable. This maximum width occurs adjacent to the gully.

With the maximum width of water defined and the crossfall and longitudinal gradient of the road known, water flow may be calculated using the formula given by Manning for channel flow. To use the formula it is necessary to know the value of the roughness coefficient; and while considerable variations in this parameter

Table 5.1 Drained area (m^2) of road under rainfall of 50 mm/h which results in a width of flow of 1 m (Manning's $n = 0.10$)[4]

CROSSFALL	GRADIENT	HEAVY DUTY GRATINGS		MEDIUM DUTY GRATINGS				KERB INLETS	
		D10-20	D11-20	E12-16	E12-20	E13-16	E13-20	E14-19	E14-19(Mod)
1/60	1/300	160	168	153	155	162	167	68	109
	1/150	225	223	209	206	209	209	66	146
	1/100	267	273	247	241	244	238	74	179
	1/80	297	304	277	274	271	264	73	198
	1/60	346	346	312	319	315	312	80	220
	1/40	410	415	382	359	359	326	84	233
	1/30	479	484	425	403	414	414	91	269
	1/20	590	590	505	564	492	499	112	308
	1/15	692	661	608	623	593	547	122	334
1/50	1/300	211	220	202	202	213	215	92	172
	1/150	297	294	275	265	275	275	84	212
	1/100	355	332	332	324	324	320	93	247
	1/80	397	393	367	363	363	359	99	268
	1/60	450	455	410	415	390	425	110	295
	1/40	514	532	471	471	490	453	104	324
	1/30	593	628	544	522	522	529	113	388
	1/20	752	778	674	708	674	648	138	415
	1/15	898	878	748	768	758	709	180	439
1/40	1/300	293	303	287	287	284	293	119	228
	1/150	415	411	389	385	385	385	119	296
	1/100	504	504	455	455	439	450	130	369
	1/80	551	545	503	491	503	491	145	382
	1/60	630	630	588	581	525	546	154	413
	1/40	764	721	652	661	644	721	146	506
	1/30	851	851	762	822	762	792	178	574
	1/20	1067	1067	933	970	933	921	230	606
	1/15	1218	1176	1064	1120	1050	1036	252	672
1/30	1/300	459	473	449	434	449	454	185	361
	1/150	642	642	593	580	573	580	186	504
	1/100	776	785	709	692	675	684	203	608
	1/80	859	850	793	765	765	746	277	651
	1/60	992	992	905	905	894	883	251	-
	1/40	1159	1159	1092	1052	1066	1066	-	-
	1/30	1355	1355	1232	1201	1140	1247	-	-
1/20	1/300	872	881	845	799	808	808	321	744
	1/150	-	-	1090	1051	1142	1077	-	-

have been observed, the Transport and Road Research Laboratory recommend a mean value of 0.01 be used.

Highway engineers have always been concerned with the efficiency of gully gratings, frequently observing that in some circumstances a proportion of the water flowing to the gully by-passes the gully inlet. As the result of an experimental programme the efficiency of heavy- and medium-duty gratings was determined for a range of crossfalls and slopes up to 1 in 15.

Calculating the efficiency as the percentage of water entering the gully to the water approaching the gully it was found that, as would be expected, most water is collected by gratings placed directly in the path of flowing water. Especially at steep longitudinal slopes, the side-inlet gully has a low efficiency. The efficiency of all gullies could be further improved if the crossfall were increased adjacent to the gully. For a heavy-duty grating and a width of flow of 1 m the maximum efficiency

Table 5.2 Drained area (m^2) of road under rainfall of 50 mm/h which results in a width of flow of 0.75 m (Manning's n = 0.10)[4]

CROSSFALL	GRADIENT	HEAVY DUTY GRATINGS		MEDIUM DUTY GRATINGS				KERB INLETS	
		D10-20	D11-20	E12-16	E12-20	E13-16	E13-20	E14-19	E14-19(Mod)
1/60	1/300	84	84	84	84	84	84	46	71
	1/150	117	117	116	113	117	117	40	88
	1/100	143	143	142	140	143	140	42	108
	1/80	146	160	152	154	154	147	47	118
	1/60	182	184	179	177	177	171	51	137
	1/40	221	225	218	212	221	209	53	154
	1/30	253	256	246	235	246	235	61	145
	1/20	308	311	295	285	282	285	71	165
	1/15	352	363	325	329	329	329	79	187
1/50	1/300	108	108	108	108	108	108	55	92
	1/150	152	152	151	148	152	142	53	117
	1/100	184	184	179	179	184	179	55	141
	1/80	193	206	202	199	199	197	61	162
	1/60	237	239	234	229	224	222	68	183
	1/40	289	289	283	280	?83	274	72	197
	1/30	334	334	323	310	320	313	83	196
	1/20	401	409	371	392	376	384	93	228
	1/15	464	478	425	444	429	434	102	249
1/40	1/300	152	152	152	152	152	152	78	128
	1/150	212	212	210	210	210	212	77	169
	1/100	257	257	257	252	254	257	73	210
	1/80	288	288	285	279	273	279	88	235
	1/60	331	331	321	314	318	314	91	274
	1/40	406	410	393	364	389	385	103	294
	1/30	464	468	454	435	445	435	115	292
	1/20	563	574	447	463	552	545	117	334
	1/15	637	664	603	597	583	590	176	339
1/30	1/300	232	234	234	234	234	234	110	201
	1/150	327	327	323	320	327	327	112	271
	1/100	400	400	388	392	384	392	125	343
	1/80	447	447	443	434	429	429	127	375
	1/60	512	517	491	491	491	496	141	428
	1/40	627	634	621	582	608	563	166	461
	1/30	716	731	701	716	694	694	162	465
	1/20	805	895	850	850	732	859	181	461
	1/15	919	1023	825	960	846	856	209	501
1/20	1/300	432	432	436	436	436	436	214	392
	1/150	610	610	598	604	604	604	203	530
	1/100	746	746	709	724	716	724	219	648
	1/80	810	836	793	793	776	802	245	751
	1/60	935	955	896	886	896	896	263	877
	1/40	1144	1144	1013	1037	1097	1061	310	906
	1/30	1321	1335	1183	1183	1238	1321	316	-
	1/20	1532	1633	1431	1548	1397	1532	-	-
	1/15	1751	1829	1537	1751	1576	1693	-	-
1/15	1/300	673	673	673	680	673	680	286	612
	1/150	952	952	933	933	827	914	317	856
	1/100	1154	1154	1107	1096	1119	1143	353	1084
	1/80	1292	1305	1226	1239	1199	1252	395	1252
	1/60	1461	1507	1370	1400	1339	1400	1	1

was noted to be 99 per cent when the road had a crossfall of 1 in 60 and a longitudinal gradient of 1 in 300. The lowest efficiency of a heavy-duty grating with a water width of 1 m was 84 per cent at a crossfall of 1 in 40 and a longitudinal gradient of 1 in 15. Medium-duty gratings at the same width of water had a maximum efficiency of 98 per cent and a minimum efficiency of 70 per cent.

By equating the water actually entering the gully (that is, the efficiency multiplied by the flow in the channel immediately upstream of the gully) with the

Table 5.3 Drained area (m²) of road under rainfall of 50 mm/h which results in a width of flow of 0.5 m (Manning's n = 0.010)[4]

CROSSFALL	GRADIENT	HEAVY DUTY GRATINGS		MEDIUM DUTY GRATINGS				KERB INLETS	
		D10-20	D11-20	E12-16	E12-20	E13-16	E13-20	E14-19	E14-19(Mod)
1/60	1/300	30	30	30	30	30	30	23	30
	1/150	44	44	44	44	44	44	22	40
	1/100	54	54	54	54	54	54	22	49
	1/80	62	62	62	62	62	61	22	55
	1/60	70	69	70	70	70	69	27	64
	1/40	84	84	84	83	84	83	31	77
	1/30	98	98	99	98	97	94	31	84
	1/20	120	118	113	120	118	117	37	89
	1/15	136	138	133	138	138	135	41	98
1/50	1/300	40	40	40	40	40	40	30	40
	1/150	58	58	58	58	58	58	29	54
	1/100	70	69	70	70	70	68	30	64
	1/80	78	76	78	78	78	75	30	70
	1/60	90	88	90	90	88	85	33	83
	1/40	110	111	110	109	110	108	39	103
	1/30	125	125	124	125	124	123	44	110
	1/20	156	155	152	155	153	153	49	117
	1/15	178	177	180	178	175	175	51	138
1/40	1/300	56	56	56	56	56	56	38	56
	1/150	78	78	78	78	78	78	43	73
	1/100	96	96	96	96	96	94	43	87
	1/80	108	107	108	108	108	106	43	98
	1/60	124	123	123	124	123	119	46	113
	1/40	150	150	150	149	149	146	52	141
	1/30	172	172	171	174	172	171	60	158
	1/20	210	210	208	205	188	208	66	160
	1/15	241	243	241	243	241	238	67	169
1/30	1/300	84	84	84	84	84	84	60	82
	1/150	118	118	118	118	118	117	64	111
	1/100	146	145	146	146	145	143	63	137
	1/80	162	160	160	162	160	159	65	144
	1/60	186	186	186	188	186	184	73	169
	1/40	228	228	225	228	225	228	85	214
	1/30	258	261	261	263	261	258	93	242
	1/20	319	323	316	319	316	316	104	251
	1/15	365	368	368	368	365	365	98	229
1/20	1/300	154	154	154	154	154	152	111	151
	1/150	218	218	216	218	216	216	118	207
	1/100	266	263	263	266	268	263	117	253
	1/80	295	295	295	298	295	292	122	280
	1/60	341	341	341	344	341	341	134	320
	1/40	414	418	414	418	418	418	156	367
	1/30	476	481	481	481	481	476	170	467
	1/20	578	590	584	584	584	584	179	519
	1/15	647	674	654	674	633	674	179	447
1/15	1/300	238	236	236	238	236	236	169	233
	1/150	336	333	333	336	333	333	185	328
	1/100	408	408	408	412	408	408	198	391
	1/80	457	457	457	462	457	457	199	434
	1/60	527	527	527	532	527	527	207	500
	1/40	639	645	645	652	639	645	235	639
	1/30	729	729	744	744	722	744	211	729
	1/20	793	867	885	876	821	885	249	774
	1/15	872	990	915	904	904	1011	277	766

product of the area draining to the gully and the rainfall intensity it is possible to calculate the area draining to each gully. Tables 5.1 to 5.3 give details of allowable contributing areas as calculated by the Transport and Road Research Laboratory[4] for widths of channel flow of 1 m, 750 mm and 500 m. Crossfalls may vary from 1/60 to 1/20 and longitudinal gradients from 1/300 to 1/15.

On steep gradients gully spacing may theoretically be increased, but if the gully becomes blocked by storm debris then the next gully downstream is likely to be very heavily overloaded. At the bottom of steep gradients the problem may become even more serious because with the decrease in gradient the width of water flow in the channel will increase to such an extent that it covers the wheel-track area. The Transport and Road Research Laboratory recommend that where the gradient is steeper than 1 in 50 the width of water flow in the channel should be designed to be not greater than 500 mm and the gully spacing used should be that appropriate to a slope of 1/50.

5.4 Drainage of Level or Nearly Level Roads

When a road is level or nearly level the drainage of surface water presents difficulties. One solution has been to produce a gradient in the channel by varying the crossfall of the carriageway. While this may be satisfactory on minor residential roads it results in an unacceptable riding surface on major roads.

On major roads a channel may be formed at the edge of the carriageway. Outlets are provided at intervals and the outlet spacing calculated so that the channel does not overflow. With level roads the maximum depth of water will occur midway between outlets but with increasing gradient the point of maximum depth moves down the slope.

The required spacing between outlets or gullies may be calculated using an experimentally derived relationship derived by Beij[5] for rectangular gutters.

$$\text{Outlet spacing (m)} = \frac{0.235 b^{12/13} h^{16/13}}{(IW)^{10/13}} \qquad (5.1)$$

where

b is the width of the rectangular gutter (mm),

h is the maximum depth of water or the depth of the gutter (mm),

I is the rainfall intensity (mm/h),

W is the width of the carriageway.

From the point of view of safety it is usual to make these gutters trapezoidal in cross-section and this makes it necessary to modify the formula by replacing b with

$$w + \frac{1}{2} kh \qquad (5.2)$$

where

w is the width of the bottom of the trapezoidal channel,

k is the sum of the cotangents of the angles of inclination of the two sides of the trapezium

An alternative form of removal of surface water is the use of the hardshoulder as a wide gutter with the water flowing against the face of a kerb. The problem in this case is to determine the spacing of the gully outlets so that the width of water flow on the hardshoulder does not exceed acceptable limits; it is assumed that the kerb is sufficiently high to retain the water level. As a result of work carried out by the Transport and Road Research Laboratory[6] it was found possible to derive the following formula for outlet spacing.

$$\text{Outlet spacing (m)} = 545 \left(\frac{N^3}{IW}\right)^{3/4} C^{23/16} \left[1 + \frac{BN^{7/4}Y^w}{(IW)^{7/8}}\right] \qquad (5.3)$$

where N is the maximum permitted width of flow across the hardshoulder (m),

   I is the rainfall intensity (mm/h),

   W is the overall width of carriageway and hardshoulder (m),

   C is the crossfall (percentage),

   B is a coefficient varying with crossfall,

   Y is the longitudinal gradient (percentage),

   w is an index varying with the crossfall and given by $2.32 - 0.13C$.

Values of B and w are given in table 5.4.

Figure 5.4 shows the relationship between outlet spacing, longitudinal gradient, rainfall intensity and crossfall obtained by the use of equation 5.3.

Table 5.4 Values of coefficient B and index w^6

Percentage Crossfall	B	w
0.5	117	2.26
1.0	190	2.19
1.5	265	2.125
2.0	326	2.06
2.5	380	1.995
3.0	416	1.93
4.0	448	1.80
5.0	448	1.67

5.5 Surface-water Run-off from Carriageways

In rural areas it is frequently adequate to discharge surface-water run-off collected by the gullies directly to a ditch alongside the highway, care being taken to ensure that the water-table beneath the highway is not adversely affected by the water level in the ditch. On other occasions a surface-water sewer will be required, which discharges into a convenient water-course and to which the gullies are connected. Sometimes, as in British motorway construction, a French drain serves the dual purpose of lowering the ground water table and also acting as a surface-water sewer. Where the highway layout permits, surface water may drain continuously

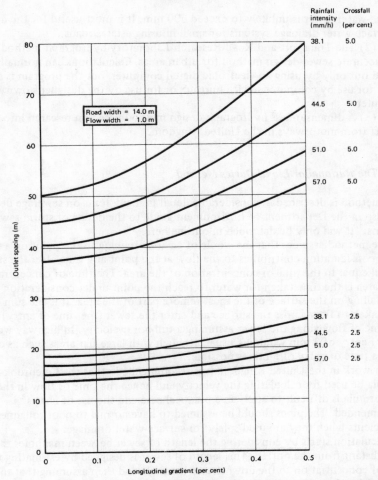

Figure 5.4 Typical curves showing relation between outlet spacing, longitudinal gradient, rainfall intensity and crossfall[6]

from the edge of the carriageway or hardshoulder and enter the porous filter media surrounding the French drain.

In urban areas it is usual for all surface water from the carriageway to be collected by road gullies and conveyed by a surface-water sewer to a convenient outfall, or alternatively in older constructions the gullies may be connected to a combined foul and surface-water sewer.

The design of these surface-water sewers requires the peak rate of run-off to be determined and there are three methods by which this may be calculated as follows.

(1) The 'Rational' (Lloyd Davies) method. Normally, because of inaccuracies in the use of this technique, it should be confined to situations where the largest

surface-water sewer is unlikely to exceed 600 mm. It is most useful for the design
of surface-water drainage systems for small-housing-estates roads.

(2) The Transport and Road Research Laboratory hydrograph method, which
is an accurate sewer-design method for urban areas. Calculations can normally be
carried out only by using an electronic digital computer, but the program is available
either for use by computer service bureaux or for use by the designer's own
computer.

(3) A dimensionless hydrograph design method based on research into the
run-off from motorways in the United Kingdom.

5.5.1 The Rational or Lloyd Davies Method

This method is described in considerable detail in many texts on sewerage design
and also in the Department of Environment guide to the design of storm-sewer
systems;[7] it will only be described in outline here.

The method assumes that the whole of an area draining to the point on a sewer
under consideration contributes to the flow at the point at a time after the start of
rainfall equal to the time of concentration of the area. The time of concentration
of an area is the time taken for water to reach the point under consideration
after falling on the surface of the most remote part of the area. It is the sum of the
time taken to flow across the surface and enter the sewer (the time of entry) and
the time of flow along the sewer assuming a full-bore velocity. In highway work a
time of entry of 2 min would be usual although with large flat areas such as car
parks a time of entry of 5 min is possible.

For work in the United Kingdom it is recommended[7] that the Colebrook–White
formula be used for calculating the velocity and hence the time of flow in the pipes.
The formula is difficult to apply in a practical case and the use of charts[8] is
recommended. The pipes should be assumed to have normal to poor roughness
coefficients when they are used solely for surface-water drainage.

Calculation starts by considering the length of sewer between manholes that is
most distant from the outfall. This length of sewer is designed by estimating the
time of concentration to the downstream manhole and then assuming that the
design storm has a duration equal to the time of concentration.

The relationship between intensity, duration and frequency of rainfall is unique
to a geographical situation but may be averaged over an area. In the United Kingdom
the formula due to Bilham has been frequently used, it has the form

$$\text{rainfall intensity, } i \text{ (m/h)} = \left(\frac{NT \times (1.21356 \times 10^5)}{10 \times 60} \right)^{1/3.55} - 2.54 \quad (5.4)$$

where N is the frequency of occurrence expressed in terms of once in N years,
          normally taken as 1 year for road drainage unless flooding would
          cause damage to adjacent property,

   T is the duration of the rainfall in min.

Equation 5.4 over-estimates intensities greater than approximately 33 mm/h and
for such intensities the following relationship, which must be solved by iteration,

should be used.

$$L_n \frac{10}{\frac{Nit}{60} \times \left(\frac{iT}{60} + 0.1\right)^{-3.55}} = 1 - 0.8i \qquad (5.5)$$

As a result of research in the United Kingdom by the Meteorological Office it is now possible to determine the rainfall and return period for any location in the United Kingdom and this information should now replace the use of equations 5.4 and 5.5.

With the rainfall intensity known, this is multiplied by the area of the carriageway to give the surface-water run-off which must be carried by the length of sewer being considered. A check should now be made to ensure that the time of flow used in the time of concentration is correct. For the design of highways the paved areas of carriageway and footpath are assumed to be completely impervious and other areas such as verges and embankments are considered to be pervious. In the design of motorway drainage this may not be correct and the third method of drainage design to be described may be more appropriate in such circumstances.

A tabular method of approach to the design of a drainage system is recommended, but except in the design of housing-estate road-drainage systems the sewerage layout for highway drainage is likely to be relatively simple.

5.5.2 The Transport and Road Research Laboratory Hydrograph Method

The unit hydrograph method of calculating run-off was first proposed in the United States in the 1930s and applied to large natural catchment areas. Subsequently the hydrograph method was investigated[9] together with other run-off calculation methods in a research project into the design of urban sewer systems carried out by the Road Research Laboratory. They proposed a modified hydrograph in which the effect of both the variation of storm intensity with time and the reservoir or storage effect of the drainage pipe system may be taken into account.

In this method a hydrograph modified for retention is constructed using the well-known time/area diagram for a drainage area. The approach is illustrated in figure 5.5, where six lengths of surface-water sewer drain to an outfall as shown diagramatically in (i); the time/area diagram is prepared in the normal manner as shown in (ii) and divided into equal time intervals. A rainfall profile for the appropriate return period — one year for highway drainage, as shown in (iii) — is also then divided into the same equal time periods.

The run-off hydrograph can be calculated from $q_1 = i_1 A_1$; $q_2 = i_1 A_2 + i_2 A_1$; $q_3 = i_1 A_3 + i_2 A_2 + i_3 A_1$; etc., as illustrated in (iv). i_1, i_2, etc., and A_1, A_2, etc., are the rainfall intensities and incremental areas respectively.

This hydrograph must then be modified for the water stored in the sewerage system. This is made by assuming that in a correctly designed sewerage system the proportional depth of water is the same throughout the system. This results in a modified hydrograph as shown in (iv). The method is difficult to apply by manual calculation for a system of any practical size. Because of this drawback the Trans-

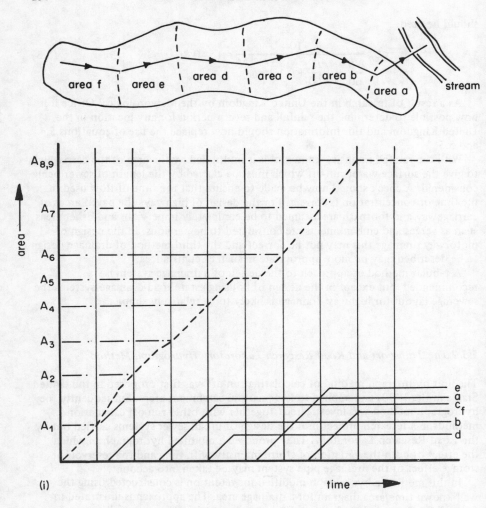

Figure 5.5 An outline of the preparation of run-off hydrographs

port and Road Research Laboratory have written a digital computer program in
which a hydrograph representing the run-off contribution from the impermeable
area contributing to the length of sewer being designed is added to the outflow
hydrograph from the upstream design length. The combined hydrograph is routed
through the reservoir formed by the pipe length under design. The peak rate of flow
is then compared with the capacity of the pipe and if inadequate the program will
increase the pipe diameter in 75 mm increments until a large enough pipe is reached.
For the analysis of existing systems this step in the procedure is not carried out,
instead a print-out giving details of surcharge conditions is produced.

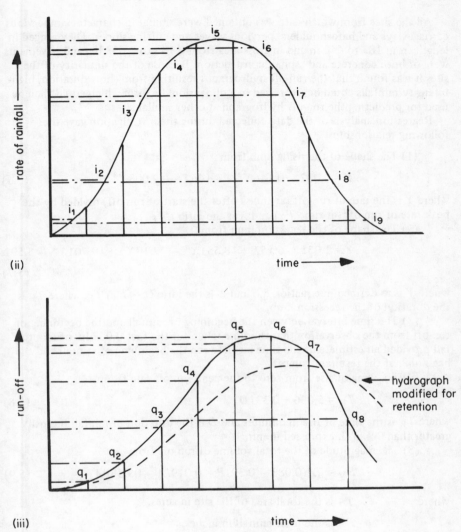

(ii)

(iii)

5.5.3 A Dimensionless Hydrograph Design Method

An investigation to derive an effective hydrological design method for motorway
drainage systems has been carried out by Imperial College of Science and
Technology, University of London,[10] under contract to the Transport and Road
Research Laboratory. Eight motorway sites were selected for study: four on the M1
motorway, two on the M45 motorway and two on the M6 motorway. Rainfall at
each of the sites was recorded and the run-off gauged by means of a standing wave
flume in the outfall pipe.

All the sites from which data was obtained were similar in character: impervious carriageways and hardshoulders, pervious verges and cutting slopes. They ranged in length from 183 to 640 m and in gross area from 0.146 to 2.633 ha, and pavements were of both concrete and asphalt construction. Because of the similarity of the sites it was found that the run-off hydrographs resulting from short duration, high-intensity rainfalls could be expressed in a dimensionless form which could then be used for predicting the run-off hydrograph at other similar sites.

Regression analysis of the data collected during the investigation gave the following relationships.

(1) The shape of the rising limb from

$$Y = 0.002 - 0.146X^2 + 3.146X^2 - 2.008X^3 \qquad (5.6)$$

where Y is the rate of run-off (at time t after the start of run-off) divided by the peak rate of run-off (at time T_R) and X is the ratio t/T_R.

(2) The shape of the recession limb from

$$Y = 1.035 - 6.15X + 18.551X^2 - 27.19X^3 + 19.701X^4 - 5.592X^5$$

$$(5.7)$$

where Y is as defined in equation 5.6 and X is the ratio $(t - T_R) T_F$, where T_F is the duration of the recession limb.

(3) The time interval between the beginning of rainfall and the beginning of run-off from the observation that the time taken for the first 0.087 in. of rain to fall provided an estimate of the time lag between the beginning of rainfall and the beginning of the resultant run-off.

(4) The time of rise from zero to the peak run off rate from

$$T_R = 5.036 + 0.331D \qquad (5.8)$$

where T_R is the time of rise in minutes and D is the duration of rainfall intensity greater than 0.2 in./h expressed in min.

(5) The magnitude of the total volume of run-off from

$$R_V = TA(0.083 - 0.391P - 0.019IA - 0.038PA) \qquad (5.9)$$

where TA is the total area of the site in acres,

              P is the total rainfall in inches,

              IA is the impervious area of the site in acres,

              PA is the pervious area of the site in acres.

(6) The magnitude of the peak rate of run-off from

$$R_P = 0.00344 I_{15}^{0.998}\, IA^{-2.51}\, TA^{3.632}\, L^{-0.253}\, S^{-0.974} \qquad (5.10)$$

where I_{15} is the maximum rainfall intensity of 15 min duration,

            L is the length of the site in feet,

            S is the longitudinal slope of the site (ft/ht).

(7) The duration of the recession limb of the hydrograph from

$$T_F = \frac{5.59}{60} \times \frac{R_V}{R_P} - 2.66 T_R \qquad (5.11)$$

where R_V is the total volume of run-off,

R_P is the peak rate of run-off.

In order to use these regression equations for design purposes the values of IA, PA, TA, L and S must be determined from the drainage area being considered. The variables I_{15}, D, P and the time taken for the first 0.087 in. of rain to fall must be obtained from the design storm profile (see section 5.5.2), the total volume of run-off R_V and the peak rate of run-off calculated. The remaining two parameters required to transform the dimensionless rising limb and recession profiles into the required dimensional form are then T_R and T_F.

5.6 Small Culverts and Flood Flows

In the construction of new highways it is frequently necessary to culvert streams passing across the line of the carriageway. To calculate the optimum dimensions of culverts it is necessary to be able to estimate peak run-offs, usually without the help of any previous stream recordings.

A simple method of estimating flood flows from natural catchments in the United Kingdom has been developed by the Transport and Road Research Laboratory.[11] As a result of observations of flood run-off and rainfall at five sites in England the following method has been proposed.

Calculate the time of concentration or the lag time when all of the catchment area is contributing to the flood flow (hours) from

$$T = 2.48(LN)^{0.39} \qquad (5.12)$$

where L is the catchment length (km) from outfall to upstream divide, being measured approximately along the middle of the catchment. A cranked line may be necessary if the shape is sufficiently irregular.

N is a dimensionless slope number equal to the ratio L/Z, where Z (km) is the rise from the outfall to the average height of the upstream divide.

The expected rainfall R_B(mm) can be obtained from the Bilham formula (section 5.5.1) for the duration T and the selected return period in years.

The flood flow can then be calculated from

$$Q_C = F_A A R_B / 3.6T \qquad (5.13)$$

where A is the catchment area (km^2),

F_A is the annual rainfall factor (dimensionless) given by $0.00127\bar{R}_A - 0.321$,

R_A is the average annual rainfall (mm).

This method was obtained from observations of catchments with an underlying stratum of clay or boulder clay. Where the catchment contains an area of pervious strata only the impervious area should be used in equation 5.13.

References

(1) ——, 'Drainage of Surface Water: Gulleys', Supplement to *Munic. Engng., Lond.,* Sept. 1964

(2) B. C. Parker and K. R. Brown, 'Housing Estate Road Design and Construction, *J. Inst. Highw. Engrs,* 15 (1968) 23–8

(3) D. J. Holland, 'Rain Intensity Frequency Relationships in Britain', *Met. Off. Hydrol. Mem.* no. 33 (1964)

(4) K. Russam, Road Research Laboratory Report LR 277, *The Hydraulic Efficiency and Spacing of British Standard Road Gulleys* (Crowthorne, 1969)

(5) K. H. Beij, 'Flow in Gutters', U.S. Bureau of Standards, Research Paper RP 644, *Bur. Standard J. Res.* 12 (1934) 193–213

(6) A. C. Whiffin and C. P. Young, Transport and Road Research Laboratory Report 602, *Drainage of Level or Nearly Level Roads* (Crowthorne, 1973)

(7) DoE, Transport and Road Research Laboratory Road Note 35, 3rd ed.: *A Guide for Engineers to the Design of Storm Sewer Systems* (HMSO, 1976)

(8) P. Ackers, *Charts for the Hydraulic Design of Channels and Pipes*, HRSP, DE2, 3rd ed. (Metric Units) (HMSO, 1969)

(9) Department of Scientific and Industrial Research, 'The Design of Urban Sewer Systems'. *Road Research Technical Paper*, no. 55 (1962)

(10) C. J. Swinnerton, M. J. Hall and T. O'Donnell, 'A Dimensionless Hydrograph Design Method for Motorway Stormwater Drainage Systems', *J. Inst Highw. Engrs,* November 1972

(11) C. P. Young and J. Prudhoe, Transport and Road Research Laboratory Report LR 565, *The Estimation of Flood Flows from Natural Catchments* (Crowthorne, 1973)

6

Earthworks

6.1 Site Investigation Procedure

A site investigation is an essential first step in the design of any highway on a new location. The information obtained by the survey assists in locating the highway to avoid adverse geological conditions and in designing earthworks, pavement thickness, drainage works and bridge foundations.

When planning a new route in a developed country, ground conditions alone are rarely a major factor in the location of the road. Avoidance of towns and villages, buildings of historic interest and areas of outstanding scenic beauty, rail and river crossings, junctions with other highways and avoidance of land severance have all to be considered. There will, however, be occasions when adverse ground conditions such as marshlands or landslip areas will profoundly change the cost of construction.

6.1.1 Sources of Preliminary Information for the United Kingdom

During the initial stages of route planning enough ground information can be obtained by a site reconnaissance and by consultation with existing records. Dumbleton and West[1] have described the following types of information, which are available and which allow more economical site investigations to be planned.

Of these sources, geological maps are probably the most important source of preliminary information. The 1:63 360 (1 in./mile) scale series with memoirs gives a good indication of the types of material and the structures occurring in the locality; 'solid' or 'drift' editions are generally available. For more detailed information the 1:10 560 (6 in./mile) series can be consulted; it contains descriptive notes and the position and brief details of many boreholes. Several smaller-scale geological maps are also published by the Institute of Geological Sciences. Whilst these maps are a useful source of information much more information is given in the Handbooks of British Regional Geology for England, Wales and Scotland, which are published by HMSO.

Information on ground-water conditions, required when cuttings are proposed, can be obtained from the Water Supply Papers of the Institute of Geological Sciences. Records are available of existing boreholes and wells, giving details of the strata encountered.

Interpretation of these geological maps and records from an engineering view-point is discussed by Dumbleton and West under the following headings: distribution and lithology of deposits; boreholes, sections and block diagrams; dip of strata; faults; dykes and sills; glacial deposits; buried channels; river terraces; springs and seepages; swallow holes and unstable ground.

A further source of ground conditions are the maps and memoirs of the Soil Survey of Great Britain, at Rothamsted Experimental Station, Harpenden, Herts, and the Soil Survey of Scotland, at the Macaulay Institute for Soil Research, Craigiebuckler, Aberdeen. Lists of published maps, memoirs and bulletins may be obtained from either section.

Surveys of land use are available from the Director of the Land Use Survey at King's College London. Agricultural-land classification maps, which show the relative value of land for agricultural use, an important consideration in route planning, are also available, on a scale of 1:63 360, and are available with explanatory notes from the Ministry of Agriculture, Fisheries and Food, London.

Mine workings and mineral deposits beneath the proposed route of a highway can lead to constructional problems or additional claims for compensation during land acquisition. It is therefore important that they should be located during the early stages of a location study. Abandoned mine workings may be difficult to locate but old maps and records may assist, and the Divisional Plans Record Offices of the National Coal Board may have information on old coal-workings.

In any preliminary location work accurate topographical maps are essential. In the United Kingdom highway location is made easier by the range of Ordnance Survey maps available. Records predating the earliest Ordnance Survey maps are also available for many areas and may be found at the Public Record Office, London, or at the local County Record Office.

Aerial photographs may be available for all or part of the route and these are a useful source of information. Enquiries should be made to air-survey firms, the Ordnance Survey, the Department of the Environment and local authorities to ascertain the extent of the records available.

6.1.2 Planning a Site Investigation

For a large-scale road scheme a preliminary site investigation using available informa-tion supplemented by site inspections will be required for several alternative road locations. This preliminary work will then assist in planning a more detailed main site investigation for the chosen line. Dumbleton and West[2] have discussed the planning and direction of site investigations. They state that 'the main investigation is the full investigation of the site using boreholes and trial pits, and includes the preparation of the site-investigation report with revised plans and sections, inter-pretation and recommendations for design'.

They consider there are two aspects: the qualitative and the quantitative. The first aspect establishes the geological structure and character of the site of the high-way and the types and distribution of the materials present. The second aspect is the testing of the soil both *in situ* and by laboratory testing of samples. In planning the main investigation they consider that the following questions should be considered.

(1) Is the succession of the strata known over the whole site; is their correlation across the site understood, including their relation to the units shown on the geological map? What measurements of depth, dip and outcrop positions are required to clarify the stratigraphy of the site? Are there key measurements of the depth of peat or soft strata or the depth to bedrock that should be made?

(2) Are the different strata fairly homogeneous over the site or may trends or local variations exist that require investigation? Are there areas of complex strata or ground structures that need examination by open excavation, or noting for closer examination in the course of excavation during the construction phase of the work? Are the characteristics of the materials present familiar and tractable, or are there unfamiliar or intractable materials present that need special examination? Are there areas where material unsuitable as fill will be excavated, where material below formation level will need to be replaced, or where levels may need to be adjusted to reduce the amounts of such materials involved? Are there areas where the ease of excavation of rock needs to be assessed so that methods of working can be planned, or levels adjusted to reduce rock excavation if this is indicated?

(3) Are there ground structures that need closer examination — for example, the position, dip and throw of faults, the geometry of folds, the extent of disturbed strata, the location and extent of natural cavities and of mine workings and their liability to cause subsidence or movement on faults, the extent and depth of surface movement and instability? Are there fractures or other structures in rocks that may give rise to instability on slopes? Are river crossings or alluvial areas present that have buried channels or layers of soft material or peat? Are there likely to be important undetected structures that need to be searched for?

(4) Will any part of the route be subject to flooding? Are there spring-lines or seepages in the area of the works? Will water-bearing strata be encountered in cuttings or excavations? Will water-bearing fissures be exposed in rock cuts? Will ground-water lowering or special drainage measures be required during excavation or to stabilise slopes? Are corrosive or sulphate-bearing ground-waters present that may affect the road or its installations and structures?

(5) Do requirements for the carrying out of special *in situ* tests or the taking of undisturbed samples affect the conduct of the qualitative investigation? For example, with forethought a single trial pit may be made to serve both for examining ground materials and structure, and for *in situ* testing and the taking of block samples.

Dumbleton and West state that these questions must be asked for the whole route, and must be related to the proposed geometry of the road and its structures. Investigations must be taken down to the depth to which ground conditions may affect the works, and must be carried out to give the degree of detail required for the design and construction of each part of the road and its structures. Costly installations and difficult engineering situations will of course call for relatively more detailed information on ground conditions.

Investigations by boring, trial pits or other ground-investigation methods must then be planned to answer any problems revealed by the previous questions. Ground investigation can be expensive and the maximum amount of information should be obtained from the points which are examined by boring or other means. Frequently such points are required to clarify the geological interpretation of the site as a whole. There will be some points which could lead to a new line for the road if geological conditions are unsatisfactory and these should be examined at an early stage in the work. Bridge sites, deep cuttings, high embankments are all points of engineering complexity and these should be examined thoroughly.

6.1.3 Methods of Ground Investigation

Information on ground conditions close to the surface can be obtained from an examination of outcrops, stream beds, quarries and surface deposits. Additional information can also be frequently obtained by shallow trial pits and excavations open for other purposes. For knowledge of ground conditions at any appreciable depth below the surface, however, their are two major methods of investigation: boring and probing, and geophysical techniques.

In sinking a borehole the engineer attempts to determine the nature of the ground in a qualitative manner and then to recover undisturbed samples for quantitative examination in the laboratory. Recovery of undistrubed samples in gravelly soils and silts and sands below the water-table is very difficult and in these circumstances *in situ* testing is frequently employed. There are five general types of boring machine which may be used for site investigation: wash-boring drills, light percussive drills, light percussive rigs, augering machines and multi-purpose machines.

Wash boring is the cheapest and most portable of all the drilling methods. It consists of a light tripod, a small power-driven capstan and a small pump. The drill casing is driven into the ground and the borehole advanced by the chiselling action of a 25 mm diameter hollow drill-pipe down through which circulating water is pumped. The debris is examined as it comes out of the top of the casing and an indication of the nature of the ground obtained by noting the penetration of the wash pipe. This method is almost entirely confined to North America and requires a considerable amount of experience by the drilling operator.

Light percussive rigs include the shell-and-auger rig. Hand-operated shell-and-auger rigs are not now used in developed countries and mechanical rigs are always used in the United Kingdom. The rig consists of a tubular tripod incorporating a power winch. In operation a casing of 150, 200 or 250 mm diameter is used to line the borehole and the hole advanced by the use of a chisel, bailer, claycutter and auger. The chisel may be repeatedly dropped down the borehole while suspended by a wire rope attached to the power winch. The debris is then removed by a bailer — a tube fitted with a cutting shoe and a hinged flap close to the shoe. In cohesive soils a clay corer (a hollow tube without a flap but with a heavy weight attached) is dropped down the casing and is then removed from the casing when filled with clay. An auger (a tubular tool with opposed cutting edges) may also be used in cohesive soils, but this requires the auger to be screwed to heavy square-section boring rods, which are then turned from the surface using hand-dogs.

In non-cohesive soils the bailer can be used to bring up loosened material, the sides of the borehole being protected by keeping the lining tubes or casing in advance of the bailer.

It is frequently necessary to drill into bedrock when it is encountered, to prove both the thickness and quality of the rock. Usually the rock is drilled and the rock core removed to a thickness of 5 m, but this may be varied according to site conditions. The mechanical shell-and-auger rig may be quickly fitted with either a gravity-fed pendant diamond drill or a hydraulically fed diamond drill. The former is used for drilling in sedimentary rocks and the latter for igneous rocks.

Augering machines have also been used to a limited extent in site investigation work. One of the simplest machines of this type is the disc auger, a short spiral digging tool frequently mounted on the rear of a lorry. The auger is rotated, lifted and lowered by a powered drill-stem. It has a rapid penetration in soft but self-supporting ground but the depth of penetration is limited by the length of the drill-stem. Deeper penetration can be achieved by the use of continuous-flight augers, which use a continuous helix of about 150 mm diameter and which is jointed in 1.5 to 2.0 m sections. Soil is cut from the bottom of the auger and is then conveyed upwards by the rotating auger. A rapid rate of penetration is achieved by this type of machine in suitable ground but it is difficult to determine the exact depth of the various strata as they are brought up to the surface.

The use of multi-purpose machines such as percussive augering machines and percussive rotary drills is somewhat limited in conventional site exploration. They are likely to be used in difficult ground conditions where the conventional shell-and-auger rigs can run into difficulties.

Geophysical methods of site investigation are normally used in site investigation for highways to aid in the interpolation of information between boreholes. These methods are best for detecting distinct changes in ground conditions, such as the depth to bedrock where the overlying conditions are reasonably uniform. They find it difficult to detect small changes in ground conditions and because of this have an advantage over a borehole, which might record a large boulder as bedrock.

The geophysical method most commonly applied to highway investigations is the seismic technique. In this process shock waves are generated close to the surface of the ground and the time taken for the energy to travel along a defined path through the ground to seismic detectors located at known distances from the point of generation of the shock wave are measured. These shock waves are generated by a small explosive charge, by a dropping weight device towed behind a small vehicle or by the blow of a sledge-hammer upon a steel plate.

Shock waves act in a similar manner to light waves: They are reflected and refracted when they come into contact with a material of differing density. Small geophones pick up the wave after its travel through the ground and relay the impulse they receive back to a control unit. This control unit produces a photographic record of the time the shock wave is fired and when the sound impulse reaches each of the geophones.

These geophones are composed of a coil suspended in a magnetic field. Upon the arrival of the shock wave the coil is vibrated, resulting in an electromotive force being set up. This current is amplified and transmitted back to the master control unit. Inside the control unit are a number of galvanometers, one for each detector. A ray of light is reflected by a small mirror set in the galvanometer. This ray of light is recorded upon the photographic record. As soon as the electrical current from the detector reaches the galvanometer the mirror is moved and the ray of light is caused to show a deflection on the photographic record. The break caused measures the time of arrival of the shock wave at each detector and the instant of finding is also marked.

The geophones are spread in a line over the terrain where it is desired to investigate the strata. The explosion or impact takes place either at the centre of the geophone spacing or at either end. Waves sent out from the explosion travel outward through the ground until they reach a differing medium, where they are partially reflected and partially refracted. Velocities through each of the media can then be calculated by comparing the travel time and the instant of firing from the record on the master controller.

From this information a graph may be drawn of time against distance. Time values are obtainable from the developed film record produced by the master controller while distance is measured on the ground. In the simplest case this curve will resolve into two intersecting straight lines. The first line represents the path of the wave through the over-burden. This wave has travelled the direct path from the shot point to the geophones spaced out over the ground. The second line indicates the shock wave which has been refracted back to the surface from the underlying bedrock. Where these two lines intersect is the distance from the shot point where the refracted waves have overtaken those travelling directly. Once this distance, D, has been determined, the depth to bedrock at the shot point may be calculated from the formula

$$H = \frac{D}{2} \frac{V_2 - V_1}{V_2 + V_1}$$ (6.1)

where H is the depth to bedrock,

V_1 is the velocity of the sound wave in the overburden,

V_2 is the velocity of the sound wave in the bedrock.

Should the formation of the strata be faulted or otherwise complicated, reverse shooting is often employed. By this means, too, it is possible to obviate the too-high velocity obtained when the sound wave is refracted along an upward bedrock slope, or the too-low velocity when the sound wave is refracted downwards.

While this technique has enjoyed considerable popularity in the United States for estimating the ease with which excavation may be carried out, the interpretation of seismic surveys of this type requires specialist knowledge. Burton[3] states that the seismic refraction method will give reliable results provided the following conditions are satisfied.

(1) The seismic velocity of successively deeper subsurface layers increases with depth below ground level.

(2) The velocity-to-thickness ratio of each subsurface layer is less than a certain critical value in relation to the overlying and underlying layers.

(3) The seismic velocities of the subsurface layers are effectively constant over the length of the geophone spread.

If condition (1) is not fulfilled and a low-velocity layer is present, critical refraction does not occur. The seismic energy is refracted towards the normal to the interface and passes downwards into a higher-velocity layer before being returned to the surface by critical refraction. Thus, the low velocity layer, called a 'blind-zone', is not detected, and consequently the calculated depths of the deeper refractors will be greater then the true depths.

If condition (2) is not satisfied, a thin layer will not be detected because the energy refracted by it will be masked by energy refracted by the underlying higher-velocity layer. This is known as the 'hidden-layer' effect, and results in the calculated depths of the deeper refractors being less than the true depths.

Condition (3) is probably fulfilled less frequently than the other two, particularly in the case of superficial deposits, and is probably the most frequent cause of depth determination errors in the interpretation of seismic refraction records. Velocity variations in the bedrock are less serious in that they affect depth calculations to a smaller degree than the velocities of overlying layers and are usually detectable.

These limitations indicate the importance of boreholes to control the interpretation of the geophysical data, not only for correlation of seismic velocities with geological strata, but to check whether the conditions mentioned above are satisfied.

6.2 Optimisation on the Horizontal and Vertical Alignment of a Highway

When a highway is planned between any two points, normally the route planner selects the shortest practical path subject to avoiding areas of development or difficult ground conditions, crossing obstacles at fixed points and a consideration of construction costs.

Keeping these considerations in mind the highway designer lays down the horizontal alignment of the road in accordance with the geometric design standards for the type of road. During this stage of the design only limited consideration is given to the vertical alignment, merely avoiding areas likely to necessitate steep vertical alignments. The vertical alignment is then designed for the previously selected horizontal line. A number of different horizontal alignments are likely to be investigated before one is selected both on cost and environmental grounds.

Usually the horizontal alignment consists of a series of straight or tangent sections joined by circular curves and transition curves, the intersections of the tangent lengths are referred to as intersection points (IPs). The vertical alignment similarly consists of straight lines joined by summit-and-valley parabolic curves which can usually be replaced by circular curves without appreciable error. The vertical alignment can thus also be represented by straights and intersection points.

The design of the vertical alignment is subjected to several constraints. These are: the minimum radius of horizontal curves, the properties of the transition curves, the minimum radius of vertical curves, the minimum length of vertical curves, maximum and minimum gradients, level-control points where the road crosses obstacles or has to meet fixed levels. In addition the vertical and the horizontal alignment must be phased together to produce a flowing alignment.

At the same time economy in construction cost is achieved by balancing excavation and filling of earthworks and minimising the haulage of material. Frequently a mass-haul curve is drawn as shown in figure 6.1, where accumulated earthwork balance (excavation positive, fill negative) is plotted against the longitudinal chainage of the highway. The curve commences with zero accumulated earthworks and the line XX' is the zero balance line; when the curve cuts this line again, cut and fill will balance. At A the road centre-line changes from cut to fill and changes back to excavation at point O. If a line is drawn parallel to the zero balance line, such as ZZ', then the excavation from Z to A balances the fill from A to Z'. Should the

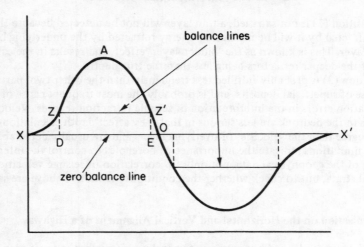

Figure 6.1 A Mass-haul diagram

distance ZZ' represent the maximum economical haul-distance then the ordinate DZ represents the volume of material that must be wasted away from the site between X and A. Also the ordinate EZ' represents the volume of material which must be imported between A and O.

In practice, the planning of earthwork is not so simple because some of the excavation material is unsuitable for embankment-filling purposes. Swell, the increase in volume of material after excavation and bulking, which is a measure of the volume excavated material takes up when compacted in embankment, has to be taken into account.

These processes require a considerable degree of engineering judgement and necessitate a great deal of routine work. In an attempt to allow the engineer to concentrate on the most creative aspects of route location a series of computer programs have been evolved for design purposes.

6.3 The Highway Optimization Program System

At the Transport and Road Research Laboratory a series of computer programs for the optimum design of the vertical elevation of a highway have been developed as part of the Highway Optimization Program System and included in the British Integrated Program System for Highway Design.

The basic data on which all these programs operate are the ground levels obtained by levelling, and it is important that these levels are accurate because they are used repeatedly in the optimisation of the vertical alignment. Because the calculations made during optimisation processes are expensive in computer time and storage it is also important for this data to be as simple as possible.

6.3.1 Program PRELUDE

To carry out these two objectives the program PRELUDE[4] has been developed and
made available to highway designers. When considering errors in the basic data
PRELUDE examines the format of the data to check errors due to re-composing,
transcribing and punching data. It also looks for errors that may have occurred in
the survey or when taking-off levels, together with the previous sources of error, by
checking whether the data is reasonable.

The program PRELUDE also simplifies the data by linearising the ground cross-
sections — that is, replacing the usual ground cross-section taken at intervals along,
and at right angles to, the centre-line as illustrated in figure 6.2. By this means the
several levels normally required to describe the cross-section are replaced by three
values: the chainage along the road centre-line, the level at the centre line, and the
gradient of the linearised line.

6.3.2 Program VENUS

The next stage in the automatic design process is carried out by program VENUS[5]
which generates a vertical alignment from the ground centre-line levels. In the
automatic design process a smoothing procedure is used to produce a longitudinal
profile with fewer undulations than the ground, as illustrated in figure 6.3. The
degree of smoothing is such that a profile is proposed which approximates to the
required vertical alignment, such that the cut-and-fill areas are approximately equal.
This profile, known as the 'quasi vertical alignment', is then modified to obey the
level control points and then approximates to the required vertical alignment.

This 'quasi vertical alignment' is then convented to the conventional engineering
form of longitudinal section by transforming it into a series of straights and vertical
parabolic curves. A preliminary alignment produced in this manner will not always
obey all the constraints on the alignment and further modifications may be necessary to produce a feasible alignment.

6.3.3 Program JANUS

This program, which phases horizontal and vertical alignment and produces the
tangent-point barrier table used subsequently in program MINERVA, has been
described by Baker.[6]

Input to this program consists of the chainages and levels of intersection points
of vertical curves and curve lengths or radii of curvature or rates of changes of
percentage gradient. Fixed conditions at the beginning and end of the scheme
must also be included. Any level control points are input as are any exceptions to
the geometric design standards. If the engineer wishes any particular vertical curves
to remain fixed in position longitudinally during the operation of the program then
fixed tangent-point barriers must be specified. Details of the horizontal alignment
are required, including transition curves and limiting values of four ranges of severity

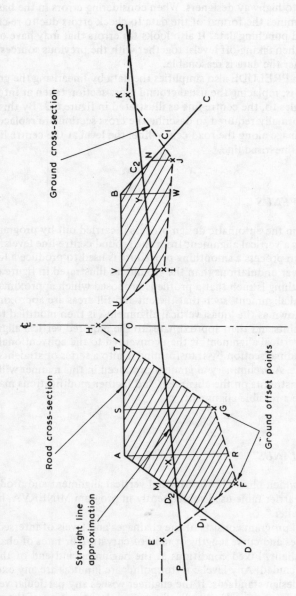

Figure 6.2 Straight-line approximation PQ fitted to cross-section offset points E, F, G, H, I, J and K

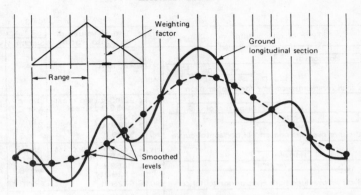

Figure 6.3 The smoothing process[5]

for horizontal radius of curvature and two ranges of severity for vertical radius of curvature together with minimum curve separation. These latter values allow the engineer to retain control over the final configuration of the vertical alignment.

The types of misphasing which are considered by the program are illustrated in figure 6.4 and are tabulated below together with the corrective action which the program takes.

(1) There is insufficient separation between the ends of the horizontal and vertical curves. It is corrected by increasing the separation between the curves.

(2) Both ends of the vertical curve lie on the horizontal curve. It is corrected by making both ends of the curves coincident or by separating them.

(3) The vertical curve overlaps both ends of the horizontal curve. The corrective action is to make both ends of the curves coincident. If, however, the horizontal curve is less sharp then a hazard may still be created if the crest occurs off the horizontal curve because the change of direction at the beginning of the horizontal curve will then occur on a downgrade, for one direction of traffic flow, where vehicles may be increasing speed. The corrective action is to make the curves coincident at one end so as to bring the crest on to the horizontal curve. No action is necessary if a vertical curve that has no crest is combined with a gentle horizontal curve. If the vertical curve is a valley curve an illusory crest or dip, depending on the 'hand' of the horizontal curve, will appear on the road alignment. The corrective action is to make both ends of the curves coincident or to separate them.

In operation the program first reads all the details of the input and makes tests on the validity of each section of the data as it is read. If an apparent error is found a message is printed immediately and the reading and testing of data is continued if possible, the program being terminated at the end of the data input. If no errors are found in the data the program proceeds to calculate the complete vertical alignment from the IP chainages, levels and curve lengths to give values of radii, rates of change of percentage gradient, percentage gradients and chainages of ends of curves. This

(1) Type of misphasing		(2) Critical values of horizontal radius		(3) Action Summits	(4) Action Valleys
I	Horizontal / Vertical — D Less than minimum recommended separation	≤ 22919 ft		A	A
II	Horizontal / Vertical — Vertical curve overlaps one end of horizontal curve	(i)	≤ 22919 ft } No crest > 11459 ft } Crest	None A or C†	A or C† ——
		(ii)	≤ 11459 ft } > 5729 ft }	A or C†	A or B†
		(iii)	≤ 5729 ft	A or B†	A or B†
III	Horizontal / Vertical — Vertical curve overlaps both ends of horizontal curve	(i)	≤ 22919 ft } No crest > 11459 ft } Crest	None A or C†	A or B† ——
		(ii)	≤ 11459 ft } > 5729 ft }	A or B†	A or B†
		(iii)	≤ 5729 ft	A or B†	A or B†
IV	Horizontal / Vertical — Both ends of vertical curve lie on horizontal curve	(i)	≤ 22919 ft } > 11459 ft }	None	None
		(ii)	≤ 11459 ft } > 5729 ft }	None	A or B†
		(iii)	≤ 5729 ft	A or B†	A or B†

Action A. Move one end of vertical curve to achieve minimum separation
Action B. Phase ends of vertical curve to ends of horizontal curve
Action C. Phase one end of vertical curve to one end of horizontal curve

   † In these cases the action taken is that which results in the least movement of the vertical curve

Vertical curves with radius greater than a critical value of 100 000 ft are not phased
Critical values of horizontal and vertical radius are decided by the engineer
Values in table are only suggestions

Metric equivalents	
100 000 ft.	30480 m
22 919 ft.	6980 m
11459 ft.	3490 m
5 729 ft.	1 740 m

Figure 6.4 Phasing criteria in Program JANUS[6]

configuration is tested to ensure that there are no overlapping vertical curves and that the constraints of level-control points and geometric design standards, including exceptions, are not violated. If no violations are found the vertical alignment is feasible and is used in the program. In the event of any constraints being violated, the intersection-point levels are varied in an attempt to find a new vertical alignment that obeys the constraints. This is often successful and the new vertical alignment is then accepted for use in the program. If unsuccessful the program prints a message that the alignment is unfeasible and then stops. The phasing action consists of moving the initial tangent point or the final tangent point of the vertical curve, or both tangent points, horizontally through the minimum distance necessary to achieve acceptable phasing. The program examines the phasing of each vertical curve with each horizontal curve. The curves are considered in sequence and are described by their start-and-finish chainages and radii. When a misphasing as classified in columns 1 and 2 of figure 6.4 is found, action is taken as shown in columns 3 and 4. The new curve length is then checked against the standard minimum length of vertical curve for acceptance. If the curve is now too short and the original action had been to fix both tangent points, nothing further can be done and an informative message is printed. If only one tangent point of the curve had been fixed the curve length is corrected by moving the other. This may cause the curve being adjusted to overlap the next curve on the vertical alignment. If so, adjustments are made to this curve and the series of checks are repeated until either no further curves are affected or no further adjustment is possible. In the latter case this is indicated in the output. Checks are made to ensure that no curves are moved outside the boundaries of the road length being considered. The chainages of one or more IPs will have been altered during this process of moving the vertical curves. Thus the gradients between the curves and also their radii may have been changed and the road may no longer obey the constraints. Adjustments are therefore made to the levels of the IPs so that all constraints are obeyed. If it proves impossible to find a feasible alignment the attempt to phase the current vertical curve is abandoned and a message is printed. This unfeasible vertical alignment is erased and replaced by the alignment that existed before this last step was attempted. The program takes each vertical curve in turn and repeats the whole process until the last vertical curve has been dealt with. As the work proceeds, some vertical-curve end-points take up positions in which either they are fixed or may be moved in only one direction without upsetting the phasing. This information is stored in the tangent-point barrier table for use by program MINERVA. The program then returns to the first vertical curve and makes a second pass along the entire road length, followed by a third and final pass. On the second and third passes the operation is governed by the tangent-point barriers originally set by the engineer together with any new ones generated during previous passes. Although program JANUS will normally be used prior to the optimisation program it can, if desired, be used as a check after optimisation or for the phasing of any alignments.

Next it is necessary to optimise the alignment by minimising and balancing the volumes of cut-and-fill to produce the final vertical alignment.

6.3.4 Program MINERVA

While the program VENUS optimises volumes of cut-and-fill it does not optimise the costs associated with vertical alignment. This process is achieved by the program MINERVA[7] which optimises on bridge costs and on five earthwork quantities each multiplied by an appropriate unit cost. These quantities are (1) excavation from cuttings, (2) compaction in embankments, (3) haulage from cuttings to embankments within the confines of the site, (4) export from and (5) import to the site (spoil and borrow).

The optimisation of the vertical alignment of the highway is described by Robinson.[5] He states that it is formulated in terms of a mathematical model, and objective function and the design constraints. The mathematical model describes the ground features using centre-line ground levels at specified chainages, and cross-sections represented as straight lines at known angles of elevation as shown in figure 6.2. The road model defines the vertical alignment as levels and chainages of the intersection points and the lengths of the vertical curves. The cross-section of the road is simplified and assumed to be horizontal.

The objective function that is minimised is the earthwork and bridge costs. It is possible to vary the amount of excavation that can be used as fill along different lengths of the route, the road width and the side slopes. A barrier to haulage of material, such as would exist if an uncompleted bridge existed along the route of the road, can also be incorporated in this program.

Design constraints include the geometric design standards for the road, level control points and the phasing of vertical and horizontal alignment to improve the visual image of the road to the driver.

Davies[7] describes the optimisation problem as follows. The solution to the optimisation problem is obtained by Univariate Search, which treats each variable separately in turn, a given variable being adjusted until the lowest value of the objective function is found while all other variables are held constant. When all variables have been adjusted independently, the search returns to the first one, and the process is repeated until no other reduction in objective function can be found. The constraints are handled by Variable Elimination, and to simplify the process mathematically the solution process is divided into two parts. In the first part the constraints on minimum curve length, the accommodation of tangent-point barriers to preserve phasing and the avoidance of curve overlapping are considered by taking each vertical curve in turn and adjusting its length and the chainage of its intersection point as appropriate. In the second part the drainage of all intersection points and the lengths of all curves are held constant and the remaining constraints satisfied by adjusting the intersection point levels.

The use of this program can result in an average reduction of 15 per cent in earthwork cost; it is sufficiently flexible to deal with the great variety of data found in different schemes; and the vertical alignments produced by the program are immediately useable by highway engineers.

6.4 Tractors in Earthmoving

Both crawler and wheeled tractors find considerable use in earthmoving work. They may be used to move earth by pushing material for relatively short distances of 100 to 200 m, or more usually by providing the motive power for other items of earthmoving equipment.

When a tractor is used for pushing earth it is fitted at the front with either a straight or an angle blade and is then referred to as a bulldozer. The blade is of heavy construction with a rectangular base and back; it has a flat leading edge of hardened steel which projects forward. The blade cuts into the ground as the tractor moves forward and breaks up the material being excavated. This loose material is pushed upwards, after which it falls forward, so producing a rotary movement of the excavated material. If the blade is used in the straight position the material is pushed forward; if in the angled position the material is moved sideways as the tractor moves forward.

Frequently the bulldozer is used for pushing other equipment and in these circumstances a reinforced blade or a specially designed pusher block may be fitted.

In operation the tractor bulldozer moves earth by successive forward and backward movements with the blade lowered and raised. Because the tractor operates more efficiently downhill, excavation is planned so that as much material as possible is moved downhill. If excavation is being carried out in hard ground the corner of the blade may be tilted downwards.

When excavation becomes difficult ripping is frequently used. A ripping attachment is a plough-like device with one or more blades that is attached to the rear of a crawler tractor. As the tractor moves forward the blade penetrates cracks and fissures in the soil and rock and breaks it up. Rippers are usually one of two types: the first type is hinged at its point of attachment to the tractor and has the ripper shank at right angles to the arm; the second is the parallelogram-type ripper in which there are two arms, one above the other, hinged at one end to the tractor and at the other end to the vertical shank. This type gives better penetration because the shank remains vertical and the two arms give a greater pull.

One of the largest track-type tractors is the Caterpillar D9H, which has an operating mass of 42 460 kg and may be equipped with several blades, straight or angled; maximum digging depth is 1130 mm. The machine is fitted with a single-stage torque converter and three forward and three reverse gears. The forward speed range in first gear is 0 to 4.0 km/h, in second gear 0 to 6.9 km/h and in third gear 0 to 10.8 km/h. Parallelogram-design rippers with hydraulic tip-angle adjustment are available for use with this machine. With this design a nearly constant penetration angle can be maintained; ripper shank cross-section is 432 x 483 mm and maximum penetration 1900 mm.

6.4.1 Tractor Loaders

A development of the bulldozer is the tractor loader, which can be used for the digging, loading and, to a limited extent, transport of material. The tractors may be crawlers or machines of two- or four-wheel drive.

The buckets are of box construction, with a heavy cutting edge along the front and some way up the sides. For digging in broken rock the cutting edge may be equipped with teeth. Some models have a side-tipping action that allows the machine to load from a windrow at the side of a carriageway and load directly into a truck standing on the carriageway.

Normally tractor loaders dig with the bucket flat or tilted at a slight downward angle. In this way good penetration into banks is achieved and a smooth level floor is obtained on which the vehicles moves forward. Care should be taken in the placing of the haul-truck in relation to the loader during the excavation process. Reduction in the cycle time of digging and loading is important, but turning of the tractor shovel between digging and loading may be important on soft ground.

Crawler tractors have small turning circles and are able to operate on soft ground. Where the ground is more stable four-wheel-drive tractor loaders are frequently used for excavation as well as material handling; they have large turning circles and so require a larger area of land for manoeuvring during the digging and loading operation. They travel faster than crawler machines so that cycle times are comparable.

The Aveling-Barford WXL 024 pivot-steer tractor-shovel combines high-speed movement with manoeuvrability by the use of drive on all four wheels and a pivot mid-way between the front and rear axles as shown in figure 6.5. This machine has a struck capacity of 3.25 m^3 with a tipping load at full reach of 14 390 kg. The loader is fitted with a Cummins six-cylinder turbo-charged diesel engine fitted with a torque converter and power shift in forward and reverse. There are four gear ratios in each direction with speeds ranging from 5.79 to 37.0 km/h. Alternative buckets

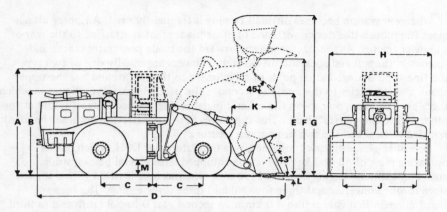

Figure 6.5 The Aveling-Barford WXL 024 pivot-steer tractor shovel

Dimensions	Symbol	Optional tyres (26.5 x 29)			Standard tyres (26.5 x 25)		
		mm	ft	in.	mm	ft	in.
Height to cab	A	3657	12	0	3606	11	10
Height to top of seat	B	2908	9	6½	2857	9	4½
Distance between wheel centre/pivot	C	1752	5	9	1752	5	9
Overall length	D	8426	27	7¾	8464	27	9¼
Height at 45° discharge	E	3083	10	1⅜	3032	9	11⅜
Maximum hinge pin height	F	4191	13	9	4140	13	7
Maximum height	G	5648	18	6⅜	5597	18	4⅜
Overall width of m/c	H	3302	10	10	3302	10	10
Track width	J	2476	8	1½	2476	8	1½
Reach at 45° discharge	K	1352	4	5¼	1407	4	7⅜
Cut below ground	L	152	0	6	152	0	6
Ground clearance	M	482	1	7	431	1	5
Alternative Buckets							
Rock bucket							
Overall length	D	8660	28	2½	8660	28	2½
Overall width	H	3365	11	0½	3365	11	0½
Light materials bucket							
Overall length	D	8780	28	9	8780	28	9
Overall width	H	3302	10	10	3302	10	10
Intermediate materials bucket							
Overall length	D	8636	28	4	8636	28	4
Overall width	H	3302	10	10	3302	10	10

Turning radius to standard bucket corner − 6 985 m (22 ft 11 in.)

are available: a heavy-material bucket with a capacity of 3.47 m³ and a light-material bucket with a capacity of 5.35 m³.

6.4.2 Motor Graders

The motor grader is an item of equipment that finds many applications in earth-moving for highway construction. It can shape or grade material or dig and transport earth over comparatively short distances. It consists of a frame running on four or six wheels with a centrally mounted blade. Blade position is extremely variable and most machines can rotate the blade to a vertical position on either side of the machine. The flexibility of the machine is further enhanced by the ability to steer both forward and rear wheels.

When the blade is in a horizontal position it can be used in a similar manner to a bulldozer blade for spreading and shaping material or for excavation by moving material ahead of the blade. Grading of embankments can be carried out by running the grader along the bottom of the embankment and lifting the blade to the side of the machine to a near vertical position.

A frequent use of motor graders is in the maintenance of haul-roads to allow more efficient operation of other earthmoving plant.

A British machine with all-wheel drive and all-wheel steer is the Aveling-Barford ASG 013 grader. The machine, illustrated in figure 6.6, has twin rear axles, an overall length of 8290 mm and an overall width of 2490 mm. Overall weight is 13 381 kg and there is the option of General Motors or Perkins diesel engines. Clark Model 13.5HR 28450 full power-shift transmission gives four speeds both forward and reverse in each of the work and travel ranges. The range of speeds varies between 2.46 and 42.82 km/h.

The grader blade has a length of 3657 mm, a height of 610 mm and a thickness of 25 mm. It can be tilted through 29° and can be shifted sideways 1143 mm by hydraulic power. For bank cutting the blade can be tilted up to 90°, can be lifted 343 mm above the ground and can cut to depth of 584 mm below the surface.

A bulldozer blade 2743 mm wide and 1082 mm high can be attached to the front of the grader, making it capable of giving useful service for the excavation and movement of soil over short distances.

6.4.3 Scrapers

Scrapers are extensively used in earthmoving for highway work. In one operation they dig, grade and haul the earth, using the bowl of the scraper. The scraper may be towed by a tractor with either crawler tracks or wheels and the combination is referred to as a tractor scraper. When the scraper with its associated prime-mover can operate without the help of any other equipment they are referred to as self-powered scrapers. Most scrapers have a single power-unit at the front of the tractor but in certain items of equipment a further power-unit is mounted at the rear of the scraper to assist by pushing.

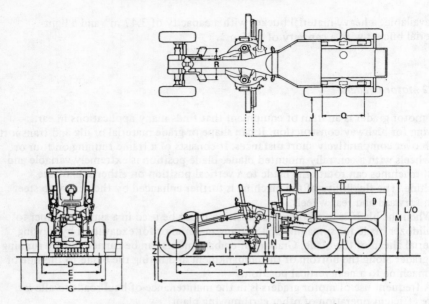

Figure 6.6 The Aveling-Barford ASG 013 grader

Dimensions	Symbol	mm	ft	in.
Front axle to blade (blade base)	A	2590	8	6
Wheelbase	B	6000	10	8¾
Overall length	C	8290	27	2⅜
Front track width	D	2016	6	7⅜
Rear track width	E	2116	6	11⁵⁄₁₆ in.
Overall width	F	2491	8	2¹⁄₁₆
Blade length	G	3657	12	0
Cut below ground (blade)	H	584	1	11
Lift above ground (blade)	I	343	1	1½
Max. blade reach beyond rear tyres	J	2223	7	3½
Max. blade reach beyond rear tyres (wheels offset)	*K	2740	9	0
Overall height with cab	L	3292	10	9⅝
Overall height without cab	M	2758	9	0⁹⁄₁₆
Height to cab base	N	1635	5	4¾
Overall height with ROPS cab	O	3292	10	9⅝
Height to steering wheel	P	—		—
Distance (tandem wheel centres)	Q	1524	5	0
Scarifier width	R	1168	3	10

* Not shown in diagram

The simplest form of scraper is the towed scraper. The bowl that carries the spoil has a cutting edge on the front edge of its bottom and this edge can be raised or lowered. The front wall of the bowl is the apron and this can be raised and lowered independently. To eject spoil from the bowl the rear wall of the bowl is moved forward, or alternatively the bowl of the scraper may be tilted forward. Operation of the scraper may be by hydraulic power or by winch action. The scraper is carried by four low-pressure pneumatic tyres that run within the path cut by the cutting edges of the bowl. A pusher block is mounted at the rear so that a following tractor may be engaged during the loading sequence.

Most towed scrapers are pulled by crawler tractors and this combination is very suitable for small earthmoving jobs where the distance that material has to be moved is relatively small. On large earthmoving schemes the towed scraper is frequently replaced by self-powered units in which the haul unit and the digging unit are combined.

The replacement of tracks with wheels became possible because of the acceptance of push-loading, which allows a tractor with insufficient traction during the loading stage to be assisted by a crawler tractor. This enables the higher speed of wheeled units to be employed to advantage during the haul stage.

There are several arrangements of the motive-power unit and the scraper unit. Four-wheel tractors may be used with a conventional towed scraper or with a single-axle scraper. In the former case traction during the loading process can be increased by a hydraulic ram on the tractor which pushes against a high point on the yoke of the scraper. In the latter case the scraper is attached to the tractor at a point over but just forward of the rear axles, so increasing the load on the driving wheels.

Attaching the scraper to the tractor by means of an over-axle king-pin makes it possible to eliminate the front wheels of the tractor, so making one unit. The scraper can be detached, but only with considerable effort as the tractor then requires to be supported. This form of construction places a large proportion of the weight of the loaded tractor scraper on the single drive axle, so increasing traction and also the maneouvrability of the machine.

The power and traction of a scraper can be greatly increased by providing an engine on the scraper to power the rear scraper wheels. These machines are able to self-load in most types of material and have a high haul speed.

Another type of tractor and scraper able to self-load without pusher assistance is the elevating scraper, typical of which is the Caterpillar 613B Elevating Scraper. The machine has a heaped capacity of 8.4 m^3, a diesel engine of 10.4 litres displacement and four forward and two reverse speeds; its top speed is 42.2 km/h. The elevator that lifts the excavated material into the bowl has an overall length of 2460 mm, a width of 146 mm and 16 flights. The elevator has two forward speeds; 69 m/min for normal material and 35 m/min for difficult soils.

6.4.4 Power Excavators

This type of equipment is mounted on crawler tracks or rubber tyres and supports a carriage on which is mounted a revolving superstructure. The superstructure contains the engine and the equipment for transmitting motive power to the actual

item of digging equipment being used as well as to the wheels and tracks. A large
range of front-end equipment may be attached to the superstructure so that in
addition to the excavating frunction the machine may be used as a crane or even as
a piling frame.

A common arrangement in highway work is the face-shovel, in which the boom
or jib carries a shorter jib or dipper stick to which is attached the digging bucket.
The machine digs into a bank with the excavator digging upwards from the level
at which it stands. As the dipper stick rotates into the bank a crowding action takes
place and the bucket moves into the bank, so assisting the digging action. The
excavated material is emptied from the bucket by opening the back of the bucket
and allowing the material to fall into the haul track beneath. In highway work the
face-shovel is frequently used to load previously drilled and blasted rock.

For excavation below ground level the backacter is used. In this arrangement
the dipper is pivoted at the top of the jib or boom and digging takes place by
moving the bucket downwards and towards the machine. Typical machines can dig
to a depth of 6 to 7 m below ground level.

For excavation over soft compressible soils, necessary when a road is being
constructed over peat deposits, a crawler-mounted dragline working on wooden
planks or mats may be employed. In this arrangement the front-end equipment is
normally a long boom from the end of which is suspended the dragline bucket.
Digging takes place by pulling the bucket through the material being excavated
towards the machine. A typical machine is the crawler-mounted E1400 dragline
manufactured by the Smith Company illustrated in figure 6.7, which has a maximum
boom length of 13.50 m. The machine has a ground pressure of approximately 0.30
kg/cm^2 and a forward travelling speed of 1.77 km/h. The upper machinery frame
rotates on a turntable with a large-diameter live ring of rollers. Power is provided
by a six-cylinder diesel engine. Dragline buckets are available for this machine with
a capacity of up to 0.5 m^3.

6.4.5 The Dump Truck

The use of loading shovels or excavators makes it necessary to use some other form
of equipment to transport the spoil. Usually dump trucks are used and they can be
divided into on-highway end-tipping trucks and off-highway dump trucks. On-
highway trucks have to comply with the legal requirements of size and weight for
vehicles used on a highway and in highway construction it is the dump truck design
designed for operation along the line of the road that is most useful in large-scale
earthmoving operations.

Typical of the off-highway dump trucks is the RD 035 manufactured by Aveling-
Barford. These machines have independent suspension and eliminate heavy springs
and the use of a front axle by using nitrogen-filled suspension units. As well as
increasing driver comfort when hauling over rough terrain the suspension is able to
cushion the shocks during loading from an excavator or shovel bucket. As is normal
with this type of equipment, the body is designed to provide a large target area for
the loading shovel and a low loading height. The wedge shape gives a quick discharge
when tipping and a heavily reinforced section gives protection to the cab from

WORKING RANGES WITH VARIOUS BOOM LENGTHS

boom length in metres and feet	9 / 29.52		10.50 / 34.45		12 / 39.37		13.50 / 44.29	
boom angle	40°	60°	40°	60°	40°	60°	40°	60°
dimension 'A' in metres and feet	7.93	5.49	9.14	6.40	10.36	7.01	11.43	7.93
	26	18	30	21	34	23	37.5	26
dimension 'B' in metres and feet	7.32	9.45	7.93	10.67	9.14	11.89	10.06	13.41
	24	31	26	35	30	39	33	44

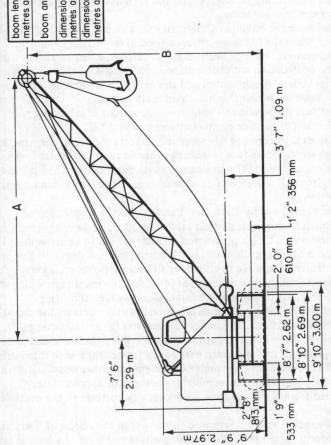

Figure 6.7 The Smith E1400 dragline

DRAGLINE SELECTION CHART

bucket size in litres and cu.yds.		type	bucket height in metres and feet		bucket weight in kgs. and lbs.		total load in kgs. and lbs.		boom length in metres and feet							
									9 / 29.52		10.50 / 34.45		12 / 39.37		13.50 / 44.29	
									dumping radius in metres and feet							
500	5/8	UL	3.12	10.25	450	1000	1300	2870	8.08	26.5	7.93	26.0	7.93	26.0		
400	1/2	Esco PMD	2.90	9.5	540	1200	1215	2700	8.23	27.0	8.08	26.5				
400	1/2	UL	2.90	9.5	315	700	1000	2200	9.14	30.0	8.84	29.0	8.53	28.0		

falling rocks. To prevent wet loads from sticking to the sides of the body, exhaust heating is employed. The RD 035 is illustrated in figure 6.8.

The largest machine in the range has a 50-ton payload and is powered by a General Motors sixteen-cylinder diesel engine with a displacement of 18.6 litres. The machine incorporates power-shift transmission and has six forward speeds and one reverse speed, giving speeds varying between 11.2 and 64 km/h. The unladen weight of the machine is 36 287 kg.

6.4.6 Belt Conveyors

An alternative to the use of tractors and scrapers, excavators and dump trucks, belt conveyors have certain advantages for the transport of spoil. In the situation where excavation and fill are widely separated the use of a conveyor allows material to be hauled by a method largely independent of weather conditions. Where haul-roads have to be maintained over cohesive soils and silts it is frequently found that earthmoving is impossible during winter months and is frequently interrupted by heavy rainfall during the summer season.

When an obstruction to the haulage of material exists along the right of way, as is frequently the case when the highway crosses a road, river or railway and an advance bridgeworks contract has not been let or completed, a belt conveyor can be bridged across the obstruction with little difficulty. This means that disturbance at crossing points can be largely eliminated and the necessity for manual or automatic signal control avoided. Whilst this has obvious advantages over earthmoving by conventional methods it also allows the highway designer a much greater flexibility in the selection of balance points between cut and fill.

Environmental issues are becoming of increasing importance in the construction of highways and highway builders face increasing pressure to reduce noise levels, dust and dirt during construction. The haulage of spoil, particularly when it must take place on the highway, is a source of considerable nuisance which can be greatly reduced by belt conveyors.

Economic studies carried out by Lewis and Parsons[8] on the application of conveyors to earthmoving have indicated that there are likely to be economic advantages in their use where a high proportion of material has to be transported over long distances, the economic choice of earthmoving method depending upon an analysis of a particular scheme. In open-tender situations, however, a great deal must depend on the availability of conventional plant and the manner in which the road builder intends to phase other constructional work with earthmoving.

An application of this method was the advance-earthworks contract for the M27 motorway at Portsmouth Harbour. The major fill-area was for an interchange situated in the upper reaches of Portsmouth Harbour between Horsea Island and the mainland. Embankments in the eastern part of the interchange were filled using hydraulically placed sand while the remainder of the embankment was filled with chalk. This chalk, which had a saturation moisture content of approximately 25 per cent, was obtained from the excavation for motorway cuttings to the north-west of the harbour.

The mean haul-distance from excavation to filling was in the region of 4 km and the line of the motorway passed through a housing estate and crossed a busy estate

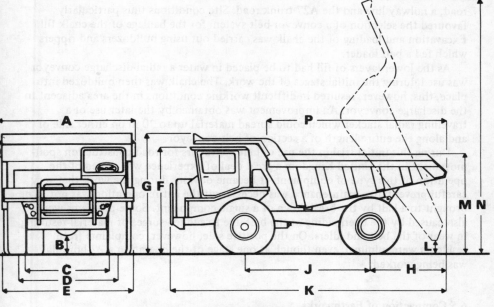

Figure 6.8 The Aveling-Barford RD 035

Dimensions	Symbol	mm	ft	in.
Overall width	A	4028	13	2½
Ground clearance	B	432	1	5
Track centres (rear wheels)	C	2480	8	1⅝
Track centres (front wheels laden)	D	2959	9	8½
Width of main body + catwalk	E	3860	12	8
Height to top of cab (unladen)	F	3193	10	5¾
Height to cab protection plate (unladen)	G	3574	11	8
Wheelbase	J	3581	11	9
Overall length	K	7722	25	4
Body ground clearance when tipped	L	381	1	3
Height to body side (unladen)	M	2994	9	9⅞
Tipped height	N	7432	24	4½

road, a railway line and the A27 trunk road. Site conditions thus particularly favoured the selection of a conveyor-belt system for the haulage of the chalk fill. Excavation and loading of the chalk was carried out using bulldozers and rippers which fed a belt loader.

As the lower layers of fill had to be placed in water a radial-discharge conveyor was used during the initial stages of the work. The chalk was then bulldozed into place, this, however, resulted in difficult working conditions in the area adjacent to the discharge conveyor. An improvement was obtained by the later use of a travelling radial stacker which could spread material up to 20 m on either side of and along the entire length of a section of belt conveyor.

During this initial trial in the use of belt conveyors for road-construction spoil-movement in the United Kingdom a great deal of experience was gained of the operation of this type of equipment. It became obvious during the work that very careful preventative maintenance was necessary if the entire operation was not to be brought to a halt by the breakdown of a single component. Some problems were also caused by the overloading of the belt due to sudden surges of material resulting in wear of the belt and idlers. On the positive side, however, complaints from residents were minimal, even though at one stage of the operation a 22-hour day was being worked.

6.5 Compaction of Earthworks

In the execution of earthworks for highway construction it is essential that adequate compaction of the soil takes place. If compaction is adequate the pavement can be immediately constructed without fear of settlement causing damage. It means that the strength of the soil is increased, so avoiding the danger of embankment slips, and that susceptibility to moisture-content changes in the subgrade is reduced, with a consequent increase of bearing capacity.

A variety of types of compacting plant are used in earthworks. These include smooth-wheeled rollers, grid rollers, tamping rollers, pneumatic-tyred rollers, vibrating rollers, vibrating-plate vibrators, vibro-tampers, power rammers and dropping-weight compactors. These items of equipment are described in detail below.

6.5.1 Smooth-wheeled Rollers

The modern smooth-wheeled roller is the descendant of the early steam-powered units that played a prominent part in highway construction in the early part of the century. Usually they have two axles, the wheel axle driving two steel rolls on either side of the driving position. This machine is referred to as a three-wheel roller. The front axle supports a smaller-diameter but greater-width steel roll, which turns to allow the roller to be steered. The roller widths are so arranged as to give compaction over the whole width of the machine. Normally the compacting effect is measured by the mass per unit width of the rolls.

A more recent development is the tandem roller, where rollers at the front and rear of the machine both have the same width as the machine. Some of these machines have three axles and are then referred to as three-axle tandem rollers.

To prevent material adhering to the rolls, scrapers are normally fitted, and when used for rolling bituminous materials the rolls are wetted by a trickle feed.

The performance of smooth-wheeled rollers for the compaction of earth fills has been investigated by Williams[9] and by Lewis.[10] Using a 8.14 Mg (8 ton) and a 2.80 Mg (2¾ ton) smooth-wheel roller in experimental work it was found that they were more efficient than the other rollers tested for compacting sand-and-gravel, sand, and clay soils. On three clay soils the 8.14 Mg (8 ton) roller had a relatively good performance but its output was generally less than that of pneumatic-tyred rollers. The optimum moisture contents for compacting clay soils with the smooth-wheel roller were rather low and, except during dry summer months, rarely occur in the United Kingdom, Provided excessive sticking does not take place, however, satisfactory compaction can be obtained at moisture contents above the optimum.

The 2.80 Mg (2¾ ton) smooth-wheel roller was less efficient on the clay soils that the 8.14 Mg (8 ton) roller because it was not heavy enough to compact the soil effectively.

The Specification for Road and Bridge Works of the Department of Transport specifies[11] the compaction requirements for three general types of soil in terms of the number of passes required with smooth-wheeled rollers, classified according to the highest value of the mass per metre width of roll. Table 6.1 contains the specified requirements for compaction by smooth-wheeled rollers.

Typical three-wheel rollers are the Aveling-Barford DC series which vary in total mass when ballasted with sand from 11 008 kg to 14 946 kg. Reduced mass can be obtained by ballasting with water or by using the roller without any ballast. A slightly greater mass can be obtained by using rear rolls 600 mm (24 in.) wide. Details of this range of machines are illustrated in figure 6.9.

Two-axle tandem rollers, also manufactured by Aveling-Barford, have ballasted weights ranging from 8721 to 10 949 kg, giving a maximum mass per metre width of roll of 3800 to 5400 kg. Details of this range of machines are illustrated in figure 6.10.

6.5.2 Tamping Rollers

Tamping rollers are defined by the Department of Transport Specification as a machine with roll or rolls from which 'feet' project. A variation of the tamping roller in which the feet have a smaller area than is specified by the Department of Transport are referred to as sheepsfoot, taper-foot or club-foot rollers. These rollers are frequently towed but they may be self-powered. In the experimental work reported by Williams and Maclean[9] a towed club-foot roller had a ballasted mass of 5005 kg (11 010 lb) and a towed taper-foot roller had a ballasted mass of 4582 kg (10 080 lb). Both types of feet had a projection of 305 mm (12 in.), the sheepsfoot had a foot size of 7742 mm^2 (12 in.^{2}) and the taper a foot size of 3266 mm^2 ($5\frac{1}{16}$ in.^{2}); in both cases the roll had a diameter of 1.067 m (42 in.) and an overall length of approximately 1.22 m (4 ft).

In their investigations it was found that sheepsfoot rollers were much less efficient than smooth-wheel rollers for compacting gravel—sand—clay soils and were unable to compact the sand effectively. Optimum moisture contents for compaction

Table 6.1 Compaction requirements for earthworks[11]

D = Maximum depth of compacted layer (mm)
N = Minimum number of passes

Type of compaction plant	Category	Cohesive soils		Well graded granular and dry cohesive soils		Uniformly graded material	
	Mass per metre width of roll:	D	N	D	N	D	N
Smooth-wheeled roller	over 2100 kg up to 2700 kg	125	8	125	10	125	10*
	over 2700 kg up to 5400 kg	125	6	125	8	125	8*
	over 5400 kg	150	4	150	8	unsuitable	
Grid roller	over 2700 kg up to 5400 kg	150	10	unsuitable		150	10
	over 5400 kg up to 8000 kg	150	8	125	12	unsuitable	
	over 8000 kg	150	4	150	12	unsuitabla	
Tamping roller	over 4000 kg	225	4	150	12	250	4
Pneumatic-tyred roller	Mass per wheel						
	over 1000 kg up to 1500 kg	125	6	unsuitable		150	10*
	over 1500 kg up to 2000 kg	150	5	unsuitable		unsuitable	
	over 2000 kg up to 2500 kg	175	4	125	12	unsuitable	
	over 2500 kg up to 4000 kg	225	4	125	10	unsuitable	
	over 4000 kg up to 6000 kg	300	4	125	10	unsuitable	
	over 6000 kg up to 8000 kg	350	4	150	8	unsuitable	
	over 8000 kg up to 12000 kg	400	4	150	8	unsuitable	
	over 12000 kg	450	4	175	6	unsuitable	
Vibrating roller	Mass per metre width of a vibrating roll						
	over 270 kg up to 450 kg	unsuitable		75	16	150	16
	over 450 kg up to 700 kg	unsuitable		75	12	150	12
	over 700 kg up to 1300 kg	100	12	125	12	150	6
	over 1300 kg up to 1800 kg	125	8	150	8	200	10*
	over 1800 kg up to 2300 kg	150	4	150	4	225	12*
	over 2300 kg up to 2900 kg	175	4	175	4	250	10*
	over 2900 kg up to 3600 kg	200	4	200	4	275	8*
	over 3600 kg up to 4300 kg	225	4	225	4	300	8*
	over 4300 kg up to 5000 kg	250	4	250	4	300	6*
	over 5000 kg	275	4	275	4	300	4*
Vibrating-plate compactor	Mass per unit area of base plate:						
	over 880 kg up to 1100 kg	unsuitable		unsuitable		75	6
	over 1100 kg up to 1200 kg	unsuitable		75	10	100	6
	over 1200 kg up to 1400 kg	unsuitable		75	6	150	6
	over 1400 kg up to 1800 kg	100	6	125	6	150	4
	over 1800 kg up to 2100 kg	150	6	150	5	200	4
	over 2100 kg	200	6	200	5	250	4
Vibro-tamper	Mass:						
	over 50 kg up to 65 kg	100	3	100	3	150	3
	over 65 kg up to 75 kg	125	3	125	3	200	3
	over 75 kg	200	3	150	3	225	3
Power rammer	Mass:						
	100 kg up to 500 kg	150	4	150	6	unsuitable	
	over 500 kg	275,	8	275	12	unsuitable	
Dropping-weight compactor	Mass of rammer over 500 kg Height of drop:						
	over 1 m up to 2 m	600	4	600	8	450	8
	over 2 m	600	2	600	4	unsuitable	

of clays with sheepsfoot rollers was lower than with other rollers and such conditions are rarely found in the United Kingdom even during the summer months For this reason this type of roller is more suited to compaction work in arid climates.

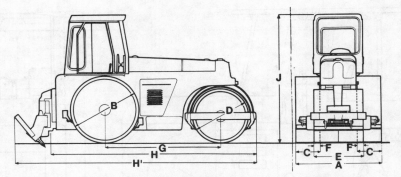

Figure 6.9 The Aveling-Barford DC Series of three-wheel rollers

Dimensions	Symbol	DC011 to DC013			DC014 to DC015		
		mm	ft	in.	mm	ft	in.
Rolling width — standard	*A	1880	6	2	2032	6	8
optional		2032	6	8			
Rear roll diameter	B	1524	5	0	1524	5	0
Rear roll width — standard	C	533	1	9	610	2	0
optional		610	2	0			
Front roll diameter	D	1219	4	0	1219	4	0
Front roll width	E	1066	3	6	1066	3	6
Overlap of rolls							
(each side)	F	127	0	5	127	0	5
Wheelbase	G	2590	8	6	2590	8	6
Length	H	4489	14	8¾	4489	14	8¾
Length with hydraulic							
scarifier	H′	5296	17	4½	5296	17	4½
Height with cab	J	2930	9	7⅜	2930	9	7⅜
Height with awning		3073	10	1	3073	10	1

* When scarifier fitted add 76 mm (3 in.) to obtain overall width. When independent asphalt cutter fitted add 216 mm (8½ in.) to obtain overall width

Table 6.1 gives compaction requirements for tamping rollers used for earthworks in the United Kingdom.

In addition to the towed rollers of this type there are a number of self-propelled rollers in use. One of these is the Aveling-Barford VS model, fitted with a vibrating padfoot roll at the front and earthmover tyres on the driving wheels at the rear. Total weight of the machine is 10 950 kg, with a weight on the padfoot vibrator roll of 6168 kg and a weight on the drive axle of 4782 kg. The centrifugal force applied to the vibrator roll is 14 515 kg, with a variable frequency up to 2300

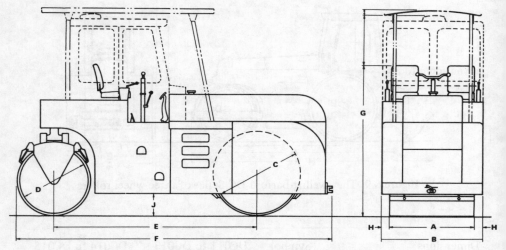

Figure 6.10 The Aveling-Barford range of two-axle tandem rollers

Dimensions	Symbol	TDC08 to TDC011			TRV, TRU, TRT, TRS		
		mm	ft	in.	mm	ft	in.
Rolling width	A	1321	4	4	1321	4	4
Overall width	B	1524	5	0	1524	5	0
Drive roll diameter	C	1321	4	4	1321	4	4
Rear roll diameter	D	1067	3	6	1066	3	6
Wheelbase	E	3048	10	0	3048	10	0
Overall length (TDC08/TRV)	F	4512	14	$9\frac{5}{8}$	4511	14	$9\frac{5}{8}$
TDC09 to TDC011/TRU etc.		4724	15	6	4724	15	6
Overall height (without cab)	G	2375	7	$9\frac{1}{2}$	2374	7	$9\frac{1}{2}$
with cab		3124	10	3	3124	10	3
with awning		3251	10	8	3263	10	$8\frac{1}{2}$
Overhang (each side)	H	101	0	4	101	0	4
Ground clearance (min)							
TDC08/TRV	J	356	1	2	355	1	2
TDC09 to TDC011/TRU etc.		279	0	11	279	0	11
Turning radius					5486	18	0

rev/min. The padfoot roll has a diameter of 1524 mm and a drum width of 2133 mm.

An investigation into the performance of a self-propelled tamping roller, the Caterpillar 815, has been carried out by Toombs.[12] The machine is based upon a conventional four-wheeled bulldozer design but it has tamping rolls instead of pneumatic-tyred wheels. The main frame is articulated between the front and rear rolls to allow the roller to be steered. The width of each roll was 965 mm and the gap between the rolls (that is, the width of the soil uncompacted by the machine) was 1.27 m. The diameter of each roll shell was 1.03 m, the height of each tamping foot was 190 mm and the coverage (that is, the sum of the projected end areas of feet expressed as a percentage of the area of the cylinder swept by the ends of the feet) was 15.3 per cent. The maximum mass per unit width of roll was 515 kg/m.

Table 6.2 Depths of layer, number of passes required and resulting outputs of the 17 Mg tamping roller operating at the restricted speed of travel used in the tests (2.4 km/h), when compacting soil to an acceptable state of compaction (50 min/h operation)[12]

Soil type	Depth of layer	Number of passes	Output
Heavy cohesive soils	250 mm	4	240 m³/h
	150 mm	1	580 m³/h
Light cohesive soils	250 mm	7	140 m³/h
	150 mm	2	290 m³/h
Well-graded granular soils	150 mm	12	50 m³/h
Uniformly graded soils	250 mm	4	240 m³/h
	150 mm	2	290 m³/h

Using the results of this investigation with the 17 Mg tamping roller and assuming that the machine is operated at the restricted speed of rolling used in the tests (2.4 km/h), the outputs of satisfactorily compacted soil have been calculated by Toombs and are given in table 6.2. The outputs given are based on the assumption that the machine is operated for 50 min/h. The calculated outputs should be regarded only as a guide to the likely performance of the machine because they are dependent upon the actual moisture content of the soil and on the site conditions.

The results obtained from the test carried out with the heavy clay, when the machine was used at a speed of travel of 4.8 km/h, showed that an output of about 390 m³/h was achieved at that speed, using a compacted layer 250 mm thick. It is concluded that, although no further tests were carried out at the higher speed of travel, substantial increases in output over those given are likely to be achieved at the more normal speeds of operation (5.10 km/h).

6.5.3 Pneumatic Rollers

A popular form of roller for the compaction of earthworks is the pneumatic roller, in which a number of pneumatic-tyred wheels are arranged along one or two axles so as to achieve a compacting effect across the whole width of the roller. For earth-work compaction they are usually towed units, where the wheels support a large box which can be ballasted. When the roller has one axle the wheels should be close enough together to produce continuous compaction across the width of the roller — a gap not exceeding 230 mm is specified in the Department of Transport Specification. With two axles the tyres on the front and rear axles overlap to give compaction over the whole width.

To equalise the loads on the wheels when travelling over uneven ground the wheels are frequently arranged in pairs on axles which are free to oscillate. In some types of roller the wheels are loosely mounted and are referred to as wobbly wheeled rollers. Because the wheels are free to move in several directions it is claimed that they produce a vibrating effect.

In an investigation carried out by Lewis[13] three pneumatic-tyred rollers were employed. Two twin-axle rollers with a mass of 12.2 Mg (12 ton) and 25.42 Mg (25 ton) each had a total of nine wheels while a single-axle roller of 45.76 Mg (45 ton) mass had four wheels. The 12.2 Mg roller had a wheel load of 1353 kg and a tyre pressure of 248.2 kN/m^2 (36 lb/in.^{2}); the 25.42 Mg roller had a wheel load of 2.258 kg and a tyre pressure of 441.3 kN/m^2 (80 lb/in.^{2}). The wheel load on the 45.76 Mg (45 ton) roller was operated with wheel loads of 5085 kg and 10 170 kg and tyre pressures of 620.5 and 965.3 kN/m^2 (90 and 140 lb/in.^{2}). The conclusions of these investigations were as follows.

(1) The contact area and contact pressure under the tyres, both of which affect the state of compaction produced, are functions of the wheel load and the inflation pressure.

(2) An increase in the wheel load or in the tyre-inflation pressure produces an increase in the maximum dry density with a corresponding lower optimum moisture content.

(3) For the compaction in the United Kingdom of soils similar to the two clays, there appears to be little point in using tyre-inflation pressures much in excess of 220.7 to 275.9 kN/m^2 (40 to 50 lb/in.^{2}) with wheel loads of about 5 tons.

(4) For the compaction of the two granular soils in the United Kingdom there appears to be some advantage in employing the highest tyre-inflation pressure and the heaviest wheel-load practicable, consistent with avoiding overstressing of the soils.

(5) The magnitudes of the wheel load and tyre-inflation pressure within the ranges used have very little influence on the general shape of the curves relating the number of passes of the roller with dry density — very little increase in the state of compaction being obtained after 16 passes.

(6) In general, about four passes of the rollers are necessary to produce states of compaction equivalent to an air-void content of 10 per cent.

(7) To achieve the greatest output of compacted soil the highest practical towing speed should be employed with, if necessary, a slight increase in the number of passes to compensate for the slight drop in the state of compaction that might result from employing the higher speed.

(8) Apart from the results obtained on the sand, which were affected by overstressing, the curves showing the change in dry density with depth below the surface of the compacted layer indicate that, in general, the higher the wheel load

and tyre-inflation pressure the higher is the state of compaction at any given depth.

(9) The maximum thickness of loose layer that can be employed in order to achieve a minimum acceptable state of compaction equivalent to an air-void content of 10 per cent ranges from 150 to 225 mm for the lightest combination of wheel load and tyre-inflation pressure to 350 to 450 mm for the heaviest combination used.

(10) It is possible to make a reasonable estimate of the likely performance of a pneumatic-tyred roller from a knowledge of the contact areas and pressures of the tyres and the relations between shear strength, dry density and moisture content of the soil.

(11) Although the output of the rollers increases with size and loading, the cost of operation is also likely to increase at a similar rate and the resulting cost per unit volume of compacted soil is not likely to be very different for the various sizes of roller.

Generally this type of roller is useful for compacting cohesive soils at relatively high moisture contents, an asset in typical British climatic conditions. They are less efficient with well-graded granular and dry cohesive soils and are unsatisfactory for the compaction of uniformly graded material. Requirements of the Standard Specification for compaction by pneumatic-tyred rollers are given in table 6.1.

6.5.4 Vibrating Rollers

A comparatively recent development in the field of compaction equipment is the use of vibrating devices in the form of vibrating smooth-wheel rollers, vibrating-plate compactors and vibro-tampers. In the Department of Transport specification a vibrating-plate compactor is defined as a machine having a base plate to which is attached a source of vibration consisting of one or two eccentrically weighted shafts. Vibro-tampers are machines in which an engine-driven reciprocating mechanism acts on a spring system through which oscillations are set up in a base plate.

Vibrating smooth-wheeled rollers may be either towed or self-propelled. An investigation into the performance of a towed vibrating smooth-wheel roller has been carried out by Toombs.[14] The roller was the Stothert and Pitt Vibroll T208 12 Mg model with a roll width of 2.08 m and a roll diameter of 1.83 m, the mass on the roll being 11.80 Mg and mass per unit width 5670 kg/m. The single vibrating roll is mounted in a welded steel chassis, at the front of which is a draw-bar extension and at the rear of which is mounted a 78 kW six-cylinder diesel engine driving an eccentric-shaft system rotating within the roll so as to produce the vibrating forces.

The results of the investigation indicated that the number of passes required to produce a state of compaction satisfactory for earthwork construction depends upon the type of soil and the speed at which the roller is towed. Table 6.3 gives, for each of the soils tested, the depth of compacted layer used, the number of passes required, and the output of compacted soil achieved for an average speed of travel of 2.4 km/h (the limitation normally imposed on this type of machine in the Department of Transport's Specification for Road and Bridge Works). The assumption has been made that the roller is operated for 50 min/h.

Relations between the outputs of heavy clay and well-graded sand, compacted to a state satisfactory for mass earthworks, and the speed of travel of the vibrating

Table 6.3 Output of compacted soil achieved with the 12 Mg vibrating roller at a towing speed of 2.4 km/h[14]

Soil type	Depth of layer (mm)	Number of passes	Output (m^3/h)
Heavy clay	300	5	250
Sandy clay	300	2	620
Well-graded sand	300	3	420
Gravel-sand-clay	300	8	160
Uniformly graded fine sand	450	2	940

roller indicated that, with both cohesive and well-graded granular soils, increases in output would be achieved when speeds of travel in excess of 2.4 km/h are used. Results suggest that outputs in the range 480 to 570 m^3/h might be expected with these soils if a speed of travel of about 6 km/h were used.

The outputs likely to be achieved on a particular project will depend on the actual moisture content of the soil and on the site conditions. The calculated outputs given in table 6.3 therefore should be regarded only as guides to the likely performance of the vibrating roller.

Investigations into the performance of another type of vibrating roller have also been carried out by Toombs.[15] The machine was the Clark Scheid DV60 6.9 Mg self-propelled roller with two vibrating rolls in tandem. It has an articulated main frame, hydrostatic transmission and a vibration system designed to produce vertically directed forces only. Each roll contains twin eccentric shafts which rotate in opposite directions and are phased so that only vertical forces are produced. The vibration frequency is normally 42 Hz. The width of each roll is 1.25 m, the diameter 1.10 m and the maximum mass per unit length of roll 2940 kg/m.

The results of the investigation showed that three passes of the roller, using a mean speed of travel of 2.2 km/h, were required to compact layers 180 mm thick of the cohesive and well-graded granular soils to a state satisfactory for earthworks construction. Thus, assuming that the machine is operated for 50 min/h, it would be possible to achieve an output of about 140 m^3/h of these soils. With the uniformly graded fine sand, where two passes were required with a compacted layer 300 m thick, an output of about 340 m^3/h would be possible.

As the double vibrating roller has hydrostatic transmission, the speed of travel can be varied infinitely, independently of the engine speed, between 0 and 10 km/h. The tests with the well-graded sand at various speeds of travel produced results from which the possible outputs of compacted soil over a wide range of speeds can be calculated. The relationship between output and speed of travel for a compacted layer 180 mm thick is shown in figure 6.11. Other relationships, of fairly similar shape but offset horizontally, can be obtained by using other thicknesses of compacted layer (for example, 150 mm), also illustrated in figure 6.11. Thus, with well-graded sand and possibly other well-graded granular and cohesive soils, by using various combinations of thickness of layer and speed of travel with the appropriate number of passes, outputs of compacted soil in the range 100 to 200 m^3/h are likely to be obtained.

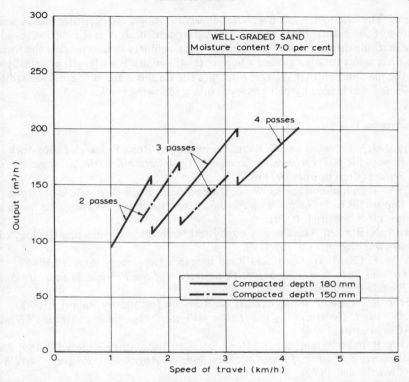

Figure 6.11 Relations between output of the well-graded sand, compacted to an air-content of 10 per cent, and speed of travel of the double-vibrating roller[15]

The calculated outputs given above should be regarded only as a guide to the likely performance of the machine, however, as they are dependent upon the actual moisture content of the soil and on the site conditions.

6.6 Subgrade Finishing

With earthworks completed it is necessary to trim the finished surface accurately to produce the desired subgrade level on which pavement construction will commence. From a performance point of view it is desirable for the pavement to have a uniform thickness and from the point of view of constructional efficiency irregularities in the formation should not be compensated for by a non-uniform sub-base.

On smaller schemes the formation can be trimmed by a grader but on larger schemes it is now usual to employ subgrade finishes which, using automatic control controls, are able to take levels from a taut line or a previously placed banquette or kerb.

Most fine-grading machines are designed with the earth-cutting mechanism extending across the width of the machine and at right angles to the direction of travel. The leading tracks on which the machine moves are normally placed well ahead of the cutting blade so as to give better control. It is in the cutting speed that the machine differs from other earthmoving machinery in that it takes the form of a helical screw rotating around a horizontal axis which has a length practically equal to the machine width. On larger machines the surplus material is automatically collected and loaded by belt conveyor into a following truck.

References

(1) M. J. Dumbleton and G. West, Transport and Road Research Laboratory Report LR 403, *Preliminary Sources of Information for Site Investigation in Britain* (Crowthorne, 1971)

(2) M. J. Dumbleton and G. West, Transport and Road Research Laboratory Report LR 625, *Guidance on Planning, Directing and Reporting Site Investigations* (Crowthorne, 1974)

(3) A. N. Burton, 'The Use of Geophysical Methods in Engineering Geology', Pt 1, *Ground Engng*, 9 (1976) 32–8

(4) M. E. Chard, Transport and Road Research Laboratory Report LR 459, *Ground Data Processing before Optimisation of the Vertical Alignment: Program Prelude* (Crowthorne, 1972)

(5) R. Robinson, Transport and Road Research Laboratory Report LR 700, *Automatic Generation of the Highway Vertical Alignment: Program VENUS* (Crowthorne, 1976)

(6) A. B. Baker, Transport and Road Research Laboratory Report LR 469, *The Design and Phasing of Horizontal and Vertical Alignments: Program JANUS* (Crowthorne, 1972)

(7) H. E. H. Davies, Transport and Road Research Laboratory Report LR 463, *Optimizing Highway Vertical Alignments to Minimize Construction Costs: Program MINERVA* (Crowthorne, 1972)

(8) W. A. Lewis and A. W. Parsons, 'The Application of Belt Conveyors in Road Earthworks', The Institution of Civil Engineers, Paper 7649 (November 1973)

(9) F. H. P. Williams, 'The Compaction of Soil', Road Research Technical Paper no. 17 (HMSO, 1950)

(10) W. A. Lewis, 'Further Studies in the Compaction of Soil and the Performance of Compaction Plant', Road Research Technical Paper, no. 33 (HMSO, 1954)

(11) *Department of Transport Specification for Road and Bridge Works* (HMSO, 1976)

(12) A. F. Toombs, Transport and Road Research Laboratory Report LR 529, *The Performance of a Caterpillar 815 17 Mg Tamping Roller in the Compaction of Soil* (Crowthorne, 1973)

(13) W. A. Lewis, 'Investigation of the Performance of Pneumatic-tyred Rollers in the Compaction of Soil', *Road Research Technical Paper*, no. 45 (1959)

(14) A. F. Toombs, Transport and Road Research Laboratory Report LR 341, *The Performance of a Stothert and Pitt Vibroll T208 12 Mg Towed Vibrating Roller in the Compaction of Soil* (Crowthorne, 1970)

(15) A. F. Toombs, Transport and Road Research Laboratory Report LR 590, *The Performance of a Clark Scheid DV60 6.9 Mg Double Vibrating Roller in the Compaction of Soil* (Crowthorne, 1973)

7
Pavement Construction

7.1 Base and Sub-base Construction

With the drainage works completed and all services and ducts crossing the carriage-way in place, the formation may be sealed to protect the subgrade from excessive moisture changes. This is because a cohesive subgrade which has become excessively dry due to evaporation during a dry construction season may swell with subsequent increases in moisture content, resulting in differential movement of the pavement. On the other hand a subgrade that has become excessively wet is difficult to compact and to overlay with sub-base material. Universal sealing of the subgrade thus will not always be the answer because it may delay evaporation and hinder the evaporation from the soil. For work in the United Kingdom the following broad recommendations have been made.[1] If the subgrade is formed during the months of October to April (inclusive) then it should be protected unless the sub-base can be laid and compacted on the same day as the subgrade is prepared. If the subgrade is cohesive and is prepared during May to September (inclusive) protection should be given if the formation is likely to be exposed for more than 4 days.

A common method of protecting the subgrade is the use of surface dressing. For it to be effective the subgrade must be shaped to a crossfall or camber so that surface-water will run off to drainage channels clear of the pavement area. Recommended[2] grades vary for road tar from A30 to A38 and for cut-back bitumen or tar-bitumen blends from 50 to 100 s, depending upon season. If construction traffic is to be carried by the subgrade then two coats are desirable, using 3 and 6 mm nominal size chippings for the first and second layers respectively. Where only light traffic is expected sand is sometimes used to blind the sealing coat. Unless the subgrade has good bearing properties the work will normally be carried out by hand spraying and spreading equipment.

Alternatively, heavy-gauge plastic sheeting may be used where weather and ground conditions make the use of a bituminous spray difficult. Adequate laps should be provided and the butt joints may be sealed with bitumen. Construction traffic cannot in these circumstances travel over the subgrade until the sub-base is placed. Proprietary fabrics are also being used to give additional stability in very difficult conditions.

Waterproofing of the subgrade is followed by the placing of the sub-base. On small jobs this may be carried out by hand, a small tractor-shovel or a grader.

Many specifications require this to be granular material, to have a specified minimum aggregate crushing value and to conform to a desired grading. Normally it is spread and compacted in layers with a thickness not exceeding 150 mm by a smooth-wheeled roller with a mass of approximately 10 Mg. Typically 16 passes of such a roller would be specified.

For major roadworks the sub-base may be formed of a variety of materials: unbound granular materials, soil cement, cement-bound granular material or lean concrete.

7.1.1 Construction of Soil—Cement Bases and Sub-bases

In suitable circumstances an economical sub-base may be formed by the incorporation of cement into the existing soil or a readily available soil which may be imported onto the site.

There are three methods by which a soil—cement sub-base may be constructed: the mix-in-place multi-pass method, the mix-in-place single-pass method, and the stationary plant-mix method.

Mix-in-place methods are used where the existing soil is suitable for stabilisation, the stationary plant-mix method is usual when the soil is imported to the site.

The mix-in-place method may be carried out either by multi-pass or single-pass techniques. In either of these methods the subgrade must be accurately shaped to the desired final levels and care taken to ensure that the soil to be treated is of uniform composition. The finished surface levels will be greatly influenced by these two factors.

Multi-pass Method

With the multi-pass technique the first operation is to break down and pulverise the soil. Normally some type of rotovating equipment is used but it should be capable of achieving the required degree of pulverisation. The soil may then be graded to the required cross-section if this is found to be necessary. When it is necessary to add water to the soil it can be done at this stage using a water sprayer, although with cohesive soils some engineers prefer to incorporate the cement before the addition of water. Accuracy in the distribution of the water from the spray-bar is essential. Frequently in the British climate it will be necessary to reduce the moisture content and additional rotovation will be necessary to assist evaporation.

The next operation is the spreading of the cement using either a mechanical spreader or by hand. Mechanical spreading is preferable on larger schemes but on smaller schemes or where labour is available it is possible to place cement bags at a predetermined spacing and then spread the contents by hand. Mixing of the cement with the soil will normally be performed by the same equipment as was used for the initial pulverisation. It is important that the depth of processing is accurately controlled and that the cement is incorporated in a uniform manner throughout the soil. Particular attention must be given to the joint with any previously stabilised strip and the pulverisation and mixing process should cut into the existing material.

Final shaping is then carried out followed by compaction with smooth-wheeled or pneumatic-tyred rollers or vibrating rollers. Curing is essential either by covering with plastic sheeting or by bituminous spraying.

Single-pass Method

In the single-pass technique the subgrade is first of all shaped up and a check on the soil uniformity carried out as with the multi-pass technique. The complete operation of pulverising, cement addition, moisture content control, mixing and compaction is then carried out in one pass. In some cases the equipment is formed into a single train while in others one machine carries out all these operations. Normally additional compaction is required before a curing membrane is applied. An advantage of this equipment is the lower risk of wet-weather damage compared with the multi-pass technique, but with the larger machines the area to be processed must be large enough for economical plant operation.

Stationary-plant Method

The stationary-plant process is normally used where the material to be stabilised is obtained at some distance from the laying site. The process is frequently used when a waste material such as pulverised fuel ash, chalk and similar materials can be improved by the addition of cement. It is a slower, more expensive form of construction than mix-in-place methods but the degree of control both of mixing and placing of the stabilised material is greater. It is normally used for small areas, such as hardstandings and car-parks.

The mixing plants used are of the power-driver paddle or pan type, either batch or continuous. When a batch-type mixer is used it is important to ensure that the cement is spread uniformly over the mixing pan and that the cement is weighed or proportioned by a separate device to that used for the soil.

7.1.2 Placing of Granular Bases and Sub-bases

Granular material, whether bound with cement or used unbound, are supplied to the site in a specified form and then are evenly spread and compacted by smooth-wheel rollers, pneumatic-tyred rollers, vibrating rollers or vibrating-plate compactors. When the material forms a roadbase, a paving machine or a spreader box will normally be required for spreading rather than a grader or bulldozer.

If dry-bound macadam is being laid it is important that as dense a layer as possible should be obtained by the use of coarse aggregate and a separately supplied fine aggregate. The coarse aggregate is laid first, using mechanical plant, to a thickness in the range 75 to 100 mm and lightly rolled. The fine aggregate, supplied or stored in a dry condition, is then spread to a depth of approximately 25 mm over the previously placed layers. Vibration is then applied to the material until as many of the voids as possible in the coarse aggregate have been filled with fine material. Surplus fine material is then removed by brushing and compaction, and completed using a smooth-wheel roller.

Joints are not provided in lean-concrete sub-bases and bases but construction joints are necessary. Longitudinal construction joints should be avoided as far as possible and all joints should be formed with a vertical face, either by compacting against substantial temporary timber 'stop ends' or by cutting back the previously placed material. Some engineers advise the painting of the joint with cement:sand grout, and in all cases special attention should be paid to compaction on these areas. Vertical joints such as these should be formed in all cases where there is an interruption in laying for a period greater than 1 h. Where the lean concrete is being used as a sub-base for a concrete pavement care must be taken to ensure that the joints in the sub-base and the slab are staggered.

All cement-bound materials require to be cured and lean-concrete and cement-bound granular material should be cured for 7 days by the use of plastic sheeting, a bituminous spray covered with fine crushed rock or sand, or an aluminium curing compound.

7.2 Kerbs and Footpaths

Where the depth of the sub-base is sufficient to allow the kerb race to be constructed to the required size without reducing the depth of the sub-base material beneath it to less than 150 mm, the next operation will be the placing of concrete support and backing to the kerb and the kerb itself. If sub-base thickness is small the kerb is frequently placed before the sub-base and forms a convenient guide to the required finished road levels.

Continuous support to the individual lengths of kerb is given by a concrete kerb race, which usually provides a 150 mm thickness of concrete beneath and at the rear of the kerb. A typical detail is shown in figure 7.1. The kerbs themselves may be natural stone but are more usually pre-cast concrete, laid so as to show a face above the road surface of 100 mm. Frequently channel blocks are used to provide a waterproof and low-friction passage to gullies for the surface water; natural stone, hard engineering bricks or pre-cast concrete blocks may be used. Where this occurs the kerb race will normally be made wider to provide a foundation for the channel.

When concrete road-slab construction is used the kerbs are likely to be placed after the completion of the main carriageway slab and may be placed directly on the completed road slab.

While in new residential development it is desirable for footpaths to be separated from carriageways, it is frequently necessary for a footpath to be constructed adjacent to the carriageway as part of the highway. A common form of construction has a width of 2 m including the kerb, and is composed of either a flexible

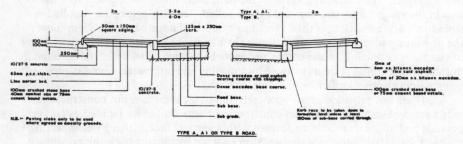

Figure 7.1 A typical flexible residential road (West Yorkshire County Council)

construction or Portland cement concrete slabs; both forms require a rolled crushed-stone base. To retain the outer edge of the footpath a precast concrete edging bedded on concrete is used.

7.3 Bituminous Paving Machines

For both minor and major roads the bituminous materials that may form the road base and surfacing are normally placed by floating-screed pavers. These machines receive hot or cold materials, which may be coated or uncoated, from a variety of trucks without spillage or damage to the vehicles. The material is then spread and compacted by the machine to a variety of depths and widths without segregation to form a hard level surface. Accurate control of the mat level both longitudinally and transversely is possible using either manual or automatic controls. At the same time the machine has to have adequate flotation and traction when working over a variety of surfaces.

The machines may be mounted on wheels or tracks: wheeled machines have an obvious speed advantage, especially when travelling while material is not being laid; tracked machines have a traction advantage that may be advantageous when the first layer of roadbase is being placed. Attached to the traction unit by arms is the screed, which tamps or vibrates and heats, if required, the material which is being laid. Material is conveyed from the hopper to an auger or spreader box, where a horizontal helical screw spreads the paving materials onto the road surface before it is compacted by the screed. An outline diagram of a typical paving machine is shown in figure 7.2. This is the Blaw-Knox BK95 paver and is a large machine suitable for use on motorways and airports and is capable of paving widths of between 1.95 and 6.75 m. The machine may be fitted with either tamping or vibrating screeds.

In floating-screed pavers the thickness of the mat can be adjusted while the machine is travelling. This is achieved by altering the angle of the screed relative to the road surface, the thickness of the mat gradually changing as the machine travels forward, until the screed is once more parallel to the road surface.

These machines are so designed that the wheels or tracks will negotiate short bumps or other irregularities in the road surface before the screed reacts, so leaving a level mat surface.

Most paving machines can be fitted with automatic controls to assist in the production of a high-quality riding surface. The most important of these controls are: auger or screw-feed control systems, longitudinal sensor controls, and crossfall controls.

The auger or screw-feed control ensures that sufficient material is presented to the front of the screed by automatically adjusting the level of material at the auger or screw. Longitudinal control over the mat surface can be maintained by the use of a taut line and sensor on the machine which is able to adjust the height of the tow point by means of hydraulic rams as illustrated in figure 7.3. The sensor can also follow a previously placed adjacent mat so as to match the joint.

A mobile reference or averaging-beam can also be used in conjunction with the sensor. This beam is towed alongside the machine and by averaging out the undulations on the surface over which it travels allows the sensor to maintain a more uniform longitudinal profile. Beams take several forms: a long skid with a length of

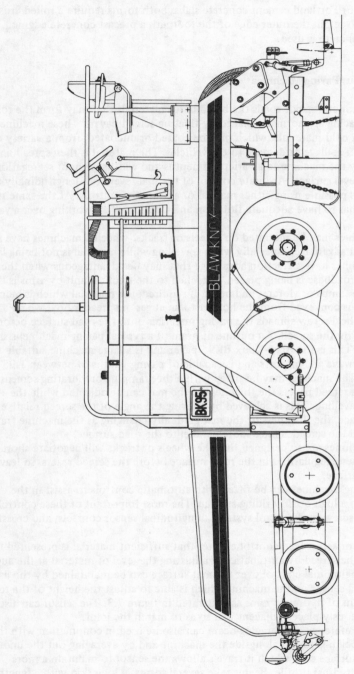

Figure 7.2 The Blaw-Knox BK 95 paving machine

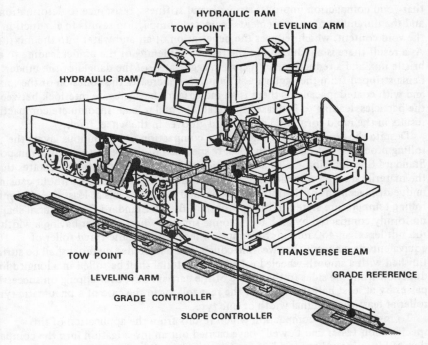

Figure 7.3 The Barber-Greene Paver levelling system

9.14 m or more, which averages over the high spots; wheeled models which follow all undulations; or one, as manufactured by Barber-Greene, with random placement of sledges as shown in figure 7.3.

The crossfall controller is a means of controlling the opposite side of the paving machine to that at which a sensor is fitted. A usual form of the device is a horizontal transverse beam attached at each end to the levelling arms onto which the slope controller is attached. Essentially the device is a form of pendulum able to detect changes from a preset crossfall when the controller detects that there has been a change from the given zero position; it automatically operates to adjust the two-point height of the appropriate levelling arm.

Speed of operation of paving machines is limited by the rate of supply of paving material and by the thickness of the mat and its laying temperature. Excessive machine speed will result in an uneven surface of poor riding quality, thick mats and/or cool material requiring a slow speed. Typical speeds are 2 to 3 m/s for base-course materials and 3 to 5 m/s for wearing-course materials.

7.4 Compaction of Bituminous Materials

Compaction of bituminous materials has a very considerable effect on the perform-ance of the material as a load-carrying highway pavement. It is generally accepted that good compaction improves strength and stiffness, resistance to deformation and the durability of the pavement. Increased compaction results in a reduction in the void content, which reduces the penetration of air and water into the mixture. As a result there is a reduction in the rate of hardening of the binder leading to a brittle mix and a reduction, with certain aggregates, of the danger of the binder being stripped from the aggregate. Compaction increases the cohesion of the mix and with coated macadams there is an increase in the aggregate interlock between the particles, leading to increased mix stability under load. Incomplete compaction results in the rapid formation of ruts and grooves in the wheel track.

Despite the obvious importance of the compaction of bituminous layers the rolling process is not particularly closely specified in the Department of Transport Standard Specification for Road and Bridge Works.[3] This specification states that the material shall be compacted as soon as rolling can be effected without causing undue displacement of the mixed material and while this has at least the minimum rolling temperature stated in the appropriate British Standard. The material shall be uniformly compacted by an 8 to 10 tonne smooth-wheeled roller having a width of roll not less than 450 mm, or by a multi-wheeled pneumatic-tyred roller of equivalent mass except that wearing-course and basecourse material shall be surface finished with a smooth-wheeled roller. The material shall be rolled in a longitudinal direction from the sides to the centre of the carriageway, overlapping on successive passes by at least half the width of the rear roll, or in the case of a pneumatic-tyred roller at least the nominal width of one tyre.

To investigate the compaction which results from the application of this specification Lister and Powell[4] have carried out an investigation into the compaction of bituminous base and basecourse material and its relation to pavement performance. Cores were removed from pavements at 12 road construction sites to determine the typical levels of compaction of dense-coated macadam bases and basecourses being achieved. They noted that the levels of compaction of dense-coated macadam achieved during construction showed that variations in binder content had a significant effect on the void content of the compacted material but not on the value of the voids in the mineral aggregate that were achieved. Ninety per cent of the values of void content were between 2 and 8 per cent whereas the range of values of voids in the mineral aggregate was considerably narrower: between 13 and 16 per cent.

Although dense macadam base and basecourses were laid to a satisfactory standard it was found that peak values of density occurred in the centre of the laid width and not in the critical wheel-path zone, which suffers the greatest wheel loading. These variations in density still existed after many years of heavy traffic, so that the initial compaction of the material was of great importance in determining pavement performance.

The temperature of the bituminous material during the rolling process has a very significant effect on the level of compaction achieved. Powell and Leech[5] report that dense bitumen macadam after 20 roller passes has a void content approximately 5 per cent higher when it has an initial temperature of 85 °C instead of 130 °C.

As bituminous materials are being rolled they lose heat by conduction to the supporting layer and to the atmosphere by convection and radiation. It is generally accepted[6] that the minimum temperature for the completion of rolling should correspond to a binder viscosity of 10^3 poise at the mid-depth of the surfacing.

For a 100-pen bitumen the appropriate minimum rolling temperature is 60 °C. If the rate of cooling of a bituminous layer can be predicted then it is possible to calculate the time available for rolling with different rates of material placing.

The approach adopted by Powell and Leech was to use computed cooling curves for different laying temperatures for differing ambient temperatures, a wind speed of 2.2 m/s, a temperature at laying of 5 °C less than the minimum specified delivery temperature, and layer thicknesses of 60 and 65 mm. Figures 7.4 and 7.5 show the cooling curves and the time available for rolling for dense roadbase macadam using 100-pen, 200-pen, 54 evt and 50 evt binders. It can be seen that with 100-pen bitumen 30 min is available for rolling even under the most adverse conditions. Less time is available for 200-pen bitumen but this grade of binder is only used for less heavily trafficked pavements. When tar is used as a binder, under adverse conditions less than 30 min is available for rolling. Powell and Leech based their proposed specification for compaction on the 30 min of rolling time available for 100-pen bitumen as they considered this was the most commonly used material.

They proposed a theoretical model of the rolling process in which the paving machine advances continuously at a uniform speed. The roller also moves continuously at a uniform speed, reversing until it reaches a fixed distance from the paver, when it moves forward until it reaches the paver. This distance is a fixed

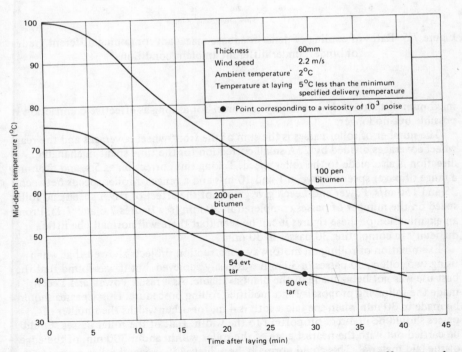

Figure 7.4 Rates of cooling of dense roadbase macadam containing different grades of binder, under adverse site conditions[5]

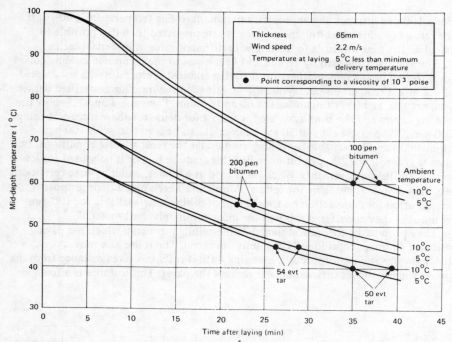

Figure 7.5 Rates of cooling of dense roadbase macadam containing different grades of binder, under different ambient conditions[5]

maximum distance such that rolling continues for as long as effective compaction is possible but no longer.

The number of roller passes is the sum of the front-wheel coverages and the rear-wheel coverages divided by 2. A small correction for the time spent in changing direction is also made to the roller speed. Taking this correction as 5 s, and assuming a range of paver speeds between 1 and 10 m/s and a range of roller speeds between 25 and 150 m/s, Power and Leech give graphs of the effect of paver speed and roller speed on the number of passes completed in 30 min (see figures 7.6 and 7.7). From an examination of these figures it can be seen that there will normally be little difficulty in completing 30 passes in 30 min.

Examination of rolling on motorway construction projects showed that when using two rollers, 30 passes in 30 min was easily achieved, but it was found that the best use was not being made of the plant available. As a result Powell and Leech made the following proposals for a modified rolling procedure. Thirty passes should be made in 30 min when the laid width is 4 m, for other widths the number of passes should be in direct proportion to the width. Half of the roller passes should be carried out with the nearest edge of the roller within about 300 mm of the edge of the laid material. This could normally be achieved if a second roller concentrates on edge rolling; preferably the second roller should be tandem. When 200-pen

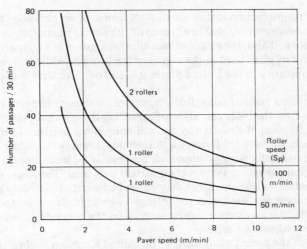

Figure 7.6 Effect of paver speed on number of roller passages completed in 30 min[5]

bitumen is used the recommended minimum delivery temperature should be increased from 80 °C to at least 90 °C.

7.5 Concrete Paving with Fixed-form Plant

An excellent review of construction methods for concrete pavements in the United Kingdom has been given by Walker and Beadle,[7] in which they describe both fixed-form and slip-form construction.

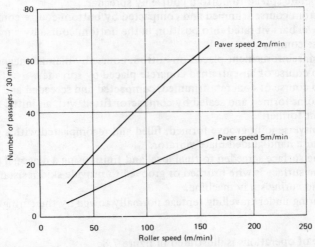

Figure 7.7 Effect of roller speed on number of passages completed by one roller in 30 min[5]

Fixed-form construction makes use of steel forms, or on occasions a permanent concrete edge-beam constructed in advance of the paving operation, to retain the plastic concrete and also, by means of machine rails, guide and support the individual items of plant used in the construction process. While this method has declined in popularity in the United States it is still of considerable importance in Europe.

In this method a train of individually operated machines run along the rails, these machines carry out the basic operation of spreading the concrete, compacting it by vibration and finishing the surface by an oscillating-beam finisher. There will be additional machines for joint-forming and inserting dowel bars, surface texturing and the application of a curing compound. Some of these machines may be operated in duplicate where two-layer construction is used. The larger machines are self-powered while smaller machines may either be towed or manually propelled. Normally machines are fitted with steel-flanged wheels for travel on the rails, but where paving against an existing slab or running on the concrete edge-beams, solid, slightly resilient wheels are used.

The width of the paving plant used in the United Kingdom is normally limited to a two-lane width of about 7 m. While greater widths of plant have been employed, there are problems with the rigidity of the supporting framework.

In the United Kingdom three-lane concrete roads are normally constructed by paving one lane and then following by constructing a further two lanes, tie bars being incorporated between the two slabs.

The sequence of events in a typical arrangement of plant for two-course construction is given below.

(1) Forms set and fixed, separation-membrane laid.

(2) Longitudinal and transverse joint crack-inducers fixed and joint assemblies fixed.

(3) Concrete spread to bottom course by spreader.

(4) Bottom course trimmed and compacted by bottom-course compactor.

(5) Dowel bars vibrated into position in the bottom course by a mechanical bottom-course compactor.

(6) Mesh reinforcement placed on bottom course by manual means.

(7) Top course of air-entrained concrete placed by spreader.

(8) Top course of concrete trimmed, compacted and screeded and the longitudinal joint formed and sealed by compactor fitted with an initial finishing beam and joint former.

(9) Transverse joint groove formed, filled and recompacted with a guillotine joint former or a hand-guided plate vibrator.

(10) The surface screeded to final level and finish using a diagonal finisher.

(11) The surface is wire-brushed or grooved to provide skid resistance, using a texturing and curing spray machine.

(12) Curing under travelling tentage normally towed by the curing spray machine.

This sequence of operations is illustrated in figure 7.8.

When single-course construction is used the concrete is placed and compacted to full depth. The compacting plant in this case must be powerful enough to

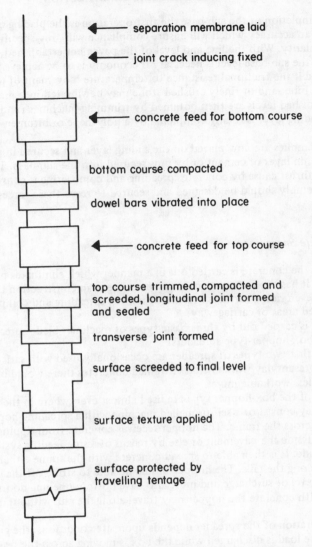

Figure 7.8 Typical plant train for fixed-form paving

compact the full depth of the slab without significantly affecting the alignment of mechanically placed dowel bars.

The availability of standard machines that are designed for two-course work together with the ease with which dowel bars may be placed in the compacted bottom course have led many contractors to use this form of construction with unreinforced concrete. An additional advantage in this case is the possibility of using only air-entrained concrete and high-quality aggregate in the upper layer.

After completion of the sub-base the first operation is the placing of the forms and rails to an accuracy which will ensure compliance with any specification for surface regularity. With the line and level of the pavement established, accurate finishing of the sub-base level is necessary if economy is to be achieved in concrete quantity and if the frictional resistance to temperature movement of the slab is to be reduced. Fine sand or finely crushed stone may be vibrated into granular sub-bases and finished levels are then obtained by trimming-machines running on the rails. The sliding layer is finally completed by a polythene or bitumen-bound paper layer.

Joint assemblies are now placed on the sliding layer and secured in position either by a thin layer of cement or by pins secured into the sub-base. The unbalanced thrust cause by concrete spreading and compacting is considerable and the joint assembly should be designed and secured to resist these forces.

7.5.1 Concrete Spreading

Spreading of the concrete is carried out in a manner which eliminates pre-compaction because it has been noted that during concrete road construction there is a danger of uneven riding surfaces because of uneven spreading and compaction of pre-compacted areas of carriageway.

Spreading is carried out by three basic types of machine: blade spreaders, screw spreaders or box-hopper-type spreaders.

While the first two types of spreader are occasionally used with satisfactory results with present-day workable air-entrained concretes there would be difficulty with harsher less-workable mixes.

Spreaders of the box-hopper type are used almost everywhere in the United Kingdom. They consist of a self-propelled machine with a spreading-hopper moving transversely across the frame. The hopper receives concrete from tipping lorries travelling alongside the pavement or else by means of a side-feeding system which travels alongside. It is then able to spread concrete with the frame either stationary or travelling along the rails. The hopper should be able to strike off the concrete to the required level of surcharge and must also have bottom-opening doors so that after filling with concrete the hopper may travel along the rails without discharging any.

Actual operation of the spreader depends upon site conditions; the greater part of the concrete load is discharged while the box is moving across the frame and the frame is moving along the rails. The return movement of the box with the frame stationary is then used for trimming the surface of the concrete and infilling. The operation of the machine is illustrated by figure 7.9.

The performance of the spreading machine is influenced to some extent by the characteristics of the concrete mix. If the mix is too cohesive it tends to stick in the hopper, causing irregularities in spreading and reduced output; on the other hand, too little cohesion results in segregation, which causes difficulty in finishing.

The depth to which the concrete must be spread to obtain a given thickness of compacted slab depends upon the workability of the concrete. For workabilities within the usual range of the 0.80 to 0.85 compacting factor the concrete should be

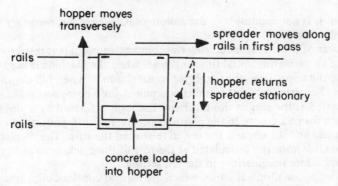

Figure 7.9 Hopper-type concrete spreader

spread to a depth between 25 and 18 per cent greater than that of the compacted slab; the amount of surcharge required decreases as the workability increases.

Although final adjustment of the level of spread concrete is made by the striking-off paddles on the finishing machine, the performance and output of the finisher is impaired if it has to carry forward too much surplus concrete. Once suitable height-settings have been determined for the spreading-hopper it is unnecessary and undesirable to make frequent adjustments.

In some instances it has been found that the spreading-hopper has developed a permanent sag due to prolonged use, resulting in waves in the spread-concrete surface. The straightness of the bottom of the hopper therefore requires checking before work starts.

If the hopper is moved erratically because of poor operation or faults in the drive or clutch mechanism the density of spread concrete will not be uniform. Similarly, irregular spreading can result from concrete sticking in the hopper. A small vibrator is sometimes fitted to one type of spreader-hopper to ease the discharge of concrete and to overcome any tendency for it to stick in the hopper. It is important that this vibrator be turned on only while the hopper is being moved, as otherwise the concrete will be compacted within the hopper and become even more difficult to discharge.

7.5.2 Compaction of Joints and Finishing

Compaction of the concrete after spreading is achieved by surface-applied vibration by a machine-mounted transverse compacting beam. The amplitude and frequency of vibration is adjustable to achieve maximum compaction with different mixes. In front of the compacting beam strike-off paddles adjust any minor irregularities in the previously levelled concrete.

After compaction of the concrete it is now almost universal to vibrate the transverse dowel bars for contraction joints and the longitudinal-joint tie bars into position. The bars are vibrated into place with a continuous carefully controlled movement. This method has now largely replaced the use of cradles attached to the sub-base but it is not applicable to expansion joints, where it is necessary to incorporate a filler board.

At the rear of the machine carrying the compacting beam it is usual to incorporate an oscillating initial finishing beam when the machine is used for compacting the upper layer for two-layer construction or when full-depth construction is used. Longitudinal-joint-forming equipment for wet-formed sealing grooves is also mounted at the rear of this machine. The joint is formed by a plough-type device which forms a groove in the plastic concrete, inserts a preformed cellular permanent seal and recompacts the concrete around the strip. The oscillating finishing beam is normally articulated at the rear of the machine so as to reduce the effect of any minor irregularities in the rail setting.

In contrast to longitudinal joints, which are formed continuously, transverse joints are formed by an intermittent process. In wet-formed joint construction this is achieved by vibrating either a permanent or temporary joint filler into position using a separate machine travelling along the rails in front of the diagonal finisher.

Where the quality of the surface regularity is important, as on major roadworks and airfield paving, final finishing is carried out by diagonal oscillating finishing beams mounted on an articulated undercarriage. A type of final finisher frequently employed uses two finishing beams working in opposing directions. Because of the skewed and articulated arrangement of the wheel bogies, vertical movement of the screed due to irregularities in the steel rails is greatly reduced.

It is considered that a diagonal finishing beam gives a more uniform profile than a transverse beam and it also has the advantage that it is less liable to displace the temporary or permanent fillers used in wet-formed sealing grooves.

Sawn concrete joints may be used but they are increasingly replaced by wet-formed joints. The choice may be influenced by the nature of the concrete aggregate — some aggregates are easily sawn while with others the process is slow and costly. A particular difficulty in large-scale concrete paving is the limited time available for the actual sawing operation. The concrete must have gained sufficient strength for the groove to be cut without ravelling, while on the other hand if the sawing operation is delayed random contraction cracking will occur. If complete sawing of the joint grooves is carried out this may entail working at night. As an alternative, partial sawing to ensure control of contraction cracking may be carried out and full-width sawing completed within 7 days.

Joint grooves must be sealed to prevent the entry of water and when wet-formed joints are employed it is usual to use a permanent preformed seal vibrated into position. Permanent compression seals at transverse joints have also been used. If this type of seal is not employed the temporary joint-filling material is removed, the groove cleared out by sawing, grinding or grit blasting, and where the depth of the groove is greater than the required depth of seal a caulking material introduced. The final seal is then achieved by either a hot-poured sealant, a two-component cold-poured sealant, or preformed compression seals.

The desirable properties of a joint sealant are that it prevents dirt and grit from entering the joint and preventing its operation, and forms a waterproof seal which prevents water standing in the joint and most of the surface-water passing into the sub-base. It must also be robust, have good ageing and weathering properties, be resilient and resistant to tearing and creep. Experimentally, some contraction joints have used narrow, 2.5 mm wide, grooves which have been left unsealed.

Joint maintenance can be a very costly operation when traffic delays are taken into account and it is therefore important to consider the life of a joint sealant in addition to its original cost. Compression seals have a longer life than poured sealants and cold-poured sealants have a longer life than hot-poured sealants.

7.6 Slip-form Paving

For many years such concrete structures as chimneys and bridge piers have been formed using continuously moving or slip forms instead of the usual fixed concrete forms, and in 1947 approximately a mile of concrete slab 6 in. thick was slip-formed in Iowa. Since that time this method of construction has gained considerable popularity, particularly in the United States where very extensive concrete paving has been carried out.

Slip-form paving consists of forming a concrete highway slab by a special machine known as a slip-form paver, which compacts the concrete fed into it by using high-frequency vibrators, screeds and/or conforming plates. The paver moves continuously forward laying, as it were, a strip of concrete. The compaction of the concrete allows the edges of the slab to stand vertically as the paver moves forward, so eliminating the need for the conventional formwork necessary for ordinary concrete road construction. The origin of the term 'slip-form paving' is attributed to the short lengths of sliding side-forms which were at one time attached to the rear of the paver, but most modern paving machines dispense with them.

A variety of slip-form pavers have been manufactured but current models can be divided into two main types. In the first the concrete surface is formed by conforming the concrete to the desired cross-section and profile beneath a single large screed, so that the concrete slab is formed as the machine moves along. The concrete is liquefied by high-frequency poker vibrators at the front of the paver. It then flows beneath the conforming screed, being contained by the side-forms within the machine and the subgrade beneath the slab.

In a second type of paver the operations of spreading, trimming, compacting and finishing are carried out in a similar manner to conventional side-form paving using surface-operating beams between travelling side-forms.

Some of the earlier machines were manually controlled, the level of the slab being fixed by the level of the running surface on which the paver is travelling, direction of travel of the paver being controlled by the operator following a guideline. Far greater control over the finished surface may be obtained, however, by the use of automatic controls such as are fitted to modern slip-form paving machines. Control is maintained by the use of two lines of piano wire, one of which is set to line to act as a steering line. Level control of both slab edges is fixed by both wires from sensing probes at the four corners of the machine. A further probe at the front of the paver controls the line of the machine.

7.6.1 The Guntert–Zimmerman Paver

Developed in the United States and now manufactured in Europe, the Guntert–Zimmerman paver was the first to be used in the United Kingdom. With an overall

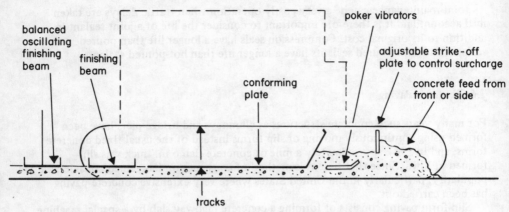

Figure 7.10 Outline of operation of Guntert–Zimmerman slip-form paver

length of approximately 6 m, the machine runs on two tracks 500 mm wide and has a chassis which will extend to make it possible to form a slab with a width of at least three lanes at one pass.

In the front hopper, which receives the concrete, is a hydraulically adjustable metering plate maintaining a constant surcharge of concrete above the level of the conforming plate. Immersed vibrators between the metering plate and the conforming plate maintain the fluidity of the concrete as it passes under the conforming plate and provide the main compaction.

The final finishing of the concrete prior to joint-groove forming and texturing is carried out by a transverse oscillating beam working across the tops of the travelling side-forms behind the conforming plate. An outline of the machine is given in figure 7.10.

Guntert–Zimmerman also manufacture a smaller machine of single-lane width that can be used for residential roads, hard shoulders or industrial roadways. It is fitted with a screw-spreader in front of the metering plate, and this together with the small width of the machine makes it possible to feed concrete from the side, using the discharge chute of truck mixers.

Side-feeding of concrete is also of importance with the larger Guntert–Zimmerman machines when reinforcement is to be incorporated in the slab. This frequently prevents concrete being loaded into the front of the slip-form paver by trucks travelling on the sub-base. In these circumstances concrete is supplied from the side of the machine using a belt conveyor system.

7.6.2 The CMI Autograde Paver

A slip-form paver differing from the Guntert–Zimmerman and the CPP 60 paver is the CMI Autograde paver, also originating from the United States. Spreading, compacting and finishing are carried out in separate operations in a similar manner to a conventional side-form machine but the operations are carried out by devices which are all attached to a long-base machine carried on four separate bogie-mounted crawler tracks. Whilst the machine cannot be easily adapted to pave different widths of carriageway it can be used for a variety of different road-construction operations, from subgrade trimming and sub-base construction to slip-form paving, by the attachment of differing items of equipment to the long-base frame.

Steering and level control is automatic, using line and level sensors mounted at the extremities of the machine, the level being given by polypropylene cords rather than the steel wires of other pavers.

Spreading of the concrete is carried out by a screw-auger, the two halves of which are powered separately, and then by an adjustable strike-off plate. A close degree of control over the surcharge level is possible with this machine — particularly useful when constructing super-elevated pavements or opposite crossfalls on either side of a centre-line. While it is possible for the machine to spread concrete placed in windrows ahead of the machine, it is better practice to use a placer-spreader travelling ahead of the slip-form paver.

Initial compaction of the concrete is achieved by means of poker vibrators placed behind the strike-off plate. The height of these vibrators can be varied and it is possible to lift them over filler boards at expansion joints. Tie bars may then be placed mechanically into the plastic concrete and the surface recompacted by means of a vibrating beam which may serve as a secondary strike-off for small amounts of concrete. Finishing is carried out by a pair of oscillating beams which move in opposite directions. Behind the finishing beams is the longitudinal-joint placer and any disturbance of the surface is corrected by means of a suspended pan float finisher.

Separate machines would normally be employed for forming transverse joints and refinishing the surface, texturing, and spraying with a curing membrane.

7.6.3 Reinforcement in Slip-formed Slabs

The incorporation of reinforcement in a concrete pavement does not lead to a reduction in slab thickness, except for lightly trafficked roads, in British practice. For this reason it is usual for slip-formed pavements, which are most economically constructed in a single layer, to be formed as unreinforced slabs. Attempts have been made to incorporate reinforcement, either by using free-standing steel or by devices which feed the reinforcement into the front of the machine.

If supported reinforcement is used then fabric reinforcement or deformed longitudinal bars, usually the latter, may be supported on cradles. Considerable labour is involved in the placing of the steel, which, together with the joint assemblies, must be placed in advance of concreting, concrete being placed by side-loading equipment.

7.7 Texturing and Curing

Once the concrete surface has been finished by the finishing beams it is necessary to texture the concrete to maintain adequate wet-road skidding resistance. Because of the relatively long life of concrete pavements and the difficulties of surface maintenance the surface texture is of considerable importance. The standard finish in the United Kingdom is imparted by means of a wire brush, either operated manually, or mechanically from a travelling bridge.

The wire brush used in the United Kingdom must have a width not less than 450 mm, with two staggered rows of 32-gauge tape wire tufts at 10 mm centres laterally and 20 mm centres in the direction of movement of the brush. As the texture should be at right angles to the direction of movement, if texturing is carried out from a travelling bridge the bridge must be skewed.

An alternative method of texturing has been developed by the Cement and Concrete Association's Construction Research Department. The machine is equipped with a profiled, vibrating traversing-plate and forms grooves in the concrete surface with random longitudinal spacings at right angles to the direction of movement.

The grooves have a nominal size of 6 by 6 mm and provide superior surface-water drainage properties. A high level of wet-road skidding resistance is given by this form of texture but problems have arisen with the tyre/road interaction noise.

Final operation in the concrete-slab construction process is the spraying of a curing compound on to the slab surface. The curing compound is normally aluminised and it is sprayed mechanically on to the concrete surface. Travelling tentage is frequently employed behind the curing sprayer so as to minimise the danger of early rainfall damaging the surface texture or regularity.

7.8 Safety Fences

One of the last site works carried out in the construction of major highways is the installation of safety fences. While the highest design and construction standards may be reached, collisions are still possible when vehicles either leave the carriageway and strike fixed objects such as bridge piers or else cross the central reservation and collide with vehicles on the other carriageway.

This danger may be reduced by the construction of safety fences or crash barriers. They have been defined[8] as structures designed and located with the following objectives.

(1) Preventing any vehicle from injuring innocent persons outside of that vehicle.

(2) Preventing passenger cars, and as far as economically possible also heavy vehicles, from entering an area hazardous to travel.

(3) Redirecting the vehicle nearly parallel to the direction of the barrier.

(4) Containing within tolerable limits the forces experienced by the vehicle occupants.

(5) Minimising property damage costs.

(6) Withstanding impact from a colliding vehicle without danger of either the vehicle or the barrier becoming a hazard to traffic.

A collision with a safety fence can cause serious damage to the colliding vehicle, so the decision to install it is a balance between preventing a probable collision when a vehicle leaves the carriageway unprotected by a safety fence and the certainty of a collision with the safety fence when a vehicle leaves a carriageway protected by it.

Warrants for the use of safety fences vary considerably from one country to another. Current criteria for the provision of safety fences in verges and central reserves of roads in the United Kingdom have been given by the Department of Transport.[9]

Safety fences are normally recommended only on major roads where speed restrictions permit 80 km/h or above and for which the circumstances below apply; there will also be a need for safety fences on less important roads where there may be exceptional hazards either affecting the layout or the roadside.

For safety fences erected in verges these exceptional hazards occur when there are embankments 6.0 m or more in height; on the outside only of curves less than about 850 m radius on embankments between 3.0 and 6.0 m in height; or at obstructions such as bridge piers or abutments, or posts to large signs.

When safety fences are erected in central reserves they give protection to bridge piers, posts to large signs, and similar obstructions that if displaced would cause danger to other vehicles or persons, but not to small signs, which should be constructed as far as possible to give minimum damage to vehicles striking them. Fences also give protection to lighting columns where the central reserve is not more than 1.75 m wide and enable adequate clearance to be provided between the face of the safety fence and the edge of the carriageway. Safety fences are to be provided on rural roads where the central reserve width is 2.5 m or less; where the difference in carriageway levels exceeds 1.0 m and the slope across the reserve is steeper than 25 per cent the doubled-sided safety fence is placed adjacent to the edge of the higher carriageway. On unlighted motorways where speed restrictions permit 100 km/h or more and which have central reserves between 2.5 m and 6.0 m wide, safety fences are to be provided as initial equipment. Existing heavily trafficked motorways are being provided with safety fences as part of a programme.

Guidance on the use of safety fences in the United States is given in highway Research Board Special Report 81.[10] It states that guard-rails may generally be omitted on embankments with 4:1 or flatter side-slopes unless other hazards are present. Current practice is for guard-rails at the edge of carriageways to be installed on major roads when the height of fill exceeds 2.4, 3.0, 3.6 and 4.6 m in conjunction with fill slopes of 1½:1, 2:1, 2½:1 and 3:1 respectively.

Safety fences in the central reserve are recommended on expressways when the central reserve has widths of 3, 6 and 9 m when the average daily traffic is 15, 30 and 45 thousand vehicles respectively. When the central reserve is equal to or greater than 12 m then barriers are generally omitted.

There are many forms of safety fence in use but they may conveniently be classified into the following general types: tensioned-beam safety fences, untensioned-beam safety fences, wire-rope safety fences, profiled concrete barriers, and proprietary fences.

In the United Kingdom two types of untensioned-beam safety fence are in common use: the open-box beam and the blocked-out beam. Both these types of fence are intended to give protection at obstructions over short lengths or where space for deflection upon impact is limited. The open-box safety fence has been developed for use on motorways and other high-speed roads; it is more effective but more expensive than the blocked-out beam. The open-box type is recommended on vertical or horizontal curves down to 30 m radius, on bridge piers or parapets. If there is a special hazard then a 2-rail open-box fence can give protection to vehicles which might normally penetrate a single beam.

There is a higher risk of colliding vehicles rolling over blocked-out beam fences and they should be installed only at situations where the consequences of this are not serious.

The open-box-beam barrier (figure 7.11) consists of a trapezoidal mild-steel beam 150 × 200 × 150 mm and 5 mm thick, mounted at a height of 710 mm. The beam is supported by 110 × 50 × 5 mm Z-section steel posts at 2400 mm centres, and posts are either bolted down to a structure or mounted in a concrete footing.

The 300 mm steel or aluminium-alloy corrugated beam is mounted at a height of 685 mm. It is attached to 150 mm by 150 mm by 1.8 m long wooden posts by means of a wooden blocking-out piece 350 mm high, 150 mm wide and 200 mm long. The posts are spaced at 2400 mm centres.

Tensioned-beam safety fences are used in preference to untensioned types, except where the length of fencing between anchorages is less than 45 m and also where the fence has a radius in plan of less than 120 m. The corrugated beams are mounted at a height of 760 mm on mild steel Z-section posts at a spacing of 3200 mm. The beam is attached to the posts by shear bolts and tensioned between anchorages sunk in the ground. When a vehicle strikes the barrier the bolts fracture, allowing the posts to be knocked down without appreciably affecting the height of the beam. The fence may be made stiffer by the use of two beams, one on each side of the vertical post; further stiffening may be obtained by halving the post spacing.

A rectangular hollow-section tensioned safety fence has been developed by the British Steel Corporation. These beams are available in two sizes: 203.2 by 101.6 mm and 101.6 by 101.6 mm. They may be used as alternatives to the tensioned corrugated beam and the open-box beam. Because of its slender construction the rectangular hollow-section fence is preferred in areas of high amenity, where appearance is important, and also where it is important to reduce the risk of snow drifting on to the carriageway.

An unusual form of guard-rail has been designed by Christiani and Nielsen Ltd. A conventional corrugated guard-rail is used but the guard-rail supports are hollow-section steel posts hinged at their bases to which hydraulic shock absorbers are connected, as shown in figure 7.12. An impact-test carried out by the Transport and Road Research Laboratory[11] showed that although in an impact there may be severe damage to the front suspension of a car which would render it uncontrollable by a driver, the barrier met the objectives of satisfactory vehicle containment and redirection for the test conditions stipulated by the Transport and Road Research Laboratory. It is considered to be most suitable for those conditions where frequent light collisions occur. In such circumstances its greater cost is justified because it can sustain frequent light impacts with less maintenance costs; its cost is expected to preclude its use, however, where long lengths of safety fence are required.

A wire-rope safety fence has been developed by the Transport and Road Research Laboratory in conjunction with British Ropes Ltd. The barrier consists of two wire ropes of 19 mm diameter, each with a breaking load of 169 kN and arranged in contact with the other, in slots cut into the tops of the steel I-section posts (75 × 37 mm) so that the centre of the lower cable is 635 mm above the level of the central reservation. The posts are a sliding fit in rectangular sockets 460 mm deep

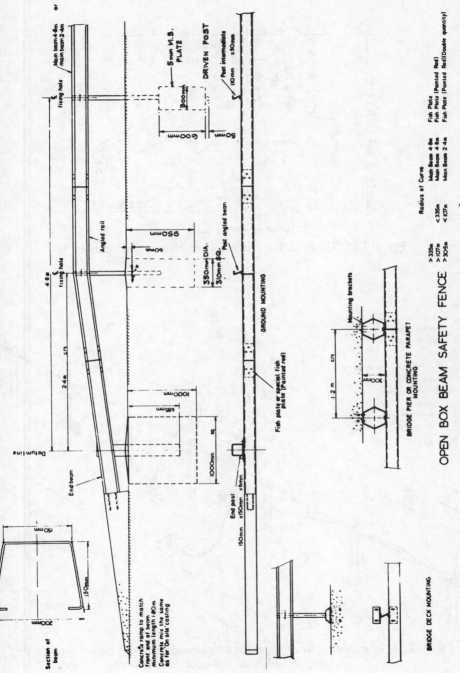

OPEN BOX BEAM SAFETY FENCE

Figure 7.11 The open-box-beam safety fence[9]

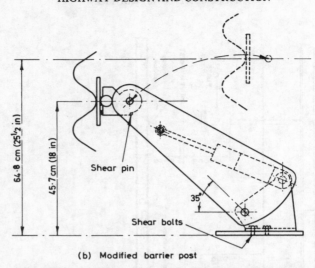

(b) Modified barrier post

Figure 7.12 The modified Christiani and Nielsen crash barrier[11]

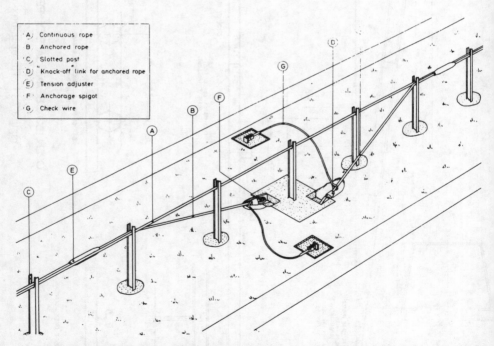

Figure 7.13 Intermediate anchorages for a tensioned wire rope barrier (courtesy of
Transport and Road Research Laboratory)

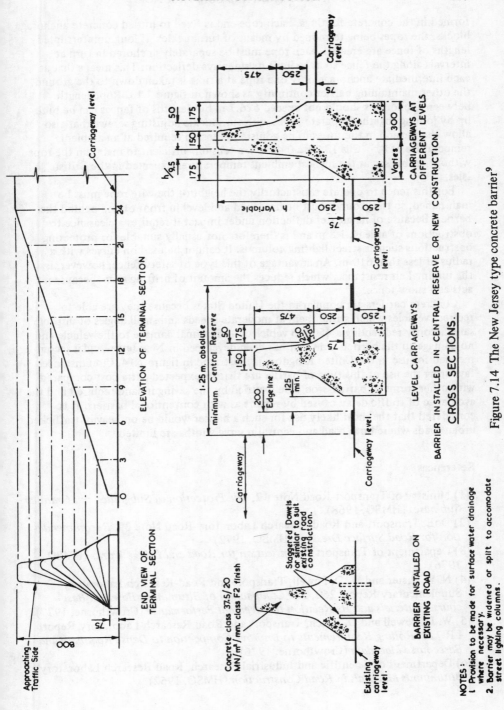

Figure 7.14 The New Jersey type concrete barrier[9]

NOTES:
1. Provision to be made for surface water drainage where necessary.
2. Barrier may be widened or split to accomodate street lighting columns.

ELEVATION OF TERMINAL SECTION

END VIEW OF TERMINAL SECTION

CARRIAGEWAYS AT DIFFERENT LEVELS.

BARRIER INSTALLED IN CENTRAL RESERVE OR NEW CONSTRUCTION.

CROSS SECTIONS.

LEVEL CARRIAGEWAYS

BARRIER INSTALLED ON EXISTING ROAD

Staggered Dowels or similar to suit existing road construction.

Concrete class 37.5/20 MN/m² / mm. class F2 finish

Approaching Traffic Side

formed in the concrete footings. Each rope-end is fixed to buried concrete anchorage blocks, the ropes being tensioned by means of turnbuckles. If long uninterrupted lengths of fence are erected, each rope must be separately anchored in turn at intervals along the fence so as to limit its sideways deflection. This means that at each intermediate anchorage only one rope at a time is taken down to the ground, the other maintaining barrier continuity as shown in figure 7.13. Rope length between anchorages should not exceed 626.7 m but lengths of fences can be built up by joining together separate ropes with turnbuckle adjusting screws that also allow the tension in the ropes to be adjusted. Tension required at an ambient temperature of 8.5 °C is 13.34 ± 0.45 kN, a tension sufficient to maintain the rope without visible sag at the highest ambient temperatures expected in the British Isles.

For this fence to operate satisfactorily the height of the wire rope must be maintained, so the ground must be hardened and level in front of and behind the barrier. Because of its greater deflection under impact it requires a clearance to obstructions of at least 1.8 m and is therefore not usually suitable for protecting obstructions such as street lighting columns. It cannot be used on curves with a radius of less than 610 m. An advantage of this type of safety fence, however, is the minimal air resistance, which reduces the amount of drifting snow because it acts as a snow fence.

Concrete barriers are popular in the United States because they are able to redirect vehicles which strike them at moderate speeds and small angles of impact, satisfactorily redirecting a 4500 lb vehicle with minimal damage to the vehicle and no damage to the barrier. One that has been developed in New Jersey and is recommended for use in the United Kingdom is illustrated in figure 7.14. Circumstances favouring the use of this type of barrier are that its expected extra cost compared with other forms of barrier would be justified by the saving in land required and the avoidance of traffic delay caused by repairs as with conventional barriers. It is considered that the most likely use for such a barrier would be on heavily trafficked urban roads where both road and central reserve widths are limited.

References

(1) Ministry of Transport Road Note 17, *The Protection of Subgrades and Granular Sub-bases* (HMSO, 1968)
(2) DoE, Transport and Road Research Laboratory Road Note 39, *Recommendation for Road Surface Dressing* (HMSO, 1972)
(3) Department of Transport, *Specification for Road and Bridge Works* (HMSO, 1976)
(4) N. W. Lister and W. D. Powell, Transport and Road Research Laboratory Supplementary Report 260, *The Compaction of Bituminous Base and Basecourse Materials and Its Relation to Pavement Performance* (Crowthorne, 1977)
(5) W. D. Powell and D. Leech, Transport and Road Research Laboratory Report LR 727, *Rolling Requirements to Improve Compaction to Dense Roadbase and Basecourse Macadam* (Crowthorne, 1976)
(6) Department of Scientific and Industrial Research, Road Research Laboratory, *Bituminous Materials in Road Construction* (HMSO, 1962)

(7) B. J. Walker and D. Beadle, *Mechanised Construction of Concrete Roads*, Cement and Concrete Association (Slough, 1975)
(8) V. J. Jehu and C. W. Prisk, *Research on Crash Barriers: Their Design, Warrants for Use, Safety Aspects, Testing and Research,* Organisation for Economic Co-operation and Development (Paris, 1967)
(9) Department of Transport, Technical Memorandum No. H9/73, *Safety Fences as Amended September 1975* (London, 1975)
(10) Highway Research Board, 'Highway Guardrail: Determination of Need and Geometric Requirements', *Spec. Rep. Highw. Res. Bd,* no. 81 (1964)
(11) J. B. Laker and G. R. Taylor, Road Research Laboratory Report 246, *Impact Test on a Modified Christiani and Nielsen Crash Barrier* (Crowthorne, 1969)

8

Pavement Maintenance

8.1 Flexible-pavement Strengthening by Overlays

The twentieth century has seen a considerable improvement in the materials and constructional techniques used for highway pavements. This has resulted in a dramatic increase in the life of a pavement from the period when an annual surface dressing was necessary to maintain the shape of the pavement to the present time when design lives of from five to twenty years are common for heavily trafficked highways.

Deterioration under heavy traffic action takes place on all highways, although the rate of deterioration is slow in a well-designed pavement. The highway will normally continue to carry traffic for many years after the termination of the design life and it follows that some form of periodic strengthening must take place.

Road strengthening that remedies a structural fault or deficiency by supplying an additional structural layer to the pavement is dealt with in this section. It should be contrasted with maintenance seeking to correct the problems of road-surface deterioration so as to maintain a given surface quality and preserve a level of service.

The principal objectives of any road-strengthening policy have been defined as (1) a minimisation of expenditure, (2) provision of a suitable level of safety, (3) production of a reasonable level of serviceability normally measured as riding comfort and (4) maximum or adequate load-carrying capacity. There must also be limited disruption to traffic during strengthening, limited disturbance of adjacent land-use and limited noise and air pollution during the strengthening process.

It is difficult to maximise each of these objectives and so any strengthening policy must be a compromise. The consideration given to each of these objectives must depend upon the importance of the road, its location, the anticipated traffic flows and the funds available for strengthening.

Expenditure, safety and serviceability are always important. Most highway authorities have inadequate funds for all their desired projects. Safety is also important: it is usually expressed in terms of skid resistance. Serviceability should maintain adequate levels of riding comfort and minimise vehicle operating costs over the design life of the pavement.

Maximising the load-carrying capacity of a pavement must be contrasted with the need to conserve highway funds and normally the compromise is the use of a standard design life. Most road-strengthening strategies attempt to minimise disruption to traffic by the use of pre-planning, while mechanised road-strengthening methods should not have adverse effects on neighbouring land-uses or contribute to noise or air pollution.

8.2 Assessment of the Need for Strengthening

Because of the need to assess the relative priority of different highways for structural strengthening and also because it is more economical to strengthen while the original pavement still has the ability to function as a structural member an objective measure of structural deficiency is required.

The usual technique used for the non-destructive testing of a pavement is deflection under load. The advantages of using such a simply determined parameter are that (1) in most cases the deflection is proportional to the applied loading, so allowing results obtained under one test condition to be compared with another, (2) it is a good indicator of structural performance and (3) it is an exceedingly simple measurement to make, machines having been developed for the rapid measurement of deflection over considerable lengths of highways.

The disadvantages have been stated to be that (1) deflection may not be related to permanent deformation in the case of a deeply rutted pavement, (2) deflection does not always vary progressively with pavement fatigue and may not give adequate advance warning of when strengthening is required and (3) it is strongly influenced by pavement type, climatic and subgrade conditions.

A considerable number of deflection-measuring devices have been developed and these have been tabulated by country of use.[1] The most frequently used device is the Benkelman beam, followed by bearing plates and the deflectograph.

8.3 The Benkelman Beam

This apparatus was developed in the United States of America by A. C. Benkelman and subsequently played an important part in the WASHO (1952–4) and AASHO (1958–60) Road Tests. The outline arrangement of the beam is shown in figure 8.1, where it can be seen that the deflection of the road surface as a loaded wheel passes over it is measured by the rotation of a long pivoted beam touching the road surface at the point where the deflection is required. Because of the length of the pivoted beam the pivot supports are not influenced by the deflection beneath the loaded wheels.

Norman, Snowdon and Jacobs of the Transport and Road Research Laboratory[2] give the following description of the beam design, which has been evolved at the Laboratory for use in the United Kingdom. 'The aluminium-alloy beam is sufficiently slender to pass between the dual rear wheels of a loading truck. It is 3.66 m in length and is pivoted at a point of 2.44 m from the tip, giving a 1:2 length ratio. The pivot is carried on a frame made of aluminium angle supported by three adjustable feet. The frame also carries, a dial gauge arranged to measure the movement of the free end of the beam.'

The dial gauge used has a 75 mm diameter face, a travel of 25 mm and is calibrated in 0.01 mm graduations. It is reverse-printed to enable it to be read from above using a 45° mirror. For travelling purposes the beam is locked by the rotating handle grip. To minimise sticking at the pivot during recording, vibration of the beam is desirable; this is provided by an electric 'buzzer' mounted on the frame close to the pivot. The battery providing the current is clamped to the rear end of the frame and the system is controlled by a hand switch. To ensure that the dial gauge is operating correctly and the beam is moving freely it is desirable to calibrate the beam before use. A simple calibration rig is supplied by the firms manufacturing the deflection beam.

8.3.1 Measurement Techniques

In general, there are two methods of measuring the deflection, which are illustrated in figure 8.1. An interesting review of these methods is given by the Road Research Group.[1]

In the first method the probe arm of the beam is inserted between the dual tyres to a distance of about $a = 1.37$ m and the initial dial reading is taken (A). The vehicle is then moved slowly forward (at creep speed) until it is at least b (3.05 m) past the tip of the beam. While the vehicle is being moved forward a maximum dial reading is recorded (B) when the dual tyres have slightly passed the beam tip. Twice the difference between the initial reading and the load reading is the 'normal' deflection, equal to $2(B - A)$. Twice the value is used because of the leverage ratio. This is equivalent to the WASHO procedure for 'total deflection'.

In the second method, the probe is inserted between the tyres to a distance of about $a = 0.46$ m, a load reading taken as the wheels passed the probe (B), and a final reading taken with the load out of range of influence (C). Here twice the difference between the two readings is the rebound deflection $= 2(B - C)$.

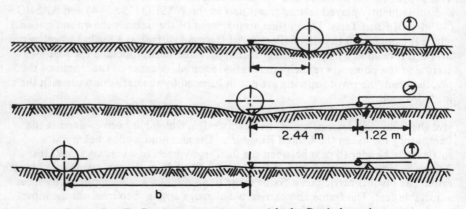

Figure 8.1 Deflection measurement with the Benkelman beam

In many countries, the method for the Benkelman beam test has been standardised in detail, including the dimensions of the apparatus, the reaction load, tyres, tyre pressure, speed and temperature measurement.[3,4,5] The load applied by the dual rear wheels of the lorry is often specified (for example, in the United Kingdom 3.175, Denmark and Finland 4, California 4.09, Japan and the Netherlands 5 and Spain 6.5 tons). There are also many differences between the various procedures. In the United Kingdom, for instance, $a = 1.30$ m and $b = 3.0$ m, the creep speed is defined as the constant speed at which a distance of 4.5 m is covered in 10 ± 1 s. The deflection is sometimes defined as the mean value of 'normal' and 'rebound' $(B - A + B - C)$. In the 'Asphalt Institute' method used by some countries, $a = 0$ m, and $b \geqslant 9.0$ m and the rebound deflection is $2(B - C)$. In France and the Netherlands the deflection of the beam tip is measured by a displacement transducer and recorded as a continuous function of the distance from the wheel load. From the recorded influence line the rebound deflection is measured as the difference between the maximum and the asymptote to the influence line. In Canada and the Netherlands measured rebound deflections are often corrected for support reaction.

Deflection measurements are not usually done in winter or summer but typically in April and October (spring and fall deflections). In most countries the spring rebound deflection is used (but not during the thawing period) and the measured value corrected to a standard temperature (20 °C) by a deflection adjustment factor (f). Sometimes a 'critical period adjustment factor' (c) is reduced to correct measurements not carried out in the most critical period. These factors are particularly related to region and climate.

Usually the representative deflection (d) of the road is calculated as the arithmetical mean of the individual values $(\bar{x})$ augmented by, for example, twice the standard deviation of the deflection values: $d = (\bar{x} + 2\sigma)fc$. In this case 2.3 per cent of the deflections are greater than the design value (97.3 percentile). In California the 80 percentile deflection is used, a value that is exceeded in only 20 per cent of the cases $(\bar{x} + 0.84\sigma)$. Others use $\bar{x} + 1.65\sigma$, where 95 per cent of the deflections have a lower value.

Details of the measuring technique used in the United Kingdom have been given in Norman, Snowdon and Jacobs.[2] The load is applied by means of a two-axle truck with a rear-axle load of 6350 kg (14 000 lb) equally divided between the twin wheel assemblies at each end of the axle, Because the load should not shift during testing, concrete-block loading is preferred and gravel is considered to be undesirable. The tyre size should be 7.50 x 20 or 8.25 x 20, with a zig-zag pattern. The inflation pressure should be 590 kN/m^2 and the spacing between the tyre walls approximately 45 mm.

The truck should be fitted with adjustable pointers carried by the chassis on the nearside and offside in line with the rear wheel tracks and directed towards a point on the road approximately 1.2 m in front of the rear axle. (The design and fixing of these pointers will depend on the type of truck used. They must be adjustable both vertically and horizontally.)

Since deflection is affected by pavement temperature this must be measured at frequent intervals (approximately 30 min) during a survey. The measurement is made at a depth of 40 mm using a suitable short-stem stirring thermometer. A percussion-type masonry drill 6 mm in diameter is used to make a hole to the appropriate depth (about 45 mm to allow for the length of the thermometer bulb), which is filled with glycerol before the thermometer is inserted.

The points at which deflection measurement are required are each marked by a cross on the road surface. Normally the points will be in the nearside and offside wheel-tracks of the road, 1 m and 2.9 m from the nearside verge. A transverse line is drawn on the pavement 1.3 m behind the point of measurement. The truck is positioned parallel with the verge, with its front wheels pointing straight ahead and its rear wheels directly over the line. The transverse positioning is such that when the vehicle is driven forward the gap between the nearside dual rear-wheel assembly will pass over the point of measurement.

With the truck in this initial position the deflection beam in the locked condition is placed with the beam tip over the point of measurement and the beam centrally located between the twin tyres. The alignment is finally adjusted by careful sighting through the tyre gap to ensure that the tyres will not foul the beam when the trunk is driven forward at creep speed. When this alignment is completed the movable pointer is adjusted to be a few millimetres directly above the shoe. Subsequent alignment can then be achieved using the pointer. When the beam is in position the lock is released, and with the vibrator running, the dial-gauge reading is set to zero by rotating the scale. At a signal from the operator the vehicle is driven forward at creep speed to a position where the rear wheels are at least 3 m beyond the test point. The speed should be such that the total time for the movement of 5 m is 10 ± 1 s. The speed should be checked against a stop-watch once or twice each day. The maximum reading of the dial gauge is noted together with the final reading after the rear wheels of the truck have reached a point 3 m from the beam tip. The magnitude of the pavement deflection is obtained by adding the maximum reading to the difference between the maximum and final readings. (The sum of deflection is not measured because of the 2:1 length ratio of the beam arms.)

Two measurements should normally be made at each point tested and the results meaned. When the deflection is greater than 25×10^{-2} mm the readings should not differ by more than 5 per cent. For deflections smaller than 25×10^{-2} mm the difference should not exceed 10 per cent. If larger differences are recorded on the same test point, fouling of the beam by the test wheels should be suspected, or alternatively friction in the beam pivot or the dial gauge. Repeat readings should be taken after attention to these matters until reliable agreement is obtained. If such agreement cannot be obtained the mean of five measurements should be taken and the variability noted.

Differential thermal expansion within the beam can cause significant errors, particularly on stiff pavements. In sunny weather the beam may pass from shade into sunshine as the vehicle moves. The thin metal shield carried by the frame of the beam and covering much of its length helps to reduce this effect.

If measurements are also required in the offside wheel track the procedure is repeated with the beam transferred to the offside rear wheel assembly of the truck.

Before or after the deflection measurements are made the structural condition of the pavement close to the point of measurement is assessed by visual inspection and by the use of a 2 m straight-edge. The latter is placed transversely across each of the wheel-tracks in turn over the points of measurement, and the rut depth is measured by a calibrated wedge or by scale. The extent of any cracking is noted and the condition classified in accordance with Table 8.1.

Table 8.1 Classification of pavement condition[2]

Classification	Visible Evidence
Sound	No cracking. Rutting under 2 m straight-edge less than 10 mm
Critical	(a) No cracking. Rutting between 10 and 20 mm (b) Cracking confined to a single crack in the wheel-tracks, with rutting less than 20 mm
Failed	Cracking extending over the area of the wheel-track and/or rutting greater than 20 mm

Deflection measurements should preferably be made when the road temperature is close to 20 °C; measurements outside the range 10 to 30 °C should be avoided because of the large temperature correction likely to be necessary. In the United Kingdom the spring months, mid-March to June, are preferable for deflection surveys, but as an alternative, measurements can be made in the autumn (September to November).

When particular urgency dictates that measurements must be made during the summer months they should be confined to the very early morning or to cool overcast weather conditions. Similarly, in the winter, any measurements made should be confined to the warmest part of the day and particular care must be taken to avoid freezing conditions. Measurements made during the summer or the winter can only be given an approximate indication of the pavement stiffness.

The spacing of points of measurement depends mainly on the purpose of the survey. To check the uniformity and potential life of an apparently sound length of road a spacing of between 20 and 50 m is recommended. Reflecting road-studs provide convenient reference points. Where the survey is being made in connection with the maintenance programme for a road already showing signs of distress a similar spacing of test points is recommended but a more detailed survey round areas of failure will be necessary.

The following information should be noted relating to the construction.

(1) The type of material below the bituminous upper layers – that is, whether unbound stone, gravel, etc., or whether cemented layers are included.

(2) The thickness and, if possible, the types of bituminous materials present. If this information is not available from reliable records it may be necessary to take cores or excavate trial pits.

(3) A broad classification of the subgrade.

A suitable form for recording deflection measurements is shown in table 8.2. The column for deflection corrected for load is intended for use where the actual test load on the truck wheel is slightly different from the standard 3175 kg. Deflection is adjusted in proportion to the wheel load for loads within the range ±10 per cent of the standard load.

The deflection measured as a loaded wheel passes over the road surface is the summation of the individual deflections in each layer of the pavement and in the foundation. The stiffness of any bituminous layer will change with the temperature

Table 8.2 Suggested form for recording deflection measurements made with the deflection beam[2]

Site & Date	Exact location of test point*	Road Temperature °C	Nearside Wheel Path						Offside Wheel Path					
			Wheel load kg	Deflection x 10^{-2} mm			Rut depth mm	Condition & remarks	Wheel load kg	Deflection x 10^{-2} mm			Rut depth mm	Condition & remarks
				Measured	Corrd to 3175 kg load	Corrd to 20°C				Measured	Corrd to 3175 kg load	Corrd to 20°C		

* Refer to site plan where applicable.

of the binder. Consequently the magnitude of the deflection measured on the surface of the pavement will vary with the temperatures of the constituent bituminous layers.

For routine measurements it is not feasible to measure temperature gradients through the pavement structure and for this reason the simple procedure of classifying temperature in terms of a measurement made at a fixed depth of 40 mm has been adopted. Using the method of defining temperature the change of deflection with temperature has been studied for pavements with a wide range of types and thickness of bituminous base and surfacing. The results are summarised in figures 8.2, 8.3, 8.4 and 8.5 which enable measured deflections at any temperature within the recommended range to be converted to 20°C for most types of pavement construction.

Figure 8.2 is for pavements with less than 135 mm of bituminous material of which less than 75 mm is dense bituminous material. Figure 8.3 also applies to pavements where there is between 135 to 195 mm of bituminous material of which less than 75 mm is dense bituminous material. Figure 8.4 is for pavements with 75 to 195 mm of bituminous material of which at least 75 mm is dense bituminous material. Figure 8.5 is for pavements with 195 to 274 mm of bituminous material. The use of these temperature charts may lead to inaccurate estimates of standard deflection when pavements known to be sited on either very strong or very weak foundations are tested at temperatures close to the extremes of the working range. In such situations a further deflection measurement at another temperature is recommended.

8.4 Travelling Deflectographs

While the deflection beam is a relatively simple piece of apparatus it has the disadvantage that only a very limited length of highway can be surveyed in one working day. In addition, carrying out the test can result in considerable traffic disruption. For these reasons more mechanised methods of measuring deflection have been developed in the form of travelling deflectographs.

One of the earliest of these machines was the California travelling deflectometer, consisting of a truck/semi-trailer unit with two Benkelman beams placed one before each dual rear wheel. Dual-wheel loading is 33 kN, the speed is 1 km/h and the reported length of road that may be measured per day is 3 to 4 km.

A deflectograph operating on similar principles has been constructed by the National Road Laboratory in Denmark. The total length of the truck/semi-trailer is about 15 m. The deflectograph travels at a constant speed of 1.5 km/h whereas the reference frame moves discontinuously. During a measurement the reference frame stands on the road on four wheels and is completely independent of the semi-trailer. Measurements are done in both tracks every 11 m (usually at 39 kN wheel load but 64 kN is possible) and the total influence line is recorded digitally on magnetic tape. A computer program is available which provides output data indicating the deformations, first as maximum deflections and then as radius of curvature. The capacity of the system is about 2000 measurements a day.

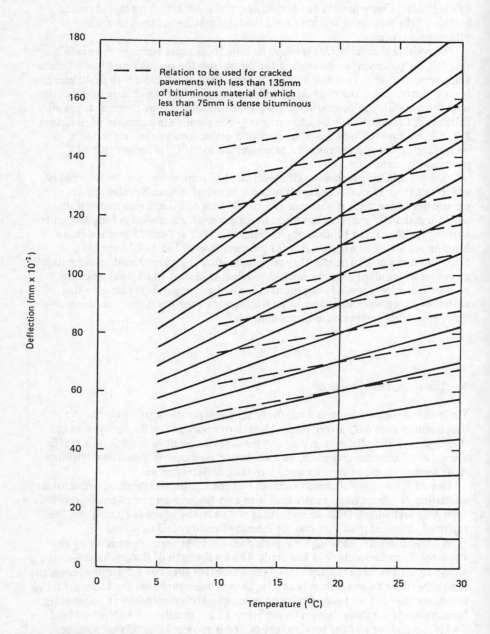

Figure 8.2 Relation between deflection and temperature for pavements with less than 135 mm of bituminous material of which less than 75 mm is dense bituminous material[12]

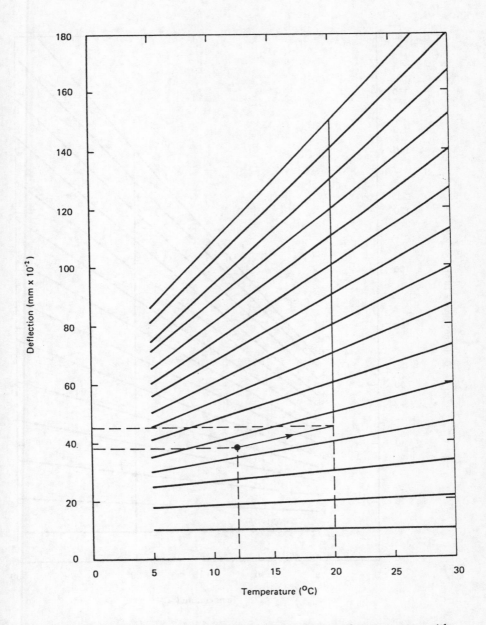

Figure 8.3 Relation between deflection and temperature for pavements with 135–195 mm of bituminous material of which less than 75 mm is dense bituminous material[12]

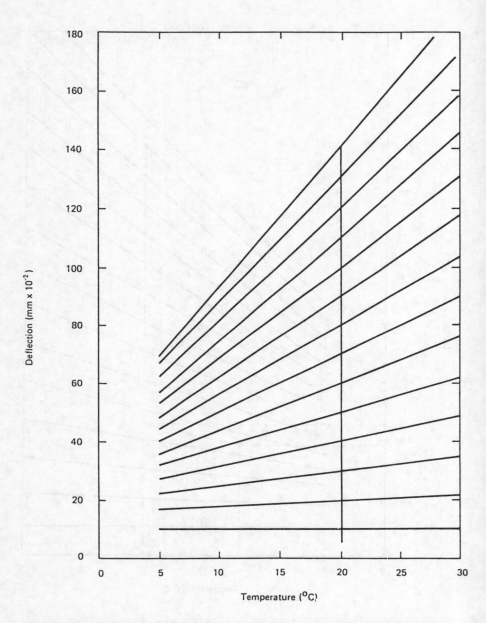

Figure 8.4 Relation between deflection and temperature for pavements with 75–195 mm of bituminous material of which at least 75 mm is dense bituminous material[12]

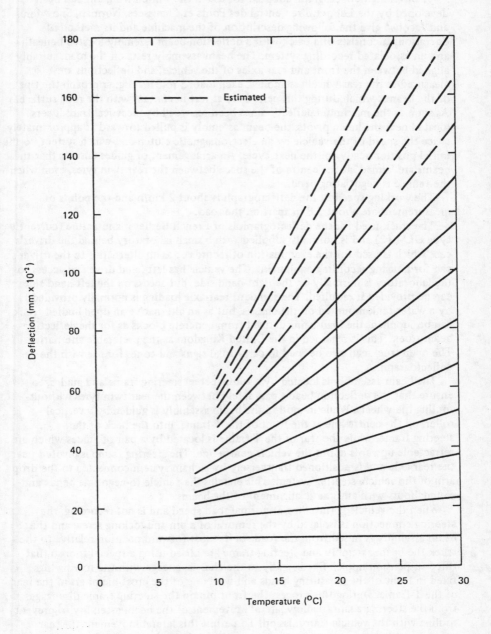

Figure 8.5 Relation between deflection and temperature for pavements with
195–274 mm of bituminous material[12]

A travelling deflectograph adopted for use in the United Kingdom has been developed by the Laboratoire Central des Ponts et Chaussées. Norman, Snowdon and Jacobs[2] give the following description of the machine and its method of operation. It consists of a truck with a deflection-beam assembly located beneath and an associated recording system. The beam assembly rests on the road, suitably aligned between the front and rear axles of the vehicle, and deflections are measured as the rear wheel assemblies, each loaded to 3175 kg, approach the tips of the beams, which during this period are at rest in contact with the road surface. As soon as the maximum deflection has been recorded by electrical transducers located near the beam pivots, the beam assembly is pulled forward at approximately twice the speed of the vehicle by an electromagnetic clutch-and-winch system, to the initial position ready for the next cycle. An arrangement of guides ensures that the beams are 'aimed' at the centre of the space between the rear twin tyres, even when the vehicle is negotiating bends.

The working speed of the deflectograph is about 2 km/h and the points of measurement are about 3.8 m apart on the road.

The truck used for the deflectograph is of French Berliet manufacture (currently type GLM 12) and is normally supplied with a small laboratory behind the driver's cab, which is used for the examination of records or as an alternative to the driver's cab for housing recording equipment. The vehicle has left-hand drive and access to the laboratory is normally on the right-hand side, but access on the left-hand side can be provided if required. The standard rear-axle loading is normally provided by a water tank mounted on the chassis, but as an alternative an open-bodied truck can be supplied, the load being derived from concrete blocks as for the deflection-beam truck. This is regarded in the United Kingdom as the preferable alternative. The open truck can also be used to carry road signs and cones for use with the deflectograph.

The beam assembly is located by a tubular-steel steering frame and guides, to ensure that the deflection beams pass safely between the rear twin tyres without fouling the wheels. While in motion the beam assembly is guided by a vertical roller, on the centre-line at the front of the T-frame, into the neck of the steering frame, while the rear of the T-frame is located by a pair of guides which are retractable upwards about the vehicle centre-line. The steering frame is pivoted near the rear axle and is positioned transversely by a chain system connected to the drop arm of the vehicle steering system. This enables the vehicle to negotiate bends and roundabouts with automatic alignment of the beams.

When the vehicle is travelling at normal road speed and is not recording, the steering connection is isolated by the removal of a pin and locking screw and the beam assembly is raised from the road. In its most forward position relative to the truck the beam assembly and steering frame are raised using a special tool so that three suspension hooks, fixed rigidly to the chassis, engage with the towing lugs fixed in front of the measuring heads and with one of the cross-members at the rear of the T-frame. During this process the front pin on the steering frame disengages from the steering chain to allow lateral movement of the beam assembly to prevent fouling with the vehicle transmission. To permit this lateral movement the rear guides must be retracted upwards. To prevent strain in the beams when the assembly is in the raised position, cables fixed to the chassis are engaged by hooks to the beam tips. A diagrammatic representation of the deflectograph with its principal dimensions is shown in figure 8.6.

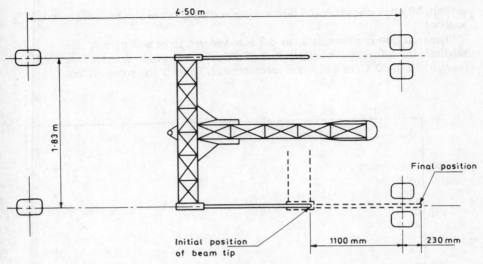

Figure 8.6   Diagrammatic representation of a deflectograph[2]

8.5 Relationship of Deflection-beam and Deflectograph Measurements

A considerable amount of research has been carried out on estimation of pavement life using deflection-beam measurements and yet at the same time the deflectograph is being used for routine investigation of pavement life. It is therefore necessary to correlate the deflection measurements obtained by each method.

The two methods use the same wheel load of 3175 kg. Tyre spacing and contact area, however, differ significantly and in the two methods the measured deflection is influenced in a differing manner by the action of both the front and rear wheels of the truck. When the deflection beam is used the front wheels of the truck have only a small influence because of their distance from the measuring point and the effect of the rear wheels decreases as the truck moves forward. With the deflectograph the beam assembly passes out of the zone of influence of the front wheels and into the zone of influence of the rear wheels as the truck moves forward.

As a result of experimental measurements made by the Transport and Road Research Laboratory the following correlation between the two types of measurement on a wide range of pavement types over the temperature range 10 to 30 °C has been reported.[12]

The correlation between the deflection measured with the Deflectograph and with the Deflection Beam is shown in figure 8.7. This relationship is based on work by the Transport and Research Laboratory[12] derived from experimental work on pavements containing crushed stone, cement-bound and bituminous-bound roadbases constructed on a wide range of subgrade types which had CBR strengths varying from 2.5 to 15 per cent. Pavements with surfacings of rolled asphalt, bitumen macadam and tarmacadam surfacings were also included in the analysis.

The relationship shown in figure 8.7 is considered to be well defined and relatively insensitive to the temperature of the pavement within the recommended range of 10 to 30°C for deflection measurement. There is also some evidence

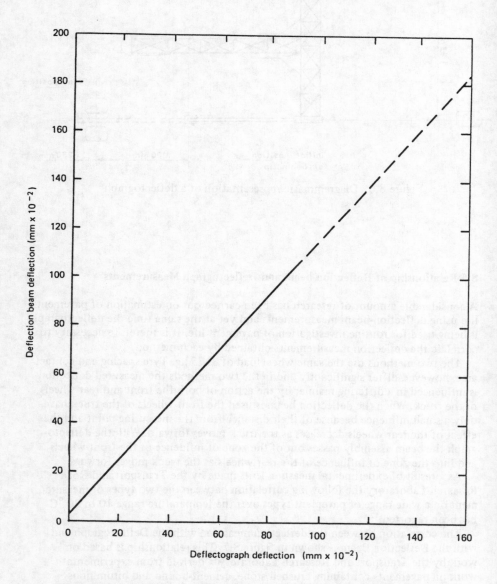

Figure 8.7 Correlation between deflection beam and deflectograph

that at temperatures which are significantly below 10°C the relation is more variable and when the pavement is weak, indicated by the dotted line in figure 8.7, the effect of temperature is more important. The Transport and Road Research laboratory consider that in this area of the relationship it may be desirable for the user to derive site-specific correlation between the two methods of measurement.

8.6 Other Means of Measuring Pavement Deflection

Dynamic deflection of pavements under the action of sinusoidally applied loads has been used as a measure of the structural adequacy of pavements in the United States[6,7] and on the continent of Europe.[8,9,10,11] The load is applied at varying frequency and the resulting deflection is represented by a curve of deflection against frequency of application. The advantages of the method are that measurements can be made with great accuracy and the deflection measurement at any one frequency is the mean value of a considerable number of observations. The disadvantages are that dynamic deflection has not been correlated as extensively with pavement deficiency as has static deflection measurements, and differing pavement types exhibit peak deflections at differing frequencies.

A variety of types of apparatus have found practical application for the measurement of dynamic deflection. The Dynafleet[6,7] is reported to be in common use in Texas and Utah. It consists of a two-wheel trailer on which two eccentrically rotating masses apply a load to the pavement through two 400 mm diameter rigid wheels with a spacing of 500 mm. A dynamic force of 227 N is superimposed on a static load of 725 kg at a constant frequency of 8 Hz. A machine that can make measurements at several frequencies is the Road Rater; the dynamic force which the machine can apply has a maximum value of 454 N and a frequency range of 10 to 60 Hz; the static load is 908 kg.

A heavier machine has been developed by Shell;[8] this has a variable weight with a maximum value of 2000 kg excited by eccentric masses and superimposed on a static weight of over 2000 kg. The load is applied over a circular area of 300 mm with a frequency range of 6 to 80 Hz. Similar apparatus, with a static load of 34.4 kN and a frequency range between 5 and 200 Hz, is used in France, the Federal Republic of Germany, the Netherlands, Sweden and the United States (9) (10 and (11).

Plate bearing tests are also used to determine the vertical deformation of the pavement and also the subgrade. While this form of test will provide the modulus of elastic deformation of the pavement layers in addition to pavement deflection it has the disadvantage that it is not possible to investigate frequent changes in pavement performance because of the length of time required.

A development of static plate tests has been the use of dynamic plate tests in which a falling mass imparts the dynamic load to the plate. This test can measure the energy absorption of the pavement and also the deflection of the pavement under the dynamic load. It has the advantage that it can be quickly carried out, but once again there is only a limited body of knowledge correlating the parameter with pavement strength. The tests are used in Denmark,[12] the Netherlands and Sweden.

The apparatus consists of a mass of 150 kg which falls through a height of 0 to 400 mm and imparts a shock to the pavement. Reported output of the apparatus is 80 measurements per day.

8.7 The Asphalt Institute Method of Overlay Design for Flexible Pavements

The Asphalt Institute method of oveflay design is based on measured pavement deflection under a 4086 kg (9000 lb) wheel load. These deflections are then corrected for pavement temperature and seasonal effects. The recommended adjustment factors to 18 °C (70 °F) are given in figure 8.8. It is recommended that deflection measurements made at the most critical period of the year should not be corrected. When measurements are made at other times of the year it is necessary to use engineering judgement or the results of a deflection measurement programme which spans the whole year.

After deflection, measurements are classified according to pavement conditions such as, on embankment, in cutting, cracked or uncracked pavements. The measured deflections are reduced to a representative deflection equal to the mean plus two standard deviations. This 95 percentile deflection is considered to be closely associated with critical pavement performance and is used with the average daily number of equivalent 8172 kg (18 000 lb) single loads (DTN) to be applied to the pavement during the future life of the pavement to determine the asphaltic concrete overlay pavement using figure 8.9.

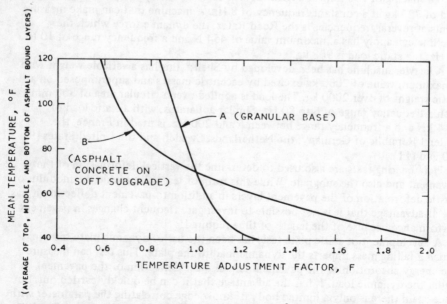

Figure 8.8 Temperature adjustment factors to 70 °F for Benkelman Beam deflections (AASHO Interim Guide for Design of Pavement Structures, 1972)

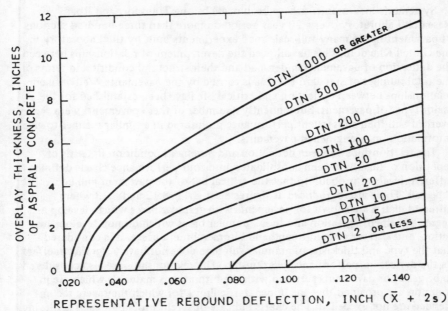

Figure 8.9 Thickness design chart (AASHO Interim Guide for Design of Pavement Structures, 1972)

8.8 The Use of the AASHO Flexible Design Guide for the Design of Flexible Overlays for Rigid Pavements

The AASHO Interim Guide for Flexible Pavements may be used to design a flexible overlay for rigid pavements by subtracting the existing pavement structure thickness required by a new design analysis. The soil support value is determined by a subgrade survey and the existing rigid pavement is given a layer coefficient of 0.3 to 0.4.

8.9 The Transport and Road Research Laboratory Method of Overlay Design for Flexible Pavements[2]

A number of experimental roads in the United Kingdom have been overlaid with asphalt when they have reached a critical condition. The reduction of deflection for various overlay thicknesses has been observed on different types of pavement and the influence of the overlay on subsequent pavement-life studied.

The design procedure is to place an overlay on the existing pavement when it is still capable of carrying the applied traffic loading and thereby to extend load-carrying life. At the critical condition, cracking is confined to a single crack or the crack extends over less than half of the width of the wheel path; rutting is less than 19 mm in depth.

Systematic measurements have been made by the Transport and Road Research Laboratory over a 20 year period on more than three-hundred sections of pavement in the many full-scale road experiments built by the Laboratory in the United Kingdom. This has allowed the development of relationships between the deflection of pavements under load and their structural condition in terms of the total number of standard axle loads carried by the pavements. Well-defined relationships between deflection and critical life have been established for the major types of pavement. Subsequently a number of these pavements were overlaid and their subsequent performance monitored in a similar manner to give information on strengthened pavements.

The relationships between deflection and pavement condition in terms of repetition of load have been consolidated into four performance charts defining different levels of probability that the critical life of the pavement will be achieved. These are reproduced as figures 8.10, 8.11, 8.12 and 8.13 where different charts are shown for pavements with granular bases which develop a degree of cementing action and those granular bases which do not develop this action, and also for cement-bound and bitumen-bound bases. It is considered that the type and thickness of granular sub-base does not have a significant effect on the deflection/performance relationship. The relationships are also considered to be valid for pavements surfaced with the bituminous materials which are in common use provided that the upper traffic limits for which they were recommended are not exceeded. The charts indicate different probabilities of achieving the desired critical life, the choice of probability depending upon the consequence of early failure.

Eight charts for the design of overlays are given in reference 12 for one each of the previously described pavement types for probabilities of 0.5 and 0.9; figure 8.14 shows the overlay design chart for pavements with bituminous roadbases and a probability of reaching the desired life of 0.5. The overlay design charts are for overlays of rolled asphalt materials; dense-coated macadam overlays containing 200 pen or B50 binder require a 30 per cent increase in thickness whilst open-textured macadams require a 100 per cent increase in thickness.

8.10 Concrete Overlays

Most pavement strengthening by the use of overlays is carried out using flexible material, but in some countries, particularly in the United States, considerable lengths of pavement have been overlaid by concrete slabs.

Design procedures have been developed by the United States Corps of Engineers primarily for use on airport runways and taxiways.

The design thickness of the overlay depends upon the degree of bond between the original pavement and the new slab, the structural condition of the old pavement and the type of overlay being used.

Three types of bond are considered in the design procedure as follows.

(1) Fully bonded, where the concrete surface is cleared of all debris and all joint sealant and may be roughened by multi-tool scabbling devices, acid etched, and coated with a bonding agent of sand-cement grout or epoxy mixture.

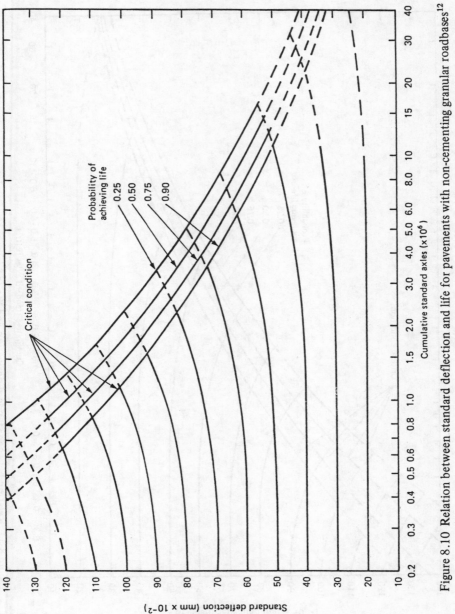

Figure 8.10 Relation between standard deflection and life for pavements with non-cementing granular roadbases[12]

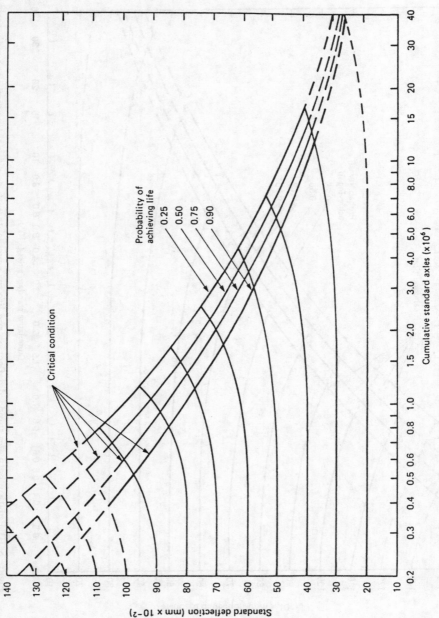

Figure 8.11 Relation between standard deflection and life for pavements with bituminous roadbases[12]

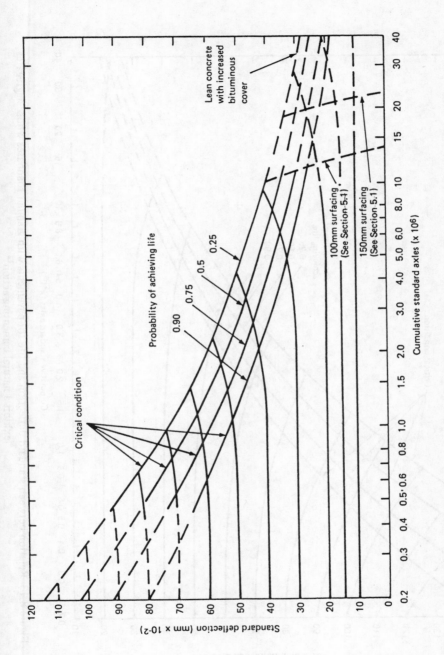

Figure 8.12 Relation between standard deflection and life for pavements with cement-bound roadbases[12]

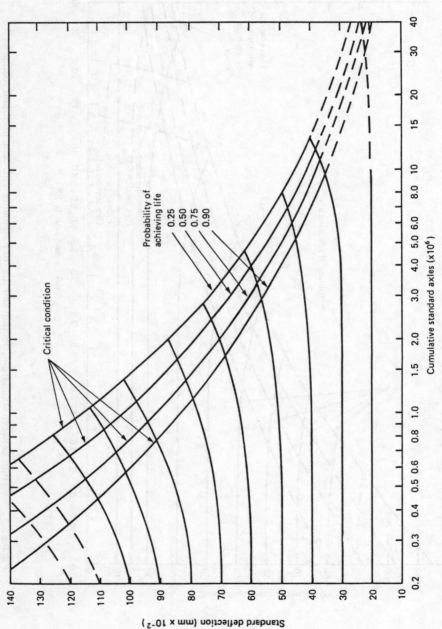

Figure 8.13 Relation between standard deflection and life for pavements with granular roadbases whose aggregates exhibit a natural cementing action[12]

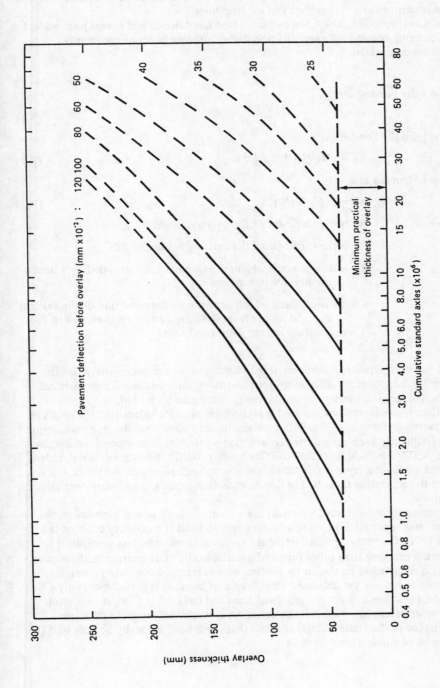

Figure 8.14 Overlay design charts for pavements with bituminous roadbases (0.50 probability)[12]

(2) Partially bonded, where the concrete surface is cleared of debris, excess joint sealant, excess tyre rubber and oil droppings.

(3) Unbonded, where the surface is cleared of debris and excess joint sealant before being covered by a layer of polythene, building paper or commonly bituminous material.

In the fully bonded case

$$h_0 = h_d - h \tag{8.1}$$

In the partially bonded case

$$h_0 = 1.4\sqrt{(h_d^{1.4} - C_h^{1.4})} \tag{8.2}$$

In the unbonded case

$$h_0 = \sqrt{(h_d^2 - C_h^2)} \tag{8.3}$$

where h_0 is the thickness of the overlaying slab,

h is the thickness of the existing pavement slab,

h_d is the thickness of a new pavement as determined by a design method for new pavements,

C_h is a coefficient which depends on the condition of the existing slab and ranges from 0.35 for a badly cracked slab to 1.0 for slabs in very good condition.

It has been reported[1] that concrete overslabs have been successfully laid in unreinforced, conventionally reinforced and steel-fibre reinforced construction. Unjointed, continuously reinforced overlays have also been used.

When jointed overslabs are used it is common practice to position the joints in the overslabs over old joints. With partially bonded construction, expansion joints have frequently been placed over contraction joints, but in new construction the same joint types must be placed over each other. Where the overslab is unbonded and the separating layer is substantial there is no need to match the joints, but where the separating layer is thin then contraction joints are necessary over all joint locations.

Continuously reinforced overslabs are a comparatively recent innovation, the oldest ones reported as being constructed in 1960 and the majority constructed since 1970. Correctly designed overslabs are considered to be less susceptible to reflection cracking than other forms of overslabs. The crack pattern in these pavements is reported to be similar to continuously reinforced concrete pavements. Experience has not yet indicated what degree of bonding is preferable. Many CRCP overslabs are thinner than conventional slabs and have 0.6 to 0.8 per cent steel.

A more recent innovation is the use of fibre-reinforced concrete overslabs. Experience in the United States suggests that these need normally be only half the thickness of conventional ones.

8.11 Surface Dressing

Surface dressing of highways is a low-cost and relatively simple form of maintenance treatment, with a life of at least 5 years. While the process is familiar to many highway engineers, careful planning is necessary and adequate supervision must be given if a satisfactory result is to be obtained.

The benefits of surface dressing are, firstly, that it seals the road surface against the entry of water, which would result in disintegration of the pavement itself and weakening of the subsoil, and, secondly, that it increases the skidding resistance of the pavement when a suitable chipping is used.

An added advantage of surface dressing is that when a light-coloured aggregate is used an improvement in light reflecting properties with road lighting is obtained.

Surface dressing is also used to form a waterproof layer over the subgrade and sub-base during the construction of the pavement.

Road Note 39[13] gives recommendations for surface dressing in the United Kingdom and states that the following factors should be considered in the design.

(1) The nature of road surfaces.
(2) The intensity of traffic.
(3) The type and condition of the stone.
(4) The quantity of binder to be used.
(5) The properties of the binder.

This Road Note identifies the following steps in the design of a surface dressing.

(1) Determine the appropriate traffic category for each lane of the pavement to be surface-dressed.
(2) Assess the hardness of the existing road surface for each lane.
(3) Choose the aggregate type and size for each lane.
(4) Consider the seasonal and weather conditions that are likely to occur.
(5) Select the binder type for the above conditions.
(6) Choose the correct binder viscosity grade.
(7) Select the rate of spread of binder.
(8) Plan traffic control measures.

These factors will now be considered in greater detail.

8.11.1 Traffic Intensity

Intensity of traffic is a major factor causing chippings to become embedded into the road surface. The measure of intensity is the number of commercial vehicles per day per lane, a commercial vehicle being defined as one having an unloaded weight greater than 1.5 tonnes unladen. Five categories of traffic are used in Road Note 39; over 2000, 1000 to 2000, 200 to 1000, 20 to 200 and less than 20 commercial vehicles per day per lane. The size of chippings used increases with traffic intensity, all other things being equal. The range of chipping sizes used for normal highway maintenance varies from 20 to 6 mm nominal size. The largest chippings are required when it is necessary to maintain large-scale surface roughness in heavily trafficked lanes. Smaller nominal-size chippings are specified with lighter traffic loads or high-speed highways.

8.11.2 The Existing Road Surface

A second important factor which influences the size of chipping to be used is the nature of the existing road surface. If the surface is very hard then the chippings are not likely to be embedded by traffic to the same extent as when the road surface is soft because of excessive binder.

Road Note 39 divides road surfaces into the following categories. (1) Very hard: the surface is concrete or dry-stone bituminous and there will be negligible penetration of chippings. (2) Hard surfaces which contain some hard bituminous mortar into which chippings will penetrate only slightly. (3) Normal surfaces into which chippings penetrate moderately under medium and heavy traffic. (4) Soft surfaces, with considerable penetration under heavy and medium traffic. (5) Very soft surfaces into which even the largest chipping will be submerged under heavy traffic.

8.11.3 Aggregate Type and Size

The nominal size of chippings employed for surface dressing in the United Kingdom depends upon the traffic intensity and the type of surface as both these factors influence the penetration of chippings into the road surface.

The recommended nominal sizes of chippings as given in Road Note 39 are reproduced in table 8.3.

Chipping grading and shape is specified by BS 63.[14] The nominal sizes of the aggregate must be one of the sizes given in BS 63 and the grading limits must fall within the specified limits. Particle shape is important for single-size roadstones and this is determined by the flakiness index of both the specified-size particles and the oversize particles.

The method of determining the flakiness index is based on the classification of an aggregate particle as flaky when the particle has a thickness (the smallest dimension) of less than 0.6 of its nominal size. The flakiness index of an aggregate sample is found by separating the flaky particles and expressing their mass as a percentage of the mass of the sample tested. The test is not applicable to material passing a 6.30 mm BS test sieve or retained on a 63.0 mm BS test sieve. The test is described in detail in BS 812, Part 1,[15] and consists of sieving the chipping particles into aggregate-size fractions and separating the flaky particles by passing them through a special slotted gauge or through special sieves.

Table 8.3 Recommended nominal size of chippings (mm)[13]

Type of surface	Lane Traffic Category				
	Approximate number of commercial vehicles currently carried per day in the lane under consideration				
	(1) Over 2000	*(2)* 1000–2000	*(3)* 200–1000	*(4)* 20–200	*(5)* Less than 20
Very hard	(10)	10	6	6	6
Hard	14	14	10	6	6
Normal	20†	14	14	10	6
Soft	*	20†	14	14	10
Very soft	*	*	20†	14	10

Note:

The size of chipping specified is related to the mid-point of lane traffic category ranges 2–5: lighter traffic conditions may make the next smaller size of stone more appropriate.

† At the discretion of the Engineer, 20mm chippings may be used for remedial treatment where traffic speeds are low. Very particular care should be taken when using 20mm chippings to ensure that no loose chippings remain on the surface when the road is opened to unrestricted traffic as there is a high risk of windscreen breakage.

* Unsuitable for surface dressing.

It is important that the chippings should be dry and free from dust when applied to the road surface. If the chippings are likely to be damp, or the weather is unsettled so that rainfall is likely upon new surface dressing, then an adhesion agent should preferably be mixed with the binder to improve the 'wetting' qualities.

When surface dressing is provided to improve the skidding resistance of a pavement it is important that the polished stone value (PSV) as determined by BS 812[15] has a suitable value.

Guidance on the choice of PSVs is given by Department of Transport in Technical Memorandum H16/76.[16] The required PSV depends upon the site conditions: there are four categories of site ranging from difficult sites to easy sites.

Difficult (A1) sites include traffic-signal approaches with 85 percentile speeds greater than 64 km/h (40 mile/h), and approaches to traffic signals, pedestrian crossings and similar hazards on main urban roads. Less than 0.1 per cent of roads in England fall into this category.

Difficult (A2) sites include certain types of priority junctions, roundabouts and their approaches, certain bends and steep gradients. Less than 4 per cent of all English roads fall into this group.

Average (B) sites are generally straight sections or large-radius curves on motorways, trunk and principal roads, and on other roads carrying more than 250 commercial vehicles per lane per day. Less than 15 per cent of all English roads are in this group.

Table 8.4 Categories of sites and minimum PSVs for flexible roads[16]

Site	Approximate Percentage of All Roads in England	Definition	Minimum Polished Stone Value	Remarks
A1 (difficult)	Less than 0.1%	(i) Approaches to traffic signals on roads with 85%ile speed of traffic greater than 40 mile/h (64 km/h) (ii) Approaches to traffic signals, pedestrian crossings and similar hazards on main urban roads	Less than 250 cv/lane/day : 60 250 to 1000 cv/lane/day: 65 1000 to 1750 cv/lane/day : 70 More than 1750 cv/lane/day : 75	Risk rating 6 Values include +5 units for braking/turning
A2 (difficult)	Less than 4%	(i) Approaches to and across major priority junctions on roads carrying more than 250 commercial vehicles per lane per day* (ii) Roundabouts and their approaches (iii) Bends with radius less than 150 m on roads with an 85%ile speed of traffic greater than 40 mile/h (64 km/h) (iv) Gradients of 5% or steeper, longer than 100 m	Less than 1750 cv/lane/day : 60 1750 to 2500 cv/lane/day: 65 2500 to 3250 cv/lane/day : 70 More than 3250 cv/lane/day : 75	Risk rating 4 Values include +5 units for braking/turning

			Risk rating 2
B (average)	Less than 15%	Generally straight sections of and large radius curves on (i) Motorways (ii) Trunk and principal roads (iii) Other roads carrying more than 250 commercial vehicles per lane per day	Less than 1750 cv/lane/day : 55 1750 to 4000 cv/lane/day : 60 More than 4000 cv/lane/day : 65
C (easy)	Less than 81%	(i) Generally straight sections of lightly trafficked roads i.e. less than 250 cv/day (ii) Other roads where wet skidding accidents are unlikely to be a problem	45 — No risk rating applied. Many local aggregates have a PSV well above 45 and normally these should be used

Note: Values should be amended where abnormal risks occur due to substandard geometric design.

* In (i) the 250 cv/lane/day applies to each approach

Finally, easy (C) sites are generally straight sections of lightly trafficked roads and other roads where wet-skidding accidents are unlikely to be a problem. Less than 81 per cent of all English roads are in this group.

For the A1 and A2 sites the minimum PSV varies according to the flow of commercial vehicle lane from a value of 75 to 60. For type B sites the required PSV value varies from 65 to 55, while for type C sites local aggregates normally having a PSV greater than 45 are required.

Complete details of required minimum PSV are given in table 8.4, which is based on Department of Transport Technical Memorandum H16/76.

8.11.4 Binder Type and Quantity

The binders used for surface dressing are normally road tar as specified in BS 76, cut-back bitumen as specified in BS 3690, bitumen emulsions as specified in BS 434, or tar—bitumen blends as specified in Technical Memorandum H10/72.[1][7]

In special circumstances cut-back bitumens incorporating natural rubber may be used. Other binders for use in difficult conditions are tar binders, modified by the addition of polymeric material — these binders are proprietary materials.

The choice of viscosity of the binder used for surface dressing depends upon the traffic intensity and also the period of the year when the surface dressing is carried out. Generally, higher-viscosity binders are used with high traffic intensities. There is the problem that it is not possible to obtain good adhesion between an uncoated chipping and a high-viscosity binder, and for this reason it is recommended in Road Note 39 that tars of viscosity grade A42 or higher, or 200 cut-back bitumen, should not be used with uncoated chippings if the air temperature during application is likely to fall below 18 °C for tar or 15 °C for cut-back bitumen. When temperatures fall below these levels traffic is likely to dislodge the stone, and it is recommended that in these circumstances coated chippings are used to secure instant adhesion.

Recommended binder viscosities for the United Kingdom are given in Road Note 39 in terms of lane traffic intensity, the time of year when the surface dressing is to be carried out, and the type of binder, road tar, cut-back bitumen and tar—bitumen blends. These values are given in table 8.5.

Table 8.5 Recommended binder viscosities[1][2]

| Lane Traffic Category | Period of the year | Viscosity grade | | |
		Road tar (BS 76 Table 1)	Cut-back bitumen (BS 3690 Table 2)	Tar-bitumen blends
1	Mid-May to Mid-July	A46	—	—
2		A46	200secs (rubberised)	200secs*
3, 4 or 5	April, May, Sept.	A34 or A38	50 or 100secs	100secs
	June, July, August	A38 or A42	1100 or 200secs	200secs

* At the discretion of the Engineer.

Having determined the viscosity of the binder it is important to spread the binder to the correct film thickness. The factors which determine the rate of spread of binder are (1) chipping size and shape, (2) the nature of the road surface and (3) the intensity of the traffic. Generally a decrease in traffic intensity results in an increase in the rate of binder speed, as does an increase in the nominal size of the chipping. The harder the road surface the less will be the penetration of chippings and the greater the thickness of binder film required. Recommended rates of spread of binder, given in Road Note 39, are given in table 8.6.

8.11.5 Application of Binder and Chippings

Before the binder is applied to the road surface and the chippings spread it is important that the surface should be prepared by strengthening any weak areas and filling in depressions that might impair the riding quality of the road. Normally repairs to the road surface are carried out by patching with coated macadam, this preferably being done in the season prior to surface dressing. The whole of the road surface should present similar binder absorption properties; patched areas should therefore receive a pre-surface dressing with small chippings. If the surface still appears porous a seal of cement slurry should be applied to the patched areas.

Road surfaces should be swept clean of all loose material before work is commenced and should if possible be dry. All reflecting studs should be masked, and ironwork covered with heavy oil or grease before the binder is sprayed.

When the binder film is applied it is essential that it has a uniform thickness, this being most easily achieved by the use of a mechanical binder distributor. This type of equipment is specified in BS 1707,[18] which gives detailed requirements for the tanks containing the binder, temperature indicators, an accurate road-speed indicator, and the construction and operation of the spray-bar and jets through which the binder is directed on to the road surface.

From the point of view of the highway engineer it is important that the rate of spread of binder film is uniform, and the Depot Tray Test specified in Appendix A of BS 1707 is normally used to check the uniformity of spread at the beginning of the surface-dressing season.

In this test it is necessary for

(1) the conditions prevailing during the test to be comparable with those occurring during normal operation as regards
   (a) binder temperature,
   (b) binder viscosity,
   (c) height of distribution gear above the test surface,
   (d) pressure in the distribution system,
   (e) speed of operation of mechanical distributing gear (when applicable);
(2) the test surface to be divided into strips of equal width, usually 50 mm, the length of the strips being parallel to the direction of travel of the distributor;
(3) the test to be so arranged that the distributor can operate for a sufficient period to obtain normal working conditions, and when this has been achieved the test surface is exposed to the discharge for a suitable period;
(4) the amount of binder delivered on each 50 mm strip is then measured and

Table 8.6 Target rates of spread of binder at spraying temperature (litre/m²); rates of spread of binder actually supplied should not vary by more than ±10 per cent of the target figure[1 2]

CRUSHED ROCK OR SLAG CHIPPINGS
Road Tar Binder

| Type of Surface | Lane Traffic Category (See Table 1) | | | | | | | | | |
| | 1 | | 2 | | 3 | | 4 | | 5 | |
	Chipping Size (mm)	Binder Rate (litre/m²)	Chipping Size (mm)	Binder Rate (litre/m²)	Chipping Size (mm)	Binder Rate (litre/m²)	Chipping Size (mm)	Binder Rate (litre/m²)	Chipping Size (mm)	Binder Rate (litre/m²)
Very Hard	—	—	10	1·4	6	1·2	6	1·4	6	1·5
Hard	14	1·2	14	1·4	10	1·2	6	1·2	6	1·3
Normal	20‡	1·2	14	1·3	14	1·2	10	1·2	6	1·2
Soft	Conditions not suitable for surface dressing		20‡	1·2	14	1·1	14	1·2	10	1·2
Very Soft					20‡	1·1	14	1·1	10	1·1

Cut-back bitumen binder

| Type of Surface | Lane Traffic Category (See Table 1) | | | | | | | | | |
| | 1 | | 2 | | 3 | | 4 | | 5 | |
	Chipping Size (mm)	Binder Rate (litre/m²)	Chipping Size (mm)	Binder Rate (litre/m²)	Chipping Size (mm)	Binder Rate (litre/m²)	Chipping Size (mm)	Binder Rate (litre/m²)	Chipping Size (mm)	Binder Rate (litre/m²)
Very Hard	Not recommended		10	1·0*	6	1·0	6	1·1	6	1·2
Hard			14	1·1†	10	1·0	6	1·0	6	1·0
Normal	(See para 7.1 p. 11)		14	1·0†	14	1·0	10	1·0	6	1·0
Soft	Conditions not suitable for surface dressing		20‡	—	14	0·9	14	1·0	10	1·0
Very Soft					20‡	0·9	14	0·9	10	0·8

Tar-bitumen binder

| Type of Surface | Lane Traffic Category (See Table 1) | | | | | | | | | |
| | 1 | | 2 | | 3 | | 4 | | 5 | |
	Chipping Size (mm)	Binder Rate (litre/m²)	Chipping Size (mm)	Binder Rate (litre/m²)	Chipping Size (mm)	Binder Rate (litre/m²)	Chipping Size (mm)	Binder Rate (litre/m²)	Chipping Size (mm)	Binder Rate (litre/m²)
Very Hard	Not recommended		10	1·2	6	1·1	6	1·2	6	1·4
Hard			14	1·2	10	1·1	6	1·1	6	1·2
Normal	(See para 7.1 p. 11)		14	1·1	14	1·1	10	1·1	6	1·1
Soft	Conditions not suitable for surface dressing		20‡	1·1	14	1·0	14	1·1	10	1·1
Very soft					20‡	1·0	14	1·0	10	1·0

* Rubberised cut-back bitumen only is recommended.
† Evidence is being sought for successful use of bitumen in these categories.
‡ At the discretion of the Engineer, 20mm chippings may be used for remedial treatment where traffic speeds are low.
Note: Crushed gravel may be used at the discretion of the Engineer for Traffic Categories 4 and 5 only. When gravel is used target rates of spread of binder should be **increased** by 10 per cent.

the results expressed as a percentage deviation from the mean for all the 50 mm units over the effective width.

8.11.6 Depot Tray Test

This apparatus consists of a wheeled trolley containing a set of removable containers. Each container is 50 mm wide, 1000 mm long and 150 mm deep and of approximately 7 litres capacity. These containers extend to a width 150 mm greater than the full spray width of the distributor; there are six containers per 300 mm of spray. The rim of each container is lipped on one side to overlap the next container and so prevent binder escaping.

The trolley runs on steel rails fastened to the top of a 1500 litre catch tank, the rails being horizontal and parallel to the sides of the tank. The rails are long enough for the trolley to lie clear of the spray before the test while the binder distributor is backed over the catch tank. After a short preliminary spray the trolley and containers are pushed beneath the spray hood and spraying recommenced until the containers are almost full. The trolley is withdrawn and the contents of each container measured by dipping with a steel rule graduated in millimetres. Each container is dipped in the same position, about 300 mm from one end, after all the froth has disappeared.

Having determined the depth of material in each container the mean depth over the effective width is determined and also the deviation from the mean. The compliance with the following requirements is then noted.

(1) The amount of binder collected on any strip surface 50 mm wide within the effective width, the length of the strip being parallel to the direction of travel of the distributor, shall not differ from the average amount over the effective width by more than 15 per cent. Furthermore, the mean of the amount collected in any four adjacent trays within the effective width shall not differ from the average over the effective width by more than 10 per cent. The effective width shall be the whole sprayed width less 150 mm at each side.

(2) The amount of binder received on the 150 mm margin at either side of the effective width of the spray shall not be less than 50 per cent or more than 100 per cent of the mean amount per 150 mm of the effective sprayed width.

When the distributor is used for surface dressing it is also important to ensure that the actual rate of spread is within ±10 per cent of the specified rate of spread for any single run of the distributor.

A method of determining the actual rate of spread achieved is to drive the distributor on to a level stretch of road and determine the contents by dipping; the position of the wheels are then marked by chalk. After 500 to 800 m^2 of pavement have been covered by binder the distributor is once again placed over the chalk marks and dipped.

An alternative method of determining the rate of spread that allows the distribution of the rate of spread over the road surface to be found uses metal trays approximately 200 mm by 200 mm by 5 mm deep, which are placed on the road surface in the path of the binder distributor.

The trays are weighed and numbered before being placed on the road surface; after the passage of the binder distributor the trays are wrapped in weighed sheets of paper and reweighed. A balance accurate to 0.1 g is necessary and if this is available at the surface-dressing site then the rate of speed can be determined very quickly.

When spraying is in progress it is important for the binder to be at the correct temperature because the rate of speed will vary with the temperature. Recommended spraying temperatures for different binder viscosities are given in Road Note 39 for differing binder types, and for best results the temperature should not fall by more than 15 °C during work.

Particular care needs to be taken when the binder film is sprayed onto the road surface where strips of binder abut. If the spray-bar on the binder distributor gives a diminished rate of spread at the edges of the strip then the strips should be overlapped by 150 mm. This means that a 150 mm strip should not be covered with chippings until it has been double sprayed. Other spray-bars give a full rate of spread to the edge of the strip and in this case particular care has to be taken to butt the strips as accurately as possible.

Chippings should be applied uniformly as soon as possible after the spraying of the binder. Metering devices attached to lorries or specially designed metering spreaders are frequently preferred. Any areas missed by the chippings are handchipped and any surplus removed by brushing.

Good contact between chippings and binder is ensured by rolling. Rubber-tyred rollers are best for ensuring adhesion as they knead the chippings into place. If a steel-wheeled roller is used a minimum number of passes should be used or crushing of the chippings will take place; in any case the maximum weight of a steel-wheeled roller is recommended as 8 tonnes.

Once surface dressing has been completed it is frequently necessary to allow traffic to run over it immediately. Vehicle speeds should be kept down to 30 km/h (20 mph) for approximately 15 to 20 min until adequate adhesion has been obtained. Any loose chippings should then be swept up before the road is open to unrestricted traffic.

8.12 Surface Dressing on Motorways and Other Heavily Trafficked High-speed Roads

The type and size of aggregate for surface dressing of these types of road are detailed in section 8.7. Selection of aggregate size is determined, as with other road types, by the weight of traffic and the road surface condition. For roads carrying high-speed traffic the size of the chipping should not exceed 14 mm because of the danger of broken windscreens. Where the traffic lanes carry only passenger cars a maximum chipping size of 10 mm is preferred.

For lane-traffic category-1 roads it is recommended in Road Note 39 that the binder should be road tar because, in the event of the chippings becoming embedded by traffic action, the binder will wear very rapidly and expose the aggregate. For lane-traffic category-2 roads either road tar or cut-back bitumen modified by the addition of rubber should be used. Tar bitumen blends may also be employed if preferred by the engineer.

A high-viscosity binder is necessary if the chippings are to resist displacement under heavy or high-speed traffic conditions. An S46 tar, a 200 s rubberised cutback bitumen or a tar bitumen blend is suitable. The rate of spread of binder is as specified in section 8.11.5.

For the surface dressing of roads of these types very careful control of work is necessary followed by control of traffic during the early stages of the trafficking. After completion of the surface dressing traffic should be restricted to a speed of 20 km/h (13 mph) for a period of not less than 20 min. This is followed by sweeping to remove any loose chippings before the road is opened to unrestricted traffic. Further sweeping may be necessary on subsequent days and if high temperature conditions occur then stone-dust or sand must be spread on to the road surface.

Because of the use of high-viscosity binders, surface dressing of these road types should be confined to the period mid-May to mid-July. If work is carried out after mid-July there is the possibility of the chippings not being properly embedded and subsequently becoming loose during the winter months.

8.13 Surface Dressing Using Calcined Bauxite and Other Artificial Polish-resistant Roadstones

There are few roadstones available that will maintain the required coefficient of friction (SFC) throughout the year under the polishing action of heavy traffic. It has emerged, however, that certain grades of bauxite heated to a temperature of 1600 °C and normally sold as an aggregate for refractory firebricks have a PSV higher than that of any natural roadstone yet tested. It is very expensive, however, and supplies are limited.

Calcined bauxite was first used in the United Kingdom adjacent to the original laboratory at Harmondsworth on the A4 Colnbrook by-pass. Areas of surface dressing were put down on this road using epoxy resin as the binder and various 1 to 3 mm grits as the aggregate.

Twelve aggregates were compared: six of them were natural roadstones and six were artificial expensive grits. One of the artificial aggregates was Demerara bauxite it was only one-quarter of the price of corundum and was found to be superior to the best natural aggregates.

Further evidence of the value of calcined bauxite was obtained on the A30 at Blackbushe, where the performance of a number of roadstones in bituminous surfacing mixtures and in tar and bitumen surface dressing was investigated. Once again calcined bauxite was proved to give superior skid resistance.

It is well known that the Greater London Council uses calcined bauxite/epoxy resin surface dressings. They have resulted in a significant reduction in personal-injury accidents at a number of London sites selected because of bad accident records.

The Shell-grip binder commonly used in this type of work is a two-component bitumen-extended epoxy resin compound. Equal parts of the two components are thoroughly mixed together and spread or sprayed on the road surface by machine at a minimum rate of 1.35 kg/m^2. The binder is then covered with an excess of small calcined bauxite chippings of 1 to 3 mm and the treatment allowed to cure.

After curing, which takes from 1 to 5 h (depending on ambient temperature), the excess aggregate is removed and the road opened to traffic.

To apply the two-component binder a special machine is required that will heat the components separately, proportion them accurately, mix them thoroughly and spray the mixture uniformily on to the road surface.

8.14 Wet-road Skidding and Accidents

Each year in the United Kingdom alone, approximately a quarter of a million highway traffic accidents involving death or injury are reported. In addition, an unknown amount of accidents involving damage take place.

Investigations carried out by the Transport and Road Research Laboratory accident investigation team[19] have shown the following main contributory causes in a group of 1164 accidents: 461 concerned road layout, visibility of junctions, adequacy of road signs and markings, weather conditions and road surface; 283 concerned the vehicle, its design and maintenance, 2218 concerned the drivers' skill, judgement, perception and fitness and also the pedestrian. This investigation showed that road factors were contributory in 27 per cent of accidents but also that the sequence of events could have been broken by a change in engineering design. Skidding in wet road conditions was one of these factors and improvements in wet-road skidding performance are one of the ways in which the chain of events can be interrupted.

Wet-road skidding accidents are of particular concern to the highway engineer because of the variability of coefficients of friction and the frequent inability of drivers to judge stopping distances under these conditions.

8.14.1 Measurement of Skidding Resistance

A great variety of test vehicles have been designed for the measurement of the skidding resistance between tyres and road surface. Any machine used for this purpose must give reliable and consistent results and the results must be capable of interpretation in relation to skidding accident risk on the highway.

In the United Kingdom the Road Research Laboratory have developed four major methods of measuring skid resistance. These techniques will now be described in detail.

8.14.2 The Sideway-force Test

In the Sideway-force test a freely rotating wheel is inclined to its direction of motion so that the wheel side-slips over the road surface. The angle of inclination of the wheel and the characteristics of the tyre affect the frictional resistance developed. If the tyre is standardised and the angle of inclination changed then a graph of the form shown in figure 8.15 is obtained.

It can be seen that even on a dry road when the coefficient of friction is high the maximum frictional resistance is reached when the angle of inclination is 20°. Initially a sideway-force testing machine was developed by the Road Research

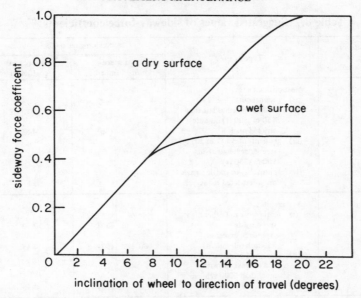

Figure 8.15 Variation of sideway-force coefficient with wheel angle

Laboratory using a motorcycle and a sidecar in which the wheel of the sidecar could be set at an angle to the direction of motion. Currently BMC 1800 saloons are being used in which a 3.00 x 20 tyre with a smooth tread is mounted within the wheelbase and inclined at an angle of 20° to the direction of travel when on test. The sideway force and also the load on the wheel are measured and recorded; the sideway-force coefficient is simply the former divided by the latter. The test is carried out on wet road surfaces, a tanker watering the road beforehand. Tests can be carried out at speeds up to 80 km/h (50 mph) or at higher speeds under more favourable conditions. The advantages of this method are considered to be

(1) past experience of the method's success,

(2) the ease with which tests can be made on roads in which short sections of experimental surfacing varying in composition are laid end to end.

(3) the ease with which difficult places such as bends, corners and rounda-bouts can be tested,

(4) the success which has been achieved in correlating the test results with the risk of skidding accidents,

(5) the considerable background of knowledge and experience built up over the many years the method has been in use.

The Road Research Laboratory has also developed a Sideway-force Coefficient Routine Investigation Machine (SCRIM), which is suitable for use on both urban and rural roads and is expected to assist in keeping a check on the skidding resistance of the whole highway network. The vehicle is a truck and beneath it, but within the wheelbase, is measuring apparatus basically similar to that of the sideway-force test-cars. The essential difference is that digital recording is used to give a direct

Table 8.7 Suggested values of sideway-force coefficients[26]

Category of site	Type of site	Skidding resistance		Sideway force coefficient
		Test speed km/h	(mile/h)	
A	Most difficult sites: (i) roundabouts (ii) bends with radius less than 150 m (500 ft) on unre- stricted roads (iii) gradients of 5% (1 in 20) or steeper or longer than 100 m (330 ft) (iv) approaches to traffic signals on unrestricted roads	50	(30)	0.55
B	Average sites: (i) motorways and other high speed roads ie speeds in excess of 95 km/h (60 mile/h) (ii) trunk and principal roads, and other roads with more than 2000 vehicles per day in urban areas	50 80 50	(30) (50) (30)	0.50 0.45 0.50
C	Other sites: Generally straight roads with easy gradients and curves, without junctions, and free from any feature such as mixed traffic especially liable to create conditions of emergency	50	(30)	0.40

print-out of results as the vehicle travels along the road. The results are printed in tabular form, giving vehicle speed and sideway-force coefficient every 10 or 20 m of travel. The vehicle carries its own supply of water, which is applied just in front of the wheel. Being self-contained it causes little inconvenience to other traffic and speeds up to motorway speed-limit are possible. Suggested minimum values of the sideway-force coefficient for various categories of highway adopted by the Marshall Committee on Highway Maintenance[20] are given in table 8.7.

8.14.3 The Braking-force Test

The second major method by which the coefficient of friction between tyre and road can be measured is by the use of a braking-force trailer. Using this apparatus it is possible to measure safely coefficients of friction between tyre and wet road surface at speeds up to 130 km/h (80 mph) on motorways and trunks roads and at speeds over 160 km/h (100 mph) on airfield runways. A small trailer with a 4.00 x 8 smooth tyre is towed behind a high-performance car and the wheel is braked so that the wheel locks for about 2 s, the brake torque is measured and the resulting coefficient of friction expressed as the braking-force coefficient.

The variation of braking-force coefficient with percentage slip is illustrated in figure 8.16.

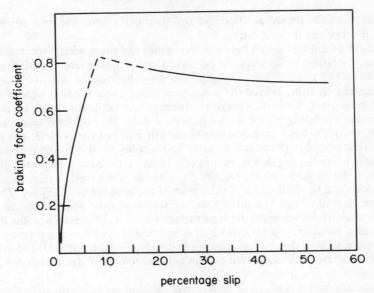

Figure 8.16 Variation of braking-force coefficient with percentage slip

It can be seen that there is a discontinuity in the curve of braking-force coefficients, the highest coefficient being obtained just as the wheel is on the point of sliding. The 'peak coefficient', as it is termed, represents the best coefficient that can be obtained using an anti-locking braking system, while the lower 'sliding coefficient' represents the conditions which prevail during skidding.

8.14.4 The Portable Skid-resistance Tester

The third method of measuring skid resistance is the Portable Skid-resistance Tester, which has been developed by the Transport and Road Research Laboratory. It provides a relatively cheap and simple method by which the highway engineer can carry out the routine measurement of skid resistance.

Essentially the apparatus consists of a pendulum arm pivoted at one end, at the other end of which is a rubber pad, which slides over the road. It gives values termed 'skid resistance', which correlate with the performance of a patterned tyre braking with locked wheels on a wet road at 50 km/h. This value is read from a scale and is indicated by a pointer showing the height to which the pendulum arm rises after being released from the horizontal position and then sliding over the road surface.

To use the tester the base is set level using the levelling screws, and the pendulum arm is lifted so that it swings clear of the road surface by the central knobs after releasing the locking knob. This allows the zero reading of the instrument to be tested by automatically locking the pendulum arm in the horizontal position and then bringing the pointer round to its stop in line with the arm. The pendulum arm is then released and as it swings it moves the pointer along with it, the arm being caught on the return swing and the pointer reading noted. The arm is returned to the automatically locked position and any error in the zero reading is corrected by adjustment of the friction rings.

Length of sliding contact between the rubber and the road surface is next checked by raising or lowering the pendulum arm until the length of sliding contact is between 125 and 127 mm. This is achieved by allowing the slider to touch the road surface on either side of the vertical and using a spacer bar as a check on the length of contact. To avoid wear of the rubber slider while this check is being carried out the lifting handle is used to lift the slider clear of the road surface during movement of the head from one side to the other side of the vertical. The pendulum arm is now placed in the release position and is ready for use on the highway.

When measuring the skid resistance of a highway the road is inspected and the section to be tested is chosen. Usually the nearside wheel track is selected although a check should be made to see if the crown of the road is more slippery. The road is swept clear of all grit, the surface wetted before measurements are made and the temperature of the water on the road surface noted. A difference in value is obtained if the reading is taken with or against the traffic flow and it is recommended that the slider swings in the direction of the traffic. If the surface has a regular pattern such as grooved or brushed concrete the slider should swing at an angle of 80° to the grooves.

The mean of five readings at each of five locations at approximately 5 to 10 m intervals along the track being tested is then taken as a representative value of the skidding resistance of that stretch of highway.

To interpret the readings from the portable tester consideration must be given to the effects of road surface and tyre characteristics, the time of year and the surface temperature of the road where the measurements were made. Since the skid resistance value given by the tester represents the performance of a patterned tyre, it may be found that, judged by accident statistics, the performance of roads where higher speeds are expected and which have smooth surfaces, is less safe than indicated by the skid resistance value when a vehicle has smooth tyres. For this reason there is the additional requirement for high-speed roads that the road surface has adequate roughness. This is ensured by requiring that the surface has a minimum texture depth of 0.65 mm. Another factor to be taken into account in interpreting the measured value is the time of year at which the measurement was taken. Readings taken in the winter months indicate values of skid resistance higher than are likely to be achieved during the summer months.

Table 8.8 Correction to skid resistance for road surface temperature (based on Road Note 27)

Test Temperatures (°C)	Correction to Skid Resistance
0	−7
10	−3
30	+2
40	+3

Table 8.9 Suggested minimum values of wet road surface skid resistance (from Table 1, Road Note 27, Instructions for Using the Portable Skid Resistance Tester, HMSO, 1969)

Category	Type of site	Minimum 'skid-resistance' (surface wet)
A	Difficult sites such as: (i) Roundabouts (ii) Bends with radius less than 150 m on unrestricted roads (iii) Gradients, 1 in 20 or steeper, of lengths greater than 100 m (iv) Approaches to traffic lights on unrestricted roads	65
B	Motorways, trunk and class 1 roads and heavily trafficked roads in urban areas (carrying more than 2000 vehicles per day)	55
C	All other sites	45

Note: For category A and B sites where speed of traffic is high (in excess of 95 km/h) an additional requirement is a minimum 'texture depth' of 0·65mm

Finally, consideration needs to be given to the effect of the water temperature on the road surface when the skid resistance value was observed. The effect of temperature on rubber resilience results in a decrease in skidding resistance as temperature rises. If the skid resistance is measured at low temperatures then the measured value is not representative of that which will exist in warmer conditions or when a warm vehicle tyre is in contact with the road surface. The effect is only significant at temperatures below 10 °C. Table 8.8 gives correction factors which should be added to the skid resistance to normalise the value to 20 °C.

Suggested minimum values of 'skid-resistance' as measured by the portable tester are given in table 8.9.

8.14.5 Passenger-car Braking Tests

A further method of estimating the skid resistance of a highway is by the use of a passenger car driven at a speed of 50 to 60 km/h on a wetted test area, the wheels of which are locked and the car allowed to slide to a standstill. The initial speed and the braking distance are noted and the average coefficient of friction f over the whole time of braking calculated from

$$f = \frac{V^2}{2gs}$$

where V is the initial velocity,

                            S is the stopping distance,

                            g is the acceleration due to gravity (9.81 m/s^2).

The advantages of this method of determining the coefficient of friction are as follows.

(1) The locked wheels closely simulate actual vehicle operation and provide an accurate measure of the average friction developed between the road and the tyre when an emergency stop has to take place.

(2) The cost of equipping a vehicle to carry out these tests is small.

(3) The test can be useful in engendering confidence in laymen.

The disadvantages of this method are as follows.

(1) There is some danger at initial speeds greater than 50 km/h.

(2) It is not a true picture of frictional performance at speeds greater than 50 km/h.

(3) Special traffic control measures are required.

(4) A large area of carriageway has to be wetted.

(5) The stopping distance depends upon braking efficiency.

(6) Vacuum brakes actuated by a hand switch are necessary for reproducible results.

(7) Normal car braking systems are not suitable for extended testing.

(8) Chalk-pellet guns are required for the accurate measurement of stopping distance, the pellet being fired when the brakes are applied.

8.14.6 The Rate-of-deceleration Test

The coefficient of friction over a short length of highway may be obtained by noting the deceleration caused by an instanteous application of vehicle brakes when

$$f = \text{deceleration}/g$$

The rate of deceleration is noted by a brake-testing meter and the coefficient of friction obtained depends to some extent on braking efficiency and the efficiency of the meter. If the wheels are locked a sliding coefficient is obtained.

8.14.7 Skidding Resistance and Road Surface Texture

The skidding resistance of a road is influenced by two characteristics of its surface: the micro- or fine-scale texture and the macro- or large-scale texture.

Microtexture — which refers to the detailed surface characteristics of the aggregate and mortar — is essential for providing friction between a vehicle tyre and a wet road surface. This level of texture assists in penetrating the last thin film of water and provides effective contact between road and tyre. Lees and Williams[21] have shown that the values of wet friction increase sharply when the relief of the aggregate topography rises above about 5×10^{-3} mm. At somewhat higher levels the rate of increase, however, reduces with further increase in the harshness of the texture, associated with a reduction in the real contact area. On the other hand, they show that an increase in the level of microtexture at such a degree of harshness results in increased tyre wear without a proportional increase in the wet friction.

Macrotexture is the second basic requirement for a pavement surface if skidding resistance is to be maintained at medium to high speeds. It is necessary to facilitate the rapid removal of water before the effect of microtexture can be brought into effect. Macrotexture also utilises the hysteresis effects of the tyre-tread rubber to absorb some of the kinetic energy of the vehicle.

These effects will not be described and illustrated by experimental work carried out by the Transport and Road Research Laboratory and reported by Sabey.[22] The extremes of surface texture met on the road are illustrated in figure 8.17, the

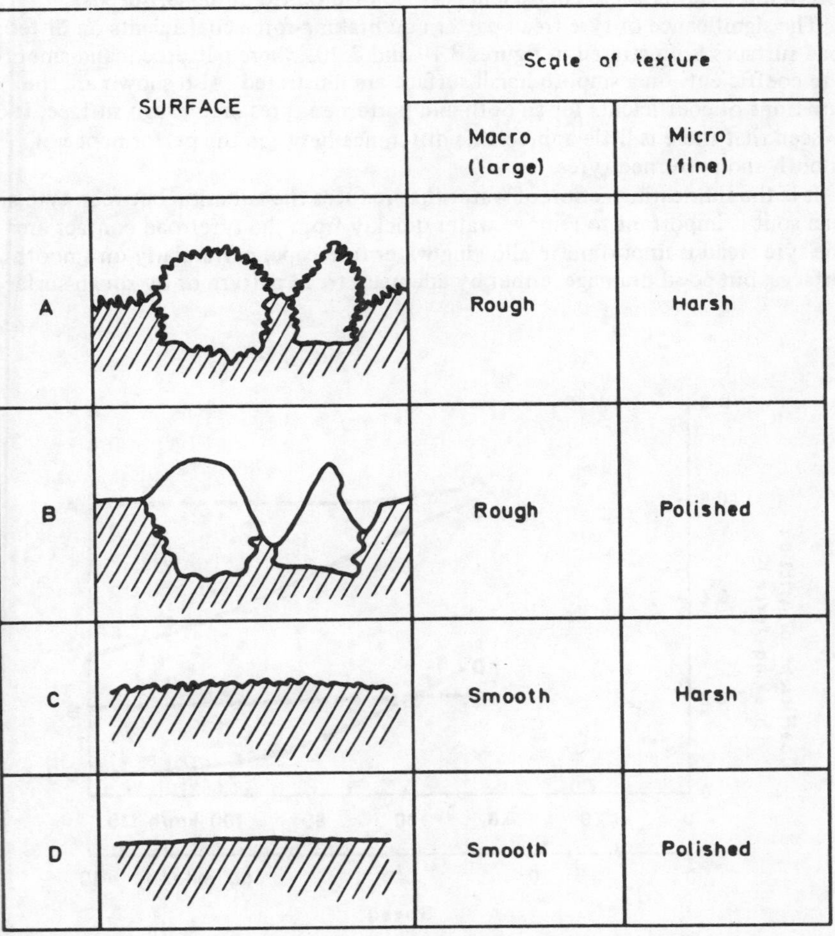

SURFACE		Scale of texture	
		Macro (large)	Micro (fine)
A		Rough	Harsh
B		Rough	Polished
C		Smooth	Harsh
D		Smooth	Polished

Figure 8.17 Terms used to describe road surface texture[22]

surfaces being categorised according to the macro surface-texture (that is, the texture visible to the eye) and the micro surface texture, which affects the harshness of the surface.

The significance of these surface-texture characteristics is illustrated by figure 8.18, which shows braking-force coefficients in which the effects of tyre tread pattern were eliminated by the use of a smooth tyre.

Surfaces A and C, which have microscopically harsh surfaces, both have high coefficients at 50 km/h, while surfaces D and B have low coefficients at 50 km/h because of their polished microtexture. As speed increases the changes in the coefficients depend upon surface texture, surfaces A and B showing little change while surfaces C and D exhibit considerable changes.

It can thus be seen that the state of polish of a road surface determines low-speed skidding resistance while the presence of large-scale asperities in the surface determine whether these coefficients can be maintained at higher speeds.

The significance of tyre tread pattern on braking-force coefficients on differing road surfaces is illustrated in figures 8.19 and 8.20, where patterned- and smooth-tyre coefficients on a smooth harsh surface are illustrated. Also shown are the variations of coefficients for smooth and patterned tyres on a rough surface. It can be seen that there is little appreciable difference between the performance of smooth and patterned tyres.

It is the lubricating action of water that reduces the adhesion between tyre and road so it is important to remove water quickly from the tyre/road contact area. The tyre tread is important in allowing water to escape, particularly on smooth surfaces, but good drainage, either by adequate tread pattern or by rough surface

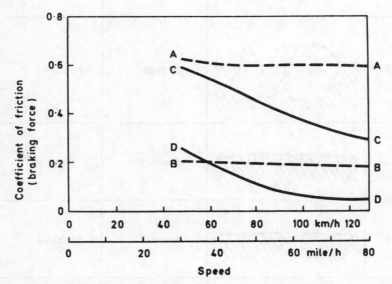

Figure 8.18 Wet road skidding resistance of surfaces, measured with a smooth tyre[22]

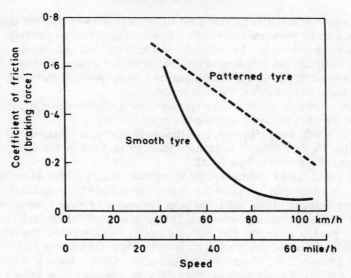

Figure 8.19 Tread pattern effect on smooth surface[22]

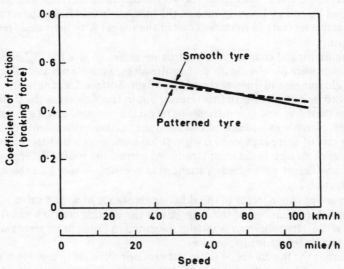

Figure 8.20 Tread pattern effect on rough surface[22]

texture, is not sufficient to provide good adhesion in the wet. The last trace of water can only be removed if the surface itself contains fine asperities on which high localised pressures (of the order of 7 MN/m^2) are built up. This means that slippery conditions will prevail even on a rough surface with a patterned tyre if the individual stones are polished. In addition, on smooth polished surfaces tread pattern cannot compensate for lack of texture.

The viscoelastic properties of the tyre tread materials have been found to make a major contribution toward improving tyre/road friction.

To gain benefit from high-hysteresis (low-resilience) tread material the road surface must have sufficiently large and angular projections in it to deform the tyre tread. This is illustrated in figure 8.21.

These results can be summarised by saying that rough surfaces discriminate between tread materials and smooth surfaces discriminate between tread patterns.

The importance of tread depth has been demonstrated using a high-speed car and the front-wheel braking technique. Test speeds up to 130 km/h (80 mph) were employed and the water film was approximately 1 mm thickness. The results for two rough surfaces and two smooth surfaces are shown in figure 8.22.

On rougher surfaces, where tread pattern is less effective because the surface itself already provides adequate drainage channels, there is a slow and gradual decrease in coefficient with wear.

On smoother surfaces there is a more marked decrease in coefficient. At 130 km/h (80 mph) even a new tyre with a tread depth of 8 mm gives little improvement in skidding resistance over a smooth tyre. This demonstrates that tyre tread cannot compensate for lack of road texture at high speeds.

The importance of the road surface texture in determining the form of the change in coefficient with speed has been demonstrated by the Transport and Road Research Laboratory. An interesting feature of this work was the way in which coefficients could rise at high speeds on very rough surfaces. This phenomenon can be explained by energy losses in rubber, the increase in coefficient being accounted for by effective increase in hysteresis loss in the rubber with increased frequency of deformation.[23]

The angularity and coarseness of texture necessary to give the higher coefficients at high speeds were obtained with surface dressings, asphalts with a high rate of spread of chippings, and open-textured macadam. Surface dressing in the fast lane was found to be outstanding in this respect, but in the slow lanes the surfaces tend to be more closed up and it is difficult to retain the required surface texture for high speeds. Notable exceptions to this are open-textured macadams and asphalts where the rate of chipping spread is high. It has been shown that the top 40 to 50 thousandths of an inch is the most significant part of the profile determining the change of coefficient with speed. Variations in coefficient noted on the A1 are given in figure 8.23.

An important single factor in the skidding resistance of a road surface under wet conditions is the behaviour of the aggregate in the wearing course when it is exposed to traffic action. Its behaviour is usually measured in terms of its resistance to polishing and its resistance to abrasion.

The reasons for the choice of these tests are not difficult to see, for if the aggregate becomes smooth under the polishing action of pneumatic-tyred vehicles then the resulting road surface will have a very poor resistance to skidding. The

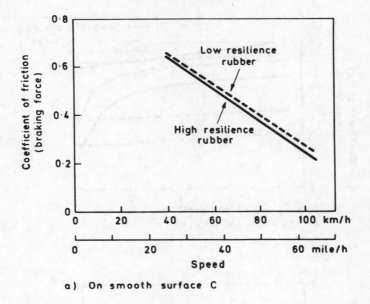

a) On smooth surface C

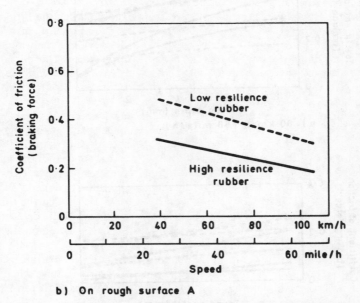

b) On rough surface A

Figure 8.21 Tread resilience effect on smooth and rough surfaces[22]

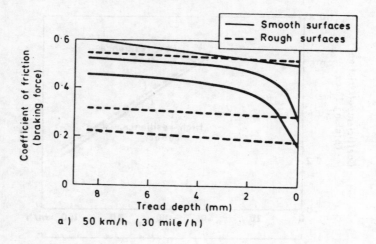

a) 50 km/h (30 mile/h)

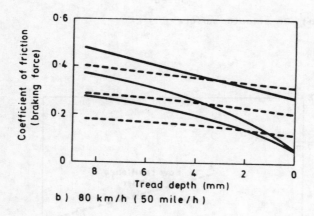

b) 80 km/h (50 mile/h)

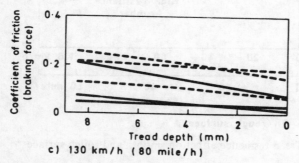

c) 130 km/h (80 mile/h)

Figure 8.22 Effect of tyre tread depth on wet-road skidding resistance[22]

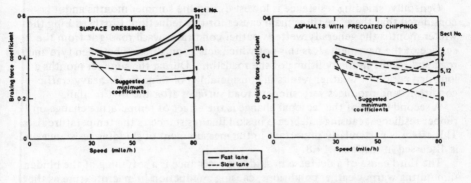

(a) VARIATION IN BRAKING FORCE COEFFICIENT WITH SPEED ON TEST SURFACES ON AI:
SURFACE DRESSINGS AND ASPHALTS WITH PRECOATED CHIPPINGS

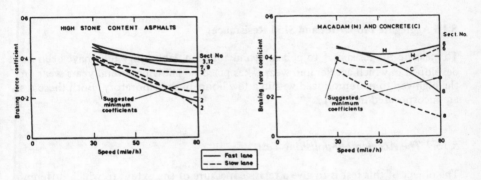

(b) VARIATION IN BRAKING FORCE COEFFICIENT WITH SPEED ON TEST SURFACES ON AI:
HIGH STONE CONTENT ASPHALTS, MACADAM AND CONCRETE

Figure 8.23 Variations of braking-force coefficient with speed[23]

rounded beach-pebbles found at Bridport, Dorset are an example of an aggregate that polishes extremely easily and it is used extensively as the aggregate when surfacing skid pans.

If, on the other hand, a polish-resistant stone abrades rapidly under traffic action the road surface will soon become slippery because of the stone loss from the carriageway. In addition, any high-speed skid resistance due to the texture of the surface will soon be lost as the aggregate is abraded.

8.14.8 Seasonal Changes in Skidding Resistance

The skidding resistance of a wet road surface exhibits considerable variation throughout the year, these seasonal changes depending upon the geometric layout of the highway and the characteristics of the traffic flow, the road surface and the weather. Considerable differences have been observed in these seasonal changes from one road to the next.

Generally, skidding resistance is lowest during the summer months and it is considered that there are three main causes for this reduction. Firstly, during the winter months the generally wetter weather conditions wash road grit from the surface of the pavement. It is this grit which acts as an abrasive between tyre and road and results in the polishing of the roadstone. During the summer months a long dry period of weather results in considerable polishing under heavy traffic conditions and produces very slippery road surfaces after the first rainfall.

A second cause of the seasonal change is the effect of temperature change on rubber resilience, causing a decrease in skidding resistance as the temperature rises. This effect is particularly important in the measurement of skidding resistance and is discussed in section 8.14.8.

The third cause of a decrease in skidding resistance is a softening of the binder film during warm weather conditions, causing a reduction in macrotexture as the aggregate is partially submerged in the binder film.

8.15 Aggregate Properties and Skid Resistance

To measure the resistance to polishing and abrasion, laboratory tests have been developed in which accelerated wear takes place, so allowing several years wear on the highway to be reproduced within a few hours in the laboratory. Both these tests are incorporated in BS 812.[24]

8.15.1 The Accelerated-polishing Test

The object of this test is to give a relative measure of the extent to which different types of roadstone in the wearing surface will polish under traffic. The test may be divided into two parts as follows.

(1) Samples of stone are subjected to an accelerated polishing action in a special machine.
(2) The state of polish reached by each sample is measured by means of a suitable friction test and is expressed as a laboratory-determined polished-stone value.

The apparatus, which is a polishing machine, has a 'road wheel' with a flat periphery and of such a size and shape that 14 specimen containers can be clamped around the periphery so as to form a continuous surface of stone particles, 45 mm (1¾ in.) wide and 406 mm (16 in.) in diameter. This 'road wheel' is rotated about its axis at a speed of 315 to 325 rev/min.

The 'road wheel' is brought to bear on a rubber-tyred wheel of 203 mm (8 in.) diameter and 50 mm (2 in.) breadth, with a total load of 390 ± 5 N (88 ± 1 lb). The tyre is an industrial 8 x 2 pneumatic 4-ply-rating smooth hand-truck tyre, specially selected and if necessary treated to obtain a true running surface. This tyre must have a hardness of 55 ± 5 IRHO (see BS 2719) and is inflated to a pressure of 310 ± 15 kN/m² (45 ± 2 lb/in.²). This wheel is not driven but rotates freely in line with that of the 'road wheel'.

A new tyre must be given a preliminary run of 6 h and a tyre has to be discarded after 20 test runs.

The specimens used to form the surface of the road wheel consist of the normal run from the plant and all the stone particles pass a 10 mm BS sieve and all are retained on a 14 to 10 mm sorting sieve. Each specimen consists of a single layer of 35 to 50 particles placed as close as possible and covering an area of 90.6 x 44.5 mm (3.57 x 1.75 in.) set in a sand-cement or resin mortar as detailed in BS 812.

To carry out an accelerated polishing test the room temperature is brought up to 20 ± 5 °C, the road wheel brought up to a speed of 315 to 325 rev/min, and the pneumatic-tyred wheel brought to bear on the surface of the specimen. Water and corn emery grit are then fed continuously onto the surface of the specimens and rotation continued within the limits of 3 h ± 1 min.

After this 3 h run the machine and specimens are thoroughly cleaned by washing and the machine then operated for a further 3 h ± 1 min with water and air-floated emery flour.

The specimens are then removed from the machine, washed, stored under water and then tested using the portable skid-resistance tester. This test must be carried out under very carefully controlled conditions and a well-defined test procedure is given in BS 812.

8.15.2 The Aggregate Abrasion Test

The object of this test is to give an indication of the extent to which different types of roadstone in the wearing surface will wear under traffic action, so reducing the macroscopic texture of the surface.

The aggregate abrasion testing machine consists of a flat circular iron or steel grinding plate of not less than 600 mm (2 ft) diameter that is rotated in a horizontal plane at a speed of 28 to 30 rev/min.

The specimens of aggregate are mounted in trays in a setting compound of polyester resin and hardener. These trays are then placed on the grinding plate with the aggregate in contact with the plate. The centres of the specimens are 260 mm (10.25 in.) from the centre of the grinding plate, the trays containing the specimens are free to move in a vertical direction and are weighed so that the total load of tray, setting compound and aggregate is 2 kg ± 10 g.

The grinding wheel is then rotated for 500 revolutions at a speed of between 28 and 30 rev/min. While rotation is taking place Leighton Buzzard sand is fed on to the wheel immediately in front of each test sample at a rate of 700 to 900 g (1.5 to 2 lb) per minute.

After abrasion the samples are removed from the machine and the loss of weight is noted. The percentage loss in weight calculated from

$$\frac{100 \text{ (weight of tray with aggregate before abrasion} - \text{ditto after abrasion)}}{\text{weight of surface dry aggregate}}$$

the mean of the two results, reported to the first decimal place, being the aggregate abrasion value.

8.16 Required Values of Sideway-force Coefficient

A relationship between the tyre/road surface coefficient and the relative likelihood of a highway to be the scene of repeated skidding accidents was proposed for the United Kingdom by Giles.[25] He found that the likelihood increased exponentially as the sideways-force coefficient measured at 50 km/h decreased. For a surface with the coefficient of 0.6 or above the risk of repeated wet-weather skidding accidents was extremely small. The risk became measurable with a coefficient of between 0.55 and 0.6 and increased rapidly by more than 20 times at values of 0.4 to 0.45 and by about 300 times when the coefficient is 0.3 to 0.35.

He also suggested tentative levels of sideway-force coefficient for various types of site. With minor amendments these proposals were accepted as target values by the Marshall Committee[20] and are reproduced in the amended form as table 8.7

While these proposals had the advantage of simplicity because there were only three broad classes of site, such a system could not take into account the many additional factors which contribute to the accident risk at a site.

In an attempt to overcome this objection a further set of standards has been proposed by Salt and Szatkowski.[26] These proposals are based on a site classification system broadly similar to the one given in table 8.7 but including a new super class of high-skid site. In place of a rigid system it is proposed that the minimum value of sideway-force coefficient for any given class of site will depend on a risk rating that depends on the accident potential of the site. If the coefficient falls below this value then the road surface is included in the maintenance programme unless the accident record indicates that the road should be reclassified with a risk rating. If the site has a coefficient equal to or greater than that indicated by the risk rating and yet has a skidding accident record higher than the average value then the risk rating must be increased.

After the scheme has been in operation for a considerable time the correct rating of every site would be indicated by the disappearance of sites having an accident level significantly different from an average value.

The proposed values for different sites are given in table 8.10.

8.17 Skidding Resistance, Traffic Flow and Polished-stone Value, Bituminous Surfacings

Research at the Transport and Road Research Laboratory has established for roads in the United Kingdom a significant connection between the sideway-force coefficient after about one year's traffication, the traffic volume and the initial nature of the aggregate as measured by the PSV.

Observations reported by Szatkowski and Hosking[27] showed that, despite the seasonal variations in skidding resistance observed during a given year, it was possible to obtain a significant relationship between the mean summer value of SFC after at least one year's wear, the volume of traffic, the PSV for the bituminous surface, and several mix and aggregate properties for concrete pavement surfaces.

It was noted that for bituminous surfacings the skid resistance fell sharply during the initial year of trafficking before reaching a constant value that depended upon the polished-stone value of the aggregate and the traffic volume. The effect of

Table 8.10 Minimum values of skidding resistance for different sites[26]

SITE	DEFINITION	SFC (at 50 km/h) Risk Rating									
		1	2	3	4	5	6	7	8	9	10
A1 (v difficult)	(i) Approaches to traffic signals on roads with a speed limit greater than 40 mile/h (64 km/h) (ii) Approaches to traffic signals, pedestrian crossings and similar hazards on main urban roads**						0.55	0.60	0.65	0.70	0.75
A2 (difficult)	(i) Approaches to major junctions on roads carrying more than 250 commercial vehicles per-lane per day (ii) Roundabouts and their approaches (iii) Bends with radius less than 150 m on roads with a speed limit greater than 40 mile/h (64 km/h) (iv) Gradients of 5% or steeper, longer than 100 m				0.45	0.50	0.55	0.60	0.65		
B (average)	(i) Generally straight sections of and large radius curves on: Motorways (ii) Trunk and principal roads (iii) Other roads carrying more than 250 commercial vehicles per lane per day	0.30	0.35	0.40	0.45	0.50	0.55				
C (easy)	(i) Generally straight sections of lightly trafficked roads (ii) Other roads where wet accidents are unlikely to be a problem	0.30	0.35	0.40	0.45						

* 'Minimum' in this context is defined on page 3.

** Main urban roads would generally be included in Marshall road categories, 1, 2 and 3.

traffic was thus not cumulative but instead the skid resistance represented an equilibrium value between natural weathering effects and the polishing action of traffic. When the traffic volume changed the equilibrium value also changed, and on one section of the A4 at Colnbrook the skidding resistance increased when the opening of a nearby section of the M4 motorway resulted in decreased traffic volumes.

Szatkowski and Hosking gave the following significant relationship (correlation coefficient 0.91) for bituminous surfaces.

$$SFC_{50} = 0.024 - 0.663 \times 10^{-4} q_{cv} + 1 \times 10^{-2} PSV \qquad (8.4)$$

where q_{cv} is the flow of commercial vehicles per lane per day in one direction.

8.17.1 Concrete Surfacings

Research into the factors affecting the skid resistance of concrete pavements requires consideration to be given to a greater number of variables. It is necessary to consider the properties of both the fine and coarse aggregate and also the strength of the concrete. Work carried out as a joint venture between the Cement and Concrete Association and the Transport and Road Research Laboratory has resulted in a limitation of the calcium carbonate content of the fine aggregate and a requirement for limestone coarse aggregate to satisfy an accelerated wear test when the concrete pavement is subjected to heavy traffic conditions.

Using a limited amount of data from the M4 motorway, Franklin, Calder and Maynard[28,29] have given the following relationship, which has a correlation coefficient of 0.84.

$$SRV = 47.05 + 0.2103x_1 - 1.106x_2 - 0.2044x_3 + 0.1889x_4 + 0.3350x_5$$

$$(8.5)$$

where
$\qquad$ SRV is the skid resistance value as measured by the portable pendulum tester,

$\qquad x_1$ $\quad$ is the PSV of the fine aggregate,

$\qquad x_2$ $\quad$ is the AAV of the fine aggregate,

$\qquad x_3$ $\quad$ is the 28-day compressive strength of the concrete (MPa),

$\qquad x_4$ $\quad$ is the fine aggregate content (percentage by weight of aggregate aggregate passing a 4.76 mm BS sieve),

$\qquad x_5$ $\quad$ is the AAV of the coarse aggregate.

A somewhat similar relationship was found for data obtained from an additional site on the A12 at Brentwood. Further work is expected to allow the skidding resistance of concrete pavements to be accurately predicted from a knowledge of aggregate properties.

8.18 Required Values of PSV for Bituminous Surfacings

From the connection developed between SFC, traffic flow and PSV it is possible to tabulate the aggregate PSV required to give specified values of SFC for varying values of traffic flow. These values are tabulated in table 8.11.

A comparison of table 8.11 with table 8.10 reveals that for category A1 and A2 sites it is necessary to consider artificial aggregates and improved binders because there are few natural aggregates with a PSV of 70.

For category B sites, which include about 15 per cent of the road network, when the traffic flow is 4000 commercial vehicles/day/lane the maintenance of a SFC of 0.45 also requires the use of a stone with a PSV of 70.

Approximately 80 per cent of roads in the United Kingdom are in category C and there is no difficulty in obtaining roadstones with the required properties.

Table 8.11 PSV of aggregate necessary to achieve the required skidding resistance in bituminous surfacings under different traffic conditions[26]

Required mean summer SFC at 50 km/h	PSV of aggregate necessary					
	Traffic in commercial vehicles per lane per day					
	250 or under	1000	1750	2500	3250	4000
0.30	30	35	40	45	50	55
0.35	35	40	45	50	55	60
0.40	40	45	50	55	60	65
0.45	45	50	55	60	65	70
0.50	50	55	60	65	70	75
0.55	55	60	65	70	75	
0.60	60	65	70	75		
0.65	65	70	75			
0.70	70	75				
0.75	75					
AAV	not greater than 12				not greater than 10	

SFC values in these traffic conditions are sometimes achievable with aggregates of extreme hardness and very high resistance to abrasion, such as certain grades of calcined bauxite.

Table 8.12 Traffic loadings and maximum aggregate abrasion values for flexible surfacings[30]

Traffic in Commercial Vehicles Per Lane Per Day	Under 250*	Up to 1000	Up to 1750	Up to 2500	Up to 3250	Over 3250
Maximum AAV for chippings	14	12	12	10	10	10
Maximum AAV for aggregate in coated macadam wearing courses	16	16	14	14	12	12

* For lightly trafficked roads carrying less then 250 commercial vehicles per lane per day, aggregate of higher AAV may be used where experience has shown that satisfactory performance is achieved by aggregate from a particular source.

Official recommendations for minimum polished stone values for bituminous surfacings to new roads in the United Kingdom are contained in Technical Memorandum H16/75.[30] These values are reproduced in table 8.4.

Because of the importance of maintaining an adequate texture depth, necessary for skid resistance at higher speeds, a minimum of 1.5 mm is specified, and to maintain this texture maximum aggregate abrasion values are specified for flexible surfacings. These values, which depend on the commercial traffic flows, are reproduced as table 8.12.

8.19 The Restoration of Skid Resistance on Highway Pavements

The maintenance of safe standards of skidding resistance on heavily trafficked high-speed roads is of considerable importance to the highway engineer. To investigate this problem the Permanent International Association of Road Congresses set up a working group which reported to the 1975 Congress held at Mexico City.[31]

Information was obtained on the restoration of rugosity from Belgium, the Federal German Republic, France, the United Kingdom, Japan, the Netherlands, Poland, Sweden, Switzerland, together with 34 of the United States.

Reasons given for the loss of road surface rugosity included increased traffic flows, excess binder, polished aggregates, penetration of chippings into rolled asphalt and the effect of wear by studded tyres.

The techniques reported as being used to restore skid resistance by the countries supplying information may be divided into two groups. In the first group are those techniques which involve the removal of material, that is

(1) bush hammering and percussion scouring using percussion tools;

(2) milling — grooving by means of hard steel discs or flails;

(3) grooving — cutting grooves by means of diamond discs;

(4) spreading of hydrochloric acid, causing a chemical reaction in the cement mortar;

(5) sanding — scouring under the action of an abrasive jet under pressure;

(6) flame scouring — shattering of cement concrete by means of high temperatures;

(7) planing, removal of a film of material from the surface using planing or milling machines.

In the second group are those techniques involving the addition of materials, that is

(8) reheating and encrusting of bituminous surfacing with chippings;

(9) application of a resinous layer with gritting;

(10) bituminous-bound surface dressing with gritting, using a traditional or modified binder;

(11) slurry sealing by the spreading of bituminous mortar filling;

(12) the spreading and rolling of granular materials (possibly pre-heated) on a bituminous surfacing or tack coat;

(13) the spreading of white spirit, removal of excess bitumen from the surface, followed by the spreading and rolling of granular materials;

(14) resurfacing with open-textured bituminous material up to a maximum thickness of 20 mm.

The application of these techniques to both bituminous and concrete surfaces will now be considered in greater detail.

8.19.1 Bush Hammering

Bush hammering consists of roughening the surface of the pavement using several types of tool. It was reported as being used experimentally on concrete surfaces in Belgium and France and experimentally on both surface types in the United Kingdom. In the Netherlands it was current practice on both types of surface and in Switzerland on concrete pavements. In the United States this technique has found little application.

It is reported that after bush hammering the resulting surface appears to be similar to sandpaper — pitted with small craters. According to reports from the Netherlands on concrete surfaces there is an increase in texture depth but on bituminous surfaces there is little change. An increase in skid resistance is also reported to have been observed at speeds between 20 and 80 km/h. Durability of treatment appears to vary from 1 year in Belgium to 4 to 6 years in the Netherlands. Environmentally it is considered that the process is noisy and produces considerable dust problems unless water sprays are also used.

A general conclusion is that bush hammering has limited application and should be avoided altogether if it causes polishable aggregates to be exposed.

8.19.2 Milling

In the milling process the pavement surface is grooved by means of hard steel discs or rings with hard-steel cutting teeth operated with a rotary or percussive action. Extensively used in the United Kingdom on concrete pavements and in Switzerland, it has been experimentally applied in Belgium and the Federal Republic of Germany.

As the process produces grooves in the road surface it is the macrotexture that is modified, resulting in a gain of adhesion at high speeds, and when the grooving is transverse, an improvement in surface drainage. Various grooving patterns have been used but there is no general conclusion as to the optimum groove pattern. The problem of the whistle produced by regularly spaced grooves is mentioned. The life of the process on bituminous surfaces is low, especially under hot-climate conditions, but on concrete surfaces Belgium reported an expected life of 3 years, while in the United Kingdom a minimum effective life of 10 years is expected.

Milling is considered to have the same environmental disadvantages as bush hammering, but with a machine jointly developed in the United Kingdom by the Department of the Environment and the Cement Association suction removal of the detritus is employed. The report concludes that this British machine has considerable promise, offering high output at reduced cost.

8.19.3 Grooving

The grooving technique consists of sawing grooves in surfacings by means of diamond cutters in the form of discs. It is reported as being current practice in the United Kingdom and France for concrete pavements and has been used experimentally in Belgium, the Federal Republic of Germany and Finland. The process is also extensively used in the United States on concrete and, with certain reservations, bituminous surfaces. When the diamond cutter discs are placed edge to edge the process is used for surface repair work.

As with milling, grooving does not affect the microtexture of the surfacing. Longitudinal grooving is practiced almost exclusively in the United States and increasingly in the Federal Republic of Germany and France, while Belgium, Switzerland and the United Kingdom favour transverse grooving. Oblique grooving is not used owing to high cost and practical difficulties.

Transverse grooving has similar effects to those observed with milling in improving skid resistance, surface drainage and water spray. Longitudinal grooving has little effect on roughness when traditional measuring devices are used. It is believed to be effective in reducing accidents on wet roads because the tyres are gripped in the grooves and follow them. This lateral stability is particularly important on curves under these conditions. Opinions appear to be divided on the merits of these two grooving methods, but longitudinal grooving is faster, causing less obstruction to traffic.

As with milling, optimum grooving patterns have not been determined. A width of 2.4 mm, depths of 5 to 6 mm and a 19 mm spacing are frequently used in the United States for longitudinal grooving. Some States believe there is a danger of rail effect and loss of steering with more widely spaced grooves.

8.19.4 Spreading of Hydrochloric Acid

The spreading of hydrochloric acid on concrete pavements is currently in use in the Netherlands; it has also found occasional use in Belgium, Switzerland and three of the United States. A solution of 50 per cent hydrochloric acid at 20° Baume and 50 per cent water is spread at a rate of 0.2 to 0.5 l/m^2. The attack on the concrete is allowed to continue for 15 min, after which the road is swilled with water. In addition to an improvement in surface texture the acid treatment also removes surface grease and oil.

It is obviously necessary to take precautions against the corrosive effects of the acid on operating staff, passing vehicles, drainage, pipes and ditches. Experience in the Netherlands indicates an increase in skid resistance which remains for 5 years for light traffic flow, but it has been reported to be as short as 1 year in the United States.

The process cannot be used where the concrete contains limestone aggregates since the acid will attack the limestone in preference to the mortar. Neither should it be used when the aggregate will polish, since it will be exposed by the action of the acid.

8.19.5 Planing

This technique consists of removing a surface layer of bituminous surfacing using a planing machine, with or without the application of heat. It is used for the removal of defective or uneven material and the removal of road markings. In some cases when hot planers are used the tailings are re-encrusted.

There are many machines available for road planing and they can be conveniently classified into the following three categories.

(1) Hot scrapers: the surface is heated and then scraped using an oscillating or non-oscillating steel blade.

(2) Hot millers: the surface is heated and then milled with a series of tungsten-carbide tools fitted with one or more tool carriers turning around a horizontal or vertical axis.

(3) Cold millers: these machines are not equipped with heaters and mill the surface using tools mounted on a carrier turning around a horizontal axis.

A comparative study carried out in Belgium indicated that for precision work, such as is required when a new surface-layer is not being placed, only milling machines with a drum on a horizontal axis and turning in the direction opposite to that of the wheels is satisfactory. These self-propelled machines move parallel to the axis of the pavement and have variable speeds which depend on the machine type, depth of planing and the nature of the surface.

The use of this technique for restoring rugosity and the removal of unevenness, in contrast to its use before applying a further surface-layer, was reported as being extensively practised in the Netherlands, Japan and Belgium. Several of the United States also reported the use of the method, but with varied success.

Generally the report concluded that the removal of thin layers by milling modified the micro- and macrotexture of the surface. It considered it an economical and effective process as long as there were no polishable aggregates present in the surfacing. It was particularly useful for removing films of bitumen, rubber and cement mortar.

8.19.6 Heating and Encrustation of Chippings

In this method a bituminous surface is heated and immediately afterwards chippings are spread and rolled into the surface. The report states that the method is in current use in the United States and France and is under test in Belgium and the Federal Republic of Germany. In the United States it is being used in Indiana, Minnesota, Colorado and North Carolina.

During treatment it is possible to fill surface cracks and increase the compaction of the surfacing; the surface appearance can also be made more uniform and to some extent the unevenness of the surface may be improved.

The process is simple to carry out. First, the surface is cleaned by brushing or compressed air and then the surface is heated using either specially designed equipment or else the heating equipment of a hot planer. Precoated chippings are then spread, either mechanically or manually, and immediately rolled into the surface. An alternative technique that has been applied in Belgium is one in which the chippings are spread on the road before heating takes place, so reducing the risk of the surface cooling before the chippings are rolled.

Care must be taken to avoid heating and too heavy a spread of chippings, while brushing-off of loose chippings on completion of the process is essential.

This process improves both the macro- and micro-structure, but a considerable increase in the macro-structure is only obtained by the use of large chippings. The successful embedment of large chippings depends upon the surfacing containing sufficient mortar. The life of the process is considered to vary between 1 year in the Federal Republic of Germany and 5 to 10 years in the United Kingdom, depending upon the traffic flow, the use of studded tyres and the size and resistance to polishing of the chippings.

Belgium, France, Colorado and Indiana consider this process to be particularly useful. The Federal Republic of Germany, the United Kingdom, Minnesota and North Carolina consider the encrustation of chippings useful for the treatment of small areas of pavement in urgent need of treatment. Tennessee does not favour the process because of difficulties with adhesion of the chippings, and Maine restricts the process to the treatment of lightly trafficked roads.

8.19.7 Resinous Layers

This technique consists of applying a layer of resinous-based binder to concrete or bituminous surfaces and then spreading chippings on the binder. Frequently the process is known under a commerical name, such as Shellgrip, Plasti-Chape (France), Spray Grip (the United Kingdom and the United States) or Hydro-Safe (Belgium).

It is currently used in the United Kingdom, France, Japan and Delaware and has been used experimentally in Oregon, Washington and Kentucky.

As well as restoring rugosity the process seals the surface and in France is used as an audible warning strip.

Spreading of the binder is carried out mechanically and the binder is obtained by mixing an epoxy resin with another component containing tar (or a mixture of bitumen and aromatic oil) with a hardener. The setting of the binder, which takes between 4 and 10 h, is the result of polymerisation between the resin and the hardener. Mechanical gritting immediately follows the application of the binder.

The chippings used vary from one country to another. In the United Kingdom only calcined bauxite is used; in Japan emery is used, while in Belgium both are used. France uses quartzite while in the United States calcined bauxite is generally used but corundum is used in Delaware.

There are considerable problems in the application of the process. The equipment must be operating in an absolutely correct manner; the road surface must be dry and have a sufficiently high temperature. It is recommended that the process should be carried out after a hot period in order that the moisture content of the road should not prevent the absorption of the resin. Protective clothing must be worn by the staff carrying out the process.

A considerable gain in rugosity was observed by all users of the process and there have not been any reports of noise problems. Spray from wet surfaces has also been noted to have been reduced.

Where studded tyres are used considerable differential wear has been noted, and in addition at very low temperatures the binder became brittle. For these reasons both Finland and the Federal Republic of Germany do not use this process.

Because of the high cost of the process, treatment is normally confined to small areas, but on bituminous surfacings a life of 3 to 10 years can be expected. On concrete surfaces the process has been infrequently used, however, as little success has been obtained.

8.19.8 Surface Dressing with Bituminous Binders

Surface dressing is an old-established process of restoring the rugosity and sealing the surface of bituminous and, to a lesser extent, concrete pavements.

The technique of surface dressing using improved binders is more recent, and in France in particular is becoming current practice. The improvement to the binders usually takes the form of the addition of 1.5 to 2.5 per cent PVC to tar or 5 to 10 per cent of synthetic thioelastomer as a fluxant to the bitumen. These binders are stated to have improved cohesion, adhesion, higher viscosity, more rapid setting and reduced thermal susceptibility.

The surface-dressing process is discussed fully in section 8.11.

8.19.9 Use of Thin-textured Wearing Courses

The technique consists of laying a thin open-textured bituminous wearing course with a thickness of between 10 and 20 mm. Many of the United States reported the use of this technique as current practice, the first applications dating from 1950 in California. Usually it is applied to bituminous surfacing, although Colorado, Illinois, Louisiana and Oregon have applied it to concrete pavements.

In Europe the technique has been used to only a limited extent as a means of restoring rugosity but experimental sections have been laid as new roads. Since 1959 it has been tested in the United Kingdom (particularly on airport runways), Belgium, France and the Netherlands.

As laid in the United States the material contains 10 to 15 per cent of sand, 2 to 5 per cent filler and 6 to 7 per cent bitumen. After laying, the void content ranges from 15 to 19 per cent. The open-textured surface obtained has a harsh microtexture obtained by the use of angular aggregates that are not easily polished and a rough macrotexture. A high degree of rugosity is obtained which is maintained at increasing speed and in addition the high internal drainage capacity of the material results in a considerable reduction of water spraying under wet conditions. The process is reported as having a life of between 5 and 20 years with no damage due to frost.

Reports from the United States indicate that they are highly satisfied with re-texturing in this manner and consider it to be one of the best methods of restoring rugosity on bituminous surfaces.

Several other techniques were stated to be used for the restoration of rugosity, including sanding and flame scouring, slurry seal treatments, the spreading and rolling of granular materials and the use of white spirit to remove excess binder, but their use is not yet widespread and no details need be given here.

References

(1) O.E.C.D., Road Research Group, *Road Strengthening* (1976)
(2) P. J. Norman, R. A. Snowdon, and J. C. Jacobs, Transport and Road Research Laboratory Report 571, *Pavement Deflection Measurements and Their Application to Structural Maintenance and Overlay Design* (Crowthorne, 1973)
(3) F. Bolivar Loco Carnero, 'Benkelman Beam, Auxiliary Instrument of the Maintenance Engineer.' *Highw. Res. Rec.* 129 (1966)
(4) Swiss Standard 670 362
(5) Asphalt Institute, 'Asphalt Overlays and Pavement Rehabilitation', Manual Series No. 17 (1969)
(6) Scrivner, G. Swift, and W. M. Moore, 'A New Research Tool for Measuring Pavement Deflection', *Highw. Res. Rec.* 129 (1966)
(7) W. J. Liddle, and D. E. Peterson, 'Utah's Use of Dynaflect Data for Pavement Rehabilitation', *Highw. Res. Rec.* 300 (1969)
(8) C. Van der Poel, 'Dynamic Testing of Pavements and Base Courses', *Proc. 2nd Int. Conf. Soil Mechanics and Foundation Engineering,* Rotterdam, 1948
(9) Ministere de l'Equipment et du Logement, Laboratorie Central des Ponts et Chaussées, 'Vibreur Goodman', *Bull. Liais. Labs Routiers, Special J.,* 1968; and R. Guillemin and J. C. Gramsammer, 'Auscultation dynamique des chaussées a l'aide du vibreur leger', *Note d'information technique LCPC* (Paris, November 1971)
(10) J. C Gramsammer, 'Grandeur et servitude de l'auscultation dynamique des chaussées', *Bull Liais. Labs des Ponts et Chaussées* 61 (Paris, September–October 1972)
(11) A. H. Joseph and J. W. Hall, 'Non-destructive Vibratory Pavement Evaluation

Techniques', *Proc. Third Int. Conf. Structural Design of Asphalt Pavement*, London, 1972

(12) C. K. Kennedy and N. W. Lister, Transport and Road Research Laboratory Report 833. *Prediction of Pavement Performance and the Design of Overlays* (Crowthorne, 1978)

(13) DoE, Road Research Laboratory Road Note 39, *Recommendations for Road Surface Dressing*, (HMSO, 1972)

(14) BS 63: 1971   Single Sized Roadstone and Chippings

(15) BS 812: 1975   Methods for Sampling and Testing of Mineral Aggregates, Sands and Fillers. Part 1. Sampling, Size, Shape and Classification

(16) Department of Transport, Technical Memorandum H16/76, *Specification Requirements for Aggregate Properties and Texture Depth for Bituminous Surfacings to New Roads* (1976)

(17) Department of Transport, Technical Memorandum H10/72, *Provisional Specification for Tar-bitumen Blends* (1972)

(18) BS 1707: 1970   Surface Dressing Binder Distributors

(19) B. E. Sabey, 'Accidents: Their Cost and Relation to Surface Characteristics', *Safety and the Concrete Road Surface-design, Specification and Construction*, Cement and Concrete Association Symposium (1973)

(20) Ministry of Transport, *Report of the Committee on Highway Maintenance* (London, 1970)

(21) G. Lees and A. R. Williams, 'The Relation between Tyre and Road Surface Design', *International Road Federation Congress*, Munich C3 (1973) 35–39

(22) B. E. Sabey, 'The Road Surface in Relation to Friction and Wear of Tyres', *Road Tar*, 28 (March 1969)

(23) B. E. Sabey, Transport and Road Research Laboratory Report LR131. *Wet Road Skidding Resistance at High Speeds on a Variety of Surfaces on A1* (Crowthorne, 1968)

(24) BS 812: 1975   Methods for Sampling and Testing Mineral Aggregates, Sands and Fillers

(25) G. C. Giles, 'The Skidding Resistance of Roads and the Requirements of Modern Traffic', *Proc. Inst. civ. Engrs*, 6 (1957)

(26) G. F. Salt and W. S. Szatkowski, Transport and Road Research Laboratory Report LR510, *A Guide to Levels of Skidding Resistance for Roads* (Crowthorne, 1973)

(27) W. S. Szatkowski and J. R. Hasking, Transport and Road Research Laboratory Report LR504. *The Effect of Traffic and Aggregate on the Resistance to Skidding of Bituminous Surfacings* (Crowthorne, 1972)

(28) R. E. Franklin and A. J. J. Calder, DoE, Transport and Road Research Laboratory Report LR640, *The Skidding Resistance of Concrete: the Effect of Materials under Site Conditions.* (Crowthorne, 1974)

(29) R. E. Franklin and D. P. Maynard, DoE, Transport and Road Research Laboratory Report SR78 UC, *The Skidding Resistance of Concrete: Relationships between Laboratory and Site Measurements* (Crowthorne, 1974)

(30) DoE, Technical Memorandum H16/76. *Specification Requirements for Aggregate Properties and Texture Depth for Bituminous Surfacings to New Roads* (London, 1976)

(31) Permanent International Association of Road Congresses General Report, *XVth World Road Congress*, Mexico, 1975

Index